Seminar on System Analysis 2017

ITM Web of Conferences Volume 10 (2017)

Moscow, Russia
14 - 15 February 2017

Editors:

E. Nikulchev
G. Bubnov

ISBN: 978-1-5108-3784-3

Printed from e-media with permission by:

Curran Associates, Inc.
57 Morehouse Lane
Red Hook, NY 12571

Some format issues inherent in the e-media version may also appear in this print version.

Printed by Curran Associates, Inc. (2017)

For additional information, please contact EDP Sciences – Web of Conferences
at the address below.

EDP Sciences – Web of Conferences
17, Avenue du Hoggar
Parc d'Activité de Courtabœuf
BP 112
F-91944 Les Ulis Cedex A
France

Phone: +33 (0) 1 69 18 75 75
Fax: +33 (0) 1 69 28 84 91

contact-edps@webofconferences.org

Additional copies of this publication are available from:

Curran Associates, Inc.
57 Morehouse Lane
Red Hook, NY 12571 USA
Phone: 845-758-0400
Fax: 845-758-2633
Email: curran@proceedings.com
Web: www.proceedings.com

TABLE OF CONTENTS

2017 Seminar on Systems Analysis

Moscow (Russia), 14–15 February 2017

Main topics:

- Control systems
- Artificial Intelligence
- Communication Networks
- Database Management & Information Retrieval
- Human Computer Interaction
- Software Engineering
- Theoretical Computer Science

Scientific Committee:

edp sciences

ITM Web of Conferences

Statement of Peer review

In submitting conference proceedings to ITM Web of Conferences, I certify to the Publisher that I adhere to the **Policy on Publishing Integrity** of the journal in order to safeguard good scientific practice in publishing.

1. All articles have been subjected to peer review administered by the proceedings editors.
2. Reviews have been conducted by expert referees, who have been requested to provide unbiased and constructive comments aimed, whenever possible, at improving the work.
3. Proceedings editors have taken all reasonable steps to ensure the quality of the materials they publish and their decision to accept or reject a paper for publication has been based only on the merits of the work and the relevance to the journal.

Title, date and place of the conference

2017 Seminar on Systems analysis
Moscow (Russia), 14–15 February 2017

Proceedings editor(s):

Evgeny Nikulchev, prof.
Gregory Bubnov, prof.

Date and editor's signature

03/03/2016

 DOI: 10.1051/itmconf/20171001001

Structural and Parametric Analysis of Robust Design Quality of Complex Technical Systems

Aleksandr Dmitriev[1, 2], *Tatyana* Mitroshkina[1, *] and *Gennady* Rogachev[3]

[1]Samara National Research University named after academician S.P. Korolev (Samara University), 443086 Samara, Russia
[2]Samara Region State Academy (Nayanova), 443010 Samara, Russia
[3]Samara State Technical University, 443100, Samara, Russia

Abstract. Discussed the approaches to robust design of complex technical systems based on Quality Function Deployment method QFD. It demonstrates how to use the matrix approach to the implementation of QFD, which enables the structural and parametric analysis of the quality of complex technical systems in conditions of uncertainty and ill-conditioning problem

1 Introduction

Effective quality design of complex technical systems based on sustainable design and methods of quality management - the basis of improving the competitiveness of products and enterprises [1-4].

The aim of this work is to improve the quality of complex engineering systems at the design stage. It is proposed to use a robust design based on modern methods of quality management, as well as approaches to the structural and parametric identification and optimization [1-6].

Product design plays a crucial role in planning and providing quality products and services. It should be noted that the evolution of quality management techniques aimed to develop effective measures against unwanted volatility. Work on the genitive Taguchi robust design is the key to this evolution [4].

The purpose of the robust approach to product design - to make the output characteristics of the product low sensitivity to environmental variability, degradation products and manufacturing imperfections. Improved product design and manufacturing process, it allows to reduce production costs and product operation.

Taguchi divided the life cycle of any commodity product into two unequal parts [4]. First – the development and implementation of products – everything that precedes the production of the product. The second – the actual production and operation. quality problems should start to engage in the first stage and the earlier, the better. It was then that it is possible not to tighten control and use a very committed, very expensive equipment, and establish a process for the design and production so that its characteristics were the least affected by the scatter / variability due to the imperfections of the manufacturing process variability of environmental conditions, heterogeneity of raw materials and other factors that are unavoidable in the manufacture and maintenance of products.

Taguchi proposes to divide the factors into groups so that one of them turned out to be the factors responsible for the primary response ("nominal"), and in another - are responsible for the spread. To identify these groups Taguchi introduces a new generic response that he calls "the signal / noise ratio." The original problem is divided into two independent optimization procedures: one for the denomination, and the other for variation.

Taguchi has developed an approach to the establishment of the nominal product and process parameters: system design and parametric design. System design – the process of the application of scientific and engineering knowledge to the development of the product structure model. The model defines the initial values of parameters of the product (or process). System design involves consideration of both customer requirements and production conditions. Robust parametric design - the process of identifying such values parameters of the product (or process), which reduce the sensitivity to design parameters change sources. The use of non-linear effects of parameters of product (or process) on the output parameters to reduce the sensitivity of Engineering to scatter sources is the essence of parametric design.

2 Robust design

In the arsenal of modern methods of transformation of customer requirements in the immediate characteristics of the new (or upgraded) product quality identification method include the quality function deployment QFD [2]. In expanded form, the process of implementing QFD includes four levels, covering all stages from conceptual design (system) design products and processes before deciding on the need to change the target parameters of manufacturing processes. On the technical level I determined (system) product characteristics, ensuring the implementation of customer requirements. Then deployed specifications / characteristics of the components are structured to product (QFD level 1, QFD level 2), further process parameters are determined that achieve the

*Corresponding author: t.mitroshkina@gmail.com

desired components and characteristics values of the product (QFD level 3), and then specifies the requirements for execution of operations in the production of (QFD level 4).

The aim of the method is the transformation of the consumer request (needs and expectations) in the technical product specifications and work instructions, visualization, documentation and planning quality. The main element of QFD is precisely the deployment of customer requirements in the production and the attainment of the relevant technical specifications that meet the expectations of the consumer. In other words, in this case it comes to the production of the preparations for the launch of a new product.

At each of the levels of QFD developed a special table, called the House of Quality (HoQ). The result of the application of QFD is to define the priorities and identifying the characteristics of products and components, process parameters and production operations, the greatest impact on the realization of customer requirements.

The traditional solution quality planning tasks products and services within the QFD method is a consistent ranking of performance in accordance with this priority (result), considering the importance of customer requirements (raw data).

The absolute priority value characteristics Θ_j at QFD level 1 is calculated as follows:

$$\Theta_i = \sum_{i=1}^{i=k} (P_i \cdot H_{ij}), \qquad (1)$$

where H_{ij} – the coefficient of correlation characteristics j and i requirements, P_i – the importance of the i-requirement for the consumer; k – the number of customer requirements; n – number of characteristics.

Characteristics are ranked by descending priority and relative value determined by the characteristics requiring clarification first. This model is the same for payments in the implementation of the method at all levels of QFD.

In the traditional approach the complexity and bulkiness of manual calculations combined with the absence of error accounting source data, resulting in low stability and reliability of the results [1, 3].

The approach to parametric identification of characteristics of complex technical systems (QFD level 1, QFD level 2) and process parameters (QFD level 3, QFD level 4), based on the matrix approach can significantly simplify the solution of practical problems of planning quality and improve the accuracy and robustness of the results to errors in the original data.

3 Structural analysis

Objectification of the design lies in the structuring of the "voice" of the consumer, structuring and defining the technical characteristics of the relationship between the "voice" of the consumer and the technical characteristics. Typically, a mathematical model of the relationship is a correlation matrix. Further analysis is given of the correlation matrix or in the matrix formulation - based on linear mathematical model. The subsequent task of parametric identification of characteristics of complex technical system using QFD method requires the use of more information and a special approach to the solution. The existing model of such information as the relationship characteristics (often negative), the error in the preparation of marketing and benchmarking information, difficulties realization of modernization (no technology) is considered in the "manual" mode that prevents the use of the existing model of QFD in full as a tool to support decision solutions.

The problem is identifying the quality of feedback and incorrect in the mathematical sense: the space of the original data is not static, for the same basic source of data, there are many solutions, etc. The incorrectness is also evident in the high variability of the requirements in time, the ambiguity of the unspoken expectations, etc.

Due to the nature of the task (reverse, incorrect) and the modern facilities of computer processing of the results of proposed solutions for sustainable use of the method of approximate solution of the matrix equation (2), allowing reasonably consider a wide range of different additional information [1, 3].

$$H \cdot \delta\Theta = \delta P, \qquad (2)$$

where $\delta\Theta$ – n-dimensional vector of relative deviations of parameters of state (evaluation of the target values of the product characteristics for level 1 of QFD), δP – k-dimensional vector of relative deviations signs state (the importance of the requirements and expectations of consumers (QFD level 1), H – matrix of size ($k \times n$) the coefficients of relationship requirements and characteristics (for QFD level 1), a linear mathematical model.

The specificity of ill-posed problems is the instability of their solution: small changes in the source data can cause large changes randomly making, that is, the error in the input data can play a crucial role. Solution of ill-posed problems is impossible without additional a priori information, which plays a key role.

It is proposed to use worked in science and engineering methods for solving ill-posed problems. Thus, by «identification» of generally understood as a set of methods for constructing mathematical models (mathematical description of the behavior) of the system or process. The problem of parametric identification is to estimate the unknown parameter vector per input and output signals [5–8].

4 Parametric analysis

To solve the practical problem of parametric identification of complex technical system performance target values of greatest interest are methods that allow resolving the ill-posed problem with a minimum of a priori information. One effective method for the approximate solution of such problems is the regularization method, which is based on the concept of a regularizing algorithm [8].

Due to the nature of the mathematical formulation of the problem of identification of quality and modern computer capabilities are encouraged to use sustainable method for the approximate solution of the matrix equation based on QFD [1, 3]. The method can reasonably be considered in addition to interconnection requirements and characteristics of additional information: the relative changes in state parameters (change the values of the product characteristics), the relative changes in the status indication (change of degree of compliance with the requirements and expectations of consumers) [1, 3].

Creating a sustainable method of identifying the mathematical model in the system design and production processes is an important task. This is primarily since the traditional identification methods (for example, using the least squares method OLS) often do not provide reliable results under practical conditions of use.

It is known that the accuracy of the OLS estimator is characterized by a covariance matrix $(H^T PH)^{-1}$. Let

$$A = (H^T PH) \quad (3)$$

It seems appropriate to explore parametric characteristics of the matrix to allow further study of the stability (robustness) the resulting estimates.

The following harmonized standards are commonly used:

$$\|A\|_1 = \max_i(\sum_j |a_{ij}|),\ \|A\|_2 = \max_j(\sum_i |a_{ij}|),$$
$$\|A\|_3 = \sqrt{\max_i \lambda^i_{AA^T}}\ . \quad (4)$$

where $\lambda^i_{AA^T}$ – the eigenvalues of the matrix AA^T.

An important characteristic parameter matrix A is the number of conditionality:

$$\rho(A) = \max_i \lambda^i / \min_i \lambda^i \quad (5)$$

where λ^i — eigenvalues A.

The study was conducted on the model of "turboshaft aircraft engine with free turbine TV 7-117A" complex technical system. It is based on a linear mathematical model (LMM) containing the factors of influence on the maximum continuous operation.

Abstract norm of the inverse matrix of normal equations and the condition number of the inverse matrix of normal equations during statistical tests (the first 20 trials). The experiment was conducted by applying to the calculated values of the linear mathematical model of random variables distributed by the normal distribution in the range of ± 20%. This variability LMM coefficients determined linearization errors, and the uncertainty of the initial state.

Results on the change of a matrix normal equations ρ depending on the mathematical model of random errors.

These results show the values of the norm of the inverse matrix of normal equations and the condition number of the inverse matrix of normal equations in the statistical tests (the first 20 trials).

Statistical data obtained after the processing results are presented in Table 1.

Similarly, research conducted for a bypass engine. It can be concluded that the picture quality in the test result is the same. However, from a quantitative point of view, the value of the sample variance in TV 7-117A study have smaller values in almost all similar cases. Ego can be explained by the fact that the original version of LMM TV 7-117A has a matrix of normal equations, not as bad as the original version due to bypass engine. In addition, the criteria of a matrix of normal equations for the LMM with superimposed random errors for TV 7-117A perform better on average than TV 7-117A. Ego again confirms the conclusion about the impact on the error status parameter estimates matrix structure of normal equations, in particular, its condition number.

Table 1. Statistical characteristics of the rules of the inverse matrix of normal theater TV 7-117A equations for modeling the original matrix H

Statistical characteristics	For the inverse matrix of the matrix norm $\|A^{-1}\|$	For the condition number ρ
Average	0,896	11800
The standard deviation	0,322	4148,05
min	0,439	5500
max	1,688	21500

5 Discussion

Using matrix approach to the implementation of QFD allows for structural and parametric analysis of the quality of complex technical systems in conditions of uncertainty and poor conditioning of the problem and be the basis of robust design. The quality of robust design proposed to estimate using the inverse matrix and the number of conditionality rules.

References

1. A.Ya. Dmitriev, T.A. Mitroshkina, Ontology of designing, **3**(17), 313-327 (2014) [In Rus]
2. Y. Akao, G.H. Mazur, International Journal of Quality & Reliability Management, **20**(1), 20-35 (2003)
3. A. Dmitriev, T. Mitroshkina. ITM Web of Conferencesm, **6**, 02005 (2016)
4. R.N. Kackar, A.C. Shoemaker, AT&T Technical Journal **65**(2), 39-50 (1986)
5. K.J. Astrom, P. Eykhoff. Automatica, **7**, 123-162, (1971)
6. L. Ljung. System identification.Theory for the User, (PTR Prentice Hall, 1999)
7. E. Pluzhnik, E. Nikulchev, Virtual Laboratories in Cloud Infrastructure of Educational Institutions, 2014 2nd International Conference on Emission Electronics (ICEE), 67-69 (2014)
8. S.K. Bochkarev, A.Y. Dmitriev, V.V. Kulagin et al. Izvestiya Vysshikh Uchebnykh Zavedenii Aviatsionaya Tekhnika, **2**, 68-70 (1993) [In Rus]

ITM Web of Conferences **10**, 01002 (2017) DOI: 10.1051/itmconf/20171001002
2017 Seminar on Systems Analysis

Automated Approach for Product Sizes Measurement on the Conveyor Belt

Vladimir V. Belov[1] and *Aleksandr K.* Lopatin[1,*]

[1] Ryazan state radio engineering University, 390005 Ryazan, Russia

Abstract. The present paper explores the concept of digital data processing algorithms' mix and outlines an approach to disclosing the relation as defined in the mix mentioned. Alongside with that we offer certain criteria for the determination of equivalence classes for the present mix in the context of automated item measurement on the conveyor belt problem.

1 Introduction

A large number of problems which arise in complex technical vision studies, as well as in optical checking scenarios etc., employ various digital image processing algorithms. The option of solving particular problems using a variety of methods can be viewed as an additional complication. Thus, the solution of the major problem is complicated by the lack of a formalized approach to the choice particular tasks' solution methods. For example, the researcher has to take great pains with a task of image processing, particularly filtering and segmentation, when it comes to creating a pattern recognition system (PRS). Ironically, fairly well developed and comprehensive toolkits, actually complicate this task. This in turn, results in either choosing the more or less 'fancy' algorithm as your number one option, or, developing a fairly complex algorithm for a task where a much simple method could suffice.

In the end, it brings us to the problem of creating an automated (and in some scenarios even automatic) image processing algorithms' development, fit for the purpose of static and motion image processing in a predefined scenario. In this paper we shall limit ourselves to the study of the problem of automated item measurement on the conveyor belt.

Suppose there is a certain structure which contains algorithms which cover 'most' methods of preliminary image processing, i.e. filtering, segmentation and morphological processing. For the sake of argument, we shall call this structure *ImPr* (acronym for Image Processing).

From hence arises a reasonable question: does this structure qualify as a set?

The answer to this question is not obvious, for reasons that historically have originated from the "naive" set theory, which allowed to define a group of any item(s) as a set only on the basis of some property, which these items possess. This approach had eventually led to a crisis in the foundations of mathematics.

So, what are the chances the use of the term 'set' will not result in Russell's Paradox [1] or, for that matter, any other paradox? Naturally, paradoxes are quite likely to occur if we stick to the 'naive' interpretation of the set concept. We shall use the following axiom: $\exists Y \forall x (x \in Y \Leftrightarrow \Phi(x))$. I.e. for the condition $\Phi(x)$ exists a set Y, comprised of the same x, which obey $\Phi(x)$.

Let us take as condition $\Phi(x)$: $x \notin \{x\}$.

Then by the axiom of separation there exists the Y set: $\forall x (x \in Y \Leftrightarrow x \notin \{x\})$.

And if it is possible for any x then, particularly, it is also true for $x=y$, i.e., the following is possible $y \in y \Leftrightarrow y \notin y$. This results in a contradiction, which shows that applying 'naive' theory of sets to all existing items is not feasible.

Moreover, there are other paradoxes which do not allow to call a collection of items that satisfy a certain condition a set.

From the mid-20th century onwards the set is defined as a model satisfying the axioms of Zermelo–Fraenkel set theory (ZFC)

We will now show that the structure consisting digital image processing algorithms is the set and give a formal description of this set, as well as some examples of relations as defined therein.

2 Check of system of axioms of Zermelo-Fraenkel

Let us make sure that the mentioned structure is a set and that it satisfies the rules of Zermelo–Fraenkel axiomatic system [1-3], and is a complete set. In all our subsequent arguments we shall assume that a, b, c are sets, the elements of which can also be sets.

1. Dimensions axiom. The set is defined by the elements: the sets consisting of the same elements are equal.

$$\forall x \forall y (\forall z (z \in x \Leftrightarrow z \in y) \Leftrightarrow x = y) \quad (1)$$

Let's define a set of algorithms of *ImPr* as the set containing image enhancement algorithms (the averaging filter, the median filter, Gauss's filter, etc.), algo-

* Corresponding author: ak_lopatin@mail.ru

rithms of selection of circuits, algorithms of morphological processing of images [4-8,9].

2. Axiom of an empty set. There is an empty set e without unit element:

$$\exists e \forall a(a \notin e) \tag{2}$$

3. Couple axiom. It is possible to construct couple of two sets

$$\forall x \forall y \exists z(z = \{x, y\}) \tag{3}$$

4. Excision axiom.

$$\forall x \exists b \forall y(y \in b \Leftrightarrow (y \in x) \wedge \Phi(x)) \tag{4}$$

This axiom is equivalent to an axiom of selection of the "naive" theory of sets: from each set it is possible to select at least one subset y, having stated judgment Φ about each element of this set of x. Formally our structure, allows to select algorithms of frequency filtering of the image, for example.

5. Substitution axiom. $\Phi(x,y)$ – the property that for every x, there exists no more than one y, that satisfies $\Phi(x,y)$. Then for every set X could be found set

$$Y = \{y : \exists x \in X : \Phi(x, y)\} \tag{5}$$

6. Foundation axiom:

$$\forall x(x = \varnothing \vee \exists y(y \in x \wedge y \cap x = \varnothing)) \tag{6}$$

In each non empty set there will be an element which is not crossed with an initial set. In other words, in a set there has to be the "minimum" element which intersection with a set is empty. There is no infinite sequence of the enclosed sets: each chain of sets $A_1 \supset A_2 \supset \ldots \supset A_n$ of course. Really, all specified structure members owing to the nature assume classification that means existence of the hierarchy allowing to select the final chain of subsets which is not including all set.

7. Axiom of infinity. There are infinite sets, such sets A, that cardinality of the A is equal to the cardinality $A \cup \{A\}$. Or using language of quantifiers: $\exists \omega(\varnothing \in \omega \wedge \forall x(x \in \omega \rightarrow x \cup \{x\}) \in \omega)$. Our structure, owing to its nature, is potentially infinite that does not contradict this axiom.

8. Choice axiom.

$$\begin{aligned} &\forall x : x \neq \varnothing \wedge \forall y(y \in x \rightarrow y \neq \varnothing) \wedge \\ &\forall y_1 \forall y_2(y_1 \neq y_2 \wedge \{y_1, y_2\} \subseteq x \rightarrow y_1 \cap y_2 \neq \varnothing) \rightarrow \\ &\exists d \forall y(y \in x \rightarrow \exists z(y \cap d = \{z\})) \end{aligned} \tag{7}$$

For any set of in pairs not crossed non-blank sets there is, at least, one set which contains precisely one element, the general with each of non-empty sets.

3 Characteristics of Sets

Since the given set *ImPr* is a naturally built set, the following characteristic of the set becomes evident:

ImPr – is a non-empty infinite enumerable set of elements required for the solution of a given image processing task.

In accordance with the nature of the set's elements, it is deemed reasonable to discriminate the following subsets:

- *AF* – image filtering algorithms' subset;
- *AS* – image segmentation algorithms' subset;
- *AMP* – morphological image processing algorithms;
- *AR* – description and representation algorithms;
- *APR* –recognition algorithms.

We can safely call any of the subsets an infinite one, as a clearly formulated proof of image processing algorithms' finiteness is non-existent.

The binary operation of algorithms' composition if defined in the original set $ImPr \times ImPr \rightarrow ImPr$. The result of the composition of the two image processing algorithms is the image processing algorithm. In the generic case this operation is neither that of association or of commutation.

The complete cycle of image x digital processing can be formally described as follows:

Let $f_1 \in AF, f_2 \in AS, f_3 \in AMP, f_4 \in AR, f_5 \in APR$.

Then the complete cycle can be represented as: $(f_1 \circ f_2 \circ f_3 \circ f_4 \circ f_5)(x)$

4 Relationships, defined in the *ImPr* set

In order to form a chain of algorithms, let us define some relations for the *ImPr* set.

1) Algorithms f and g are qualitatively equivalent if for the same set of input parameters there exist the same output parameters. Analogous to that we can introduce the concept of performance equivalence (a key feature - the number of processor cycles), by complexity.

2) Algorithms f and g are strictly equivalent if they are qualitatively equivalent, as well as equivalent in complexity and speed.

There is a clear relation between quality and strict equivalence. This clarity is manifested in complete consistency in the algorithms' output: $Result(f) = Result(g)$. In particular, for the algorithms, the execution of which results in images, quality and strict equivalence means full output image congruence, and, consequently, correlation coefficient equaling one: $r_{f,g} = 1$, where

$$r_{f,g} = \frac{\sum_{x=0}^{M-1}\sum_{y=0}^{N-1}\left[f(x,y)-\bar{f}\right]\left[g(x,y)-\bar{g}\right]}{\sqrt{\sum_{x=0}^{M-1}\sum_{y=0}^{N-1}\left[f(x,y)-\bar{f}\right]^2 \sum_{x=0}^{M-1}\sum_{y=0}^{N-1}\left[g(x,y)-\bar{g}\right]^2}}, \tag{8}$$

$f(x,y), g(x,y)$ $x = \overline{0; M-1}$; $y = \overline{0, N-1}$ – brightness values in the pixels with coordinates x, y of output images generated by algorithms f, g, respectively; $\bar{f}, \bar{g}$ – mean pixel brightness value for images, generated algorithms f, g, respectively; M, N – number of pixels in the images vertically and horizontally, respectively.

Often it is quite sensible to exploit fuzzy similarity relations of alternative algorithms when conducting a search for an adequate image processing algorithm. Let us define one of the fuzzy similarity types 'a visual similarity' and define it as follows: algorithms f and g are visually similar, if the correlation coefficient between the output images of these algorithms is larger than λ: $r_{f,g} > \lambda$. λ value may vary depending on the application. It is possible to set a 'default value': $\lambda = 0{,}95$.

DOI: 10.1051/itmconf/20171001002

Note that the ratio of visual similarity is reflexive, since $r_{f,g} = 1$ and symmetrical, as $r_{f,g} = r_{g,f}$ and therefore, $(r_{f,g} > \lambda) \rightarrow (r_{g,f} > \lambda)$. At the same time the relation of visual similarity is not transitive, as the validity of the predicate $(r_{f,g} > \lambda) \wedge (r_{g,h} > \lambda)$ does not guarantee the validity of $r_{f,h} > \lambda$ in the generic case.

Let us define an additional relation of visual similarity to overcome the intransitivity mentioned. We shall call this relation a transitive one: algorithms f_i and f_j are connected by the relation of transitive visual similarity, if the following relation is true: $r^*_{f_i,f_j} > \lambda$, where

$$r^*_{f_i,f_j} = \max(r_{f_i,f_j}, \min_{l \in L}(\min_{(k_1,k_2,...,k_l) \in D}(\max(r_{i,k_1}, r_{k_1,k_2}, ..., r_{k_l,j}))))$$

m – the number of alternative algorithms for the solution of a certain task; $L = \{1, 2, ..., m-2\}$ a set of integers from 1 to $m-2$; $D = Disp(V, l)$ – a set of placements l of integers from the set V; $V = \{1, 2, ..., m\} \setminus \{i, j\}$ – a set of integers from 1 to m, excluding numbers i and j.

The present relations allow to create mixes (compositions) of algorithms which can be used to solve a variety of practical tasks: from improving image quality to pattern recognition and the task similar to it, i.e. parts geometry measurement.

5 The example of the subsets' structure of for the formation of the digital image processing algorithms' mixes

We restrict ourselves to the minimum composition of the sets of algorithms that allows to demonstrate the ideas outlined above

Consider the problem of preprocessing the image details for the subsequent measurement of product dimensions. Preprocessing process consists in performing sequential filtering and edge detecting.

The compassion of each subset is given in Table 1.

Table 1. Composition of the subsets for the choice of mixes

AS	Canny operator [4], Sobel operator, Prewitt operator [5], Roberts operator [7,9]
AF	averaging filter[9], Gaussian filter [6]

To solve a particular problem we have to determine the composition of the subsets of *ImPr* set and then having selected a particular criterion or criteria, choose the set of mixes for subsequent testing.

In this case by defining image preprocessing algorithm, we will create all possible mixes (with the total number being 8) and evaluate the quality of the outcome for a particular image by enumerating the possibilities.

To assess the quality necessary:

1. Determine the equivalence classes of asymptotic complexity among algorithms.
2. Identify visually similar algorithms.
3. Using the results of paragraphs 1 and 2 to make a judgment about the choice of the optimum in terms of the ratio of "quality of impact / performance" combination of algorithms

6 Algorithms' Mixes Test

The results of the tests conducted in the Matlab environment for the algorithms mentioned are shown in Fig. 1. For demonstration purposes we employed the 'photocopy effect' available in Microsoft Word package.

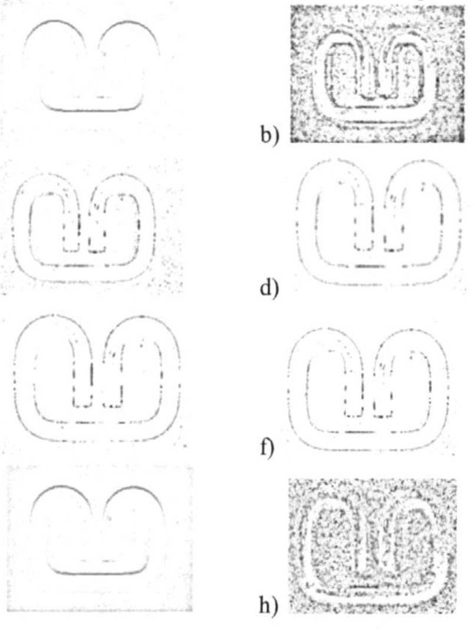

Fig. 1. Filter combinations: A) Gauss and Sobel operator, B) Gauss and Canny, C) Gauss and Prewitt, D) averaging and Prewitt. E) averaging and Roberts F) averaging and Sobel G) Gauss and Roberts H) averaging and Canny

The results of evaluation time of the mixtures are shown in Fig. 2. In addition to the choice of pre-image processing method, this chart allows, for example, to draw a conclusion about equivalence by complexity of algorithms of the Sobel operator and the Prewitt operator [5]. The diagram illustrates that multiple launches show the same time processing the image data operators. In addition, the relative complexity by equivalence of these operators also is result of similarity of masks of these operators [5, 8, 9], which are differs only by constants.

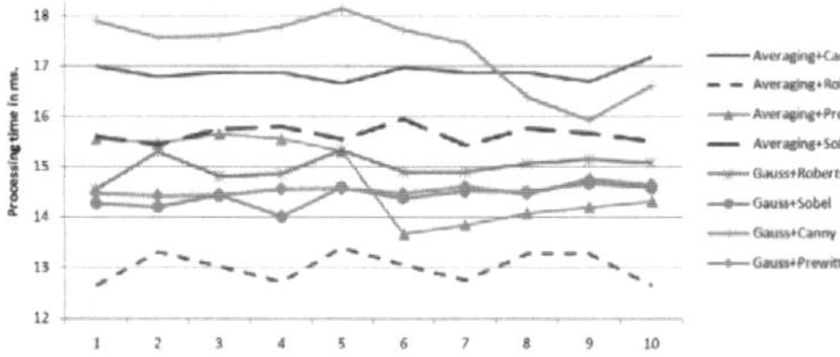

Fig. 2. The result of the correlation analysis of the Gauss's filter and the averaging filter for the different radius of filtering.

The following chart shows that the relations given can be applied for the Gauss and averaging filters. By

DOI: 10.1051/itmconf/20171001002

calculating the correlation for various sets of input parameters (filter window radius) we get various combinations of parameters which create a visual effect similar to that of the filter. It allows us to get a different set of parameters that provide the visual similarity of the results of applying filters.

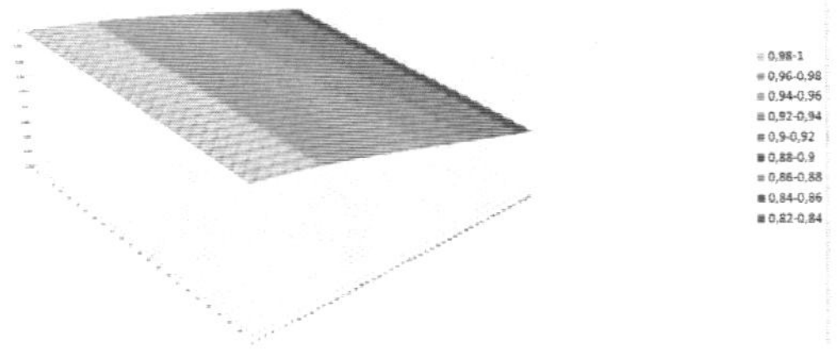

Fig. 3. The results of correlation analysis of Gaussian filter and averaging filter for the filtration of various radius

Thus, we obtain similar results using filters having different computational complexity. As a result, there is ability of optimization, that consists in the selection of algorithms and their parameters, the most appropriate specific conditions. And only if was proved that chosed mix of algorithms is optimum in some meaning (for example in terms of performance) we have reason to believe that the task of the image preprocessing solved.

7 Conclusions

The key findings of this paper are the following:
1. It has been established that there exists a formal set of digital image processing algorithms;
2. The relations in the set of digital image processing algorithms have been defined;
3. An approach to algorithm's mixes for digital data processing in the scenario of automated item geometry measurement on the conveyor belt has been proposed.
4. A mechanism of visual similarity classes search in real-life applications has been shown. As the result of the practical uses of this mechanism it was shown:

– In the context of a given task even the algorithms which are considered to be among the best (Gauss filter and Canny operator [6, 9]) do not guarantee a consistently good outcome.
– Experimental data shows that the following three mixes can be deemed the most effective: averaging filter and Sobel operator, averaging filter and Prewitt operator and averaging filter and Roberts operator.
– By expert opinion the most roubust algorithm mix for the given scenario was the one on averaging filter and Sobel operator. However, in terms of speed this mix loses out to that of averaging filter with Roberts operator [9].

References

1. I. V. Yaschenko, *Paradoksy teorii množestv* (Moskow, 2002)
2. http://lib.usue.ru/resource/free/10/MelnikovAlgebra3/00SetC.pdf
3. A.V. Koganov, Computer Research and Modeling, **1**(4), 367–380 (2009)
4. Canny J., IEEE Trans. PAMI, **8**, 679–698 (1986)
5. J.M.S. Prewitt, B. Lipkin, A. Rosenfeld, *Object enhancement and extraction in Picture Processing and Psychopictorics* (New York, Academic Press, 1970)
6. L.A. Iverson, S.W. Zucker IEEE Trans. PAMI, **17**, 982–996 (1995)
7. L.G. Roberts, *Machine Perception Of Three-Dimensional Solids* (MIT, 1965).
8. I. Sobel, G. Feldman A 3x3 Isotropic Gradient Operator for Image Processing (2015).
9. R. Gonsales, R. Vuds, *Cifrovaya obrabotka izobrazhenij* (Tehnosfera, 2012)

Aircraft Group Coordinated Flight Route Optimization Using Branch-and-Bound Procedure in Resolving the Problem of Environmental Monitoring

Georgy Lebedev[1], *Vladimir* Goncharenko[1], *Denis* Mikhaylin[1], and *Alena* Rumakina[1, *]

[1] Moscow Aviation Institute (National Research University), 125080 Moscow, Russia

Abstract. The solution of a travelling salesman problem (TSP) for the case of two-dimensional flight routing is suggested. Unlike the case of one-dimensional routing, this solution implies the formation of two initial matrices of the distances between the points for two unlinked routes. The routes are analyzed alternately with the coordinated selection of the minimal length element in each of them. Examples of calculations demonstrating the proposed approach efficiency are provided indicating the reduction of overflights by more than two times.

1 Introduction

At the current time, more attention is paid to increasing efficiency of in-flight group action for various operation and control tasks. These include services for a given set of monitoring land points. The problem is solved by group of aircrafts (*AC*), which routes should be predetermined based on the criteria of minimum total length.

Many works are devoted to the optimal one-dimensional routing problem [1–3], among which the branch-and-bound algorithm plays a specific role [4]. Group flight action penalties should be taken into consideration when crossing one-dimensional flight routes [5]. Otherwise, predictable flight control is required to ensure mutual safe approach. In this article the problem of routing of two AC coordinated flight is considered [6].

2 Statement of the problem

1. The problem of two horizontal flight open loop routes for two flying vehicles with common preset initial and finite points A and B, respectively, is solved. (Example in figure 1).

2. The set of fixed monitoring points is given. Coordinates of their location and total number (number $n = 5$ in figure 1). It allows to form the parent matrix M_0 of distances between them, the beginning 0 and the end $(n + 1)$ according to branch-and-bound procedure. In table 1 this matrix has the following form.

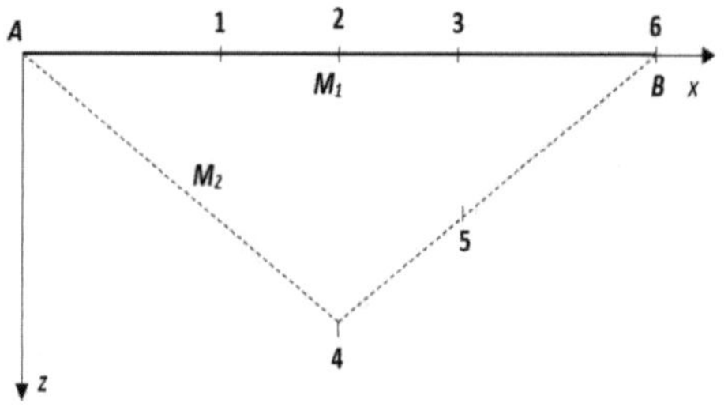

Fig. 1. Location of monitoring land points with the indication of calculated routes M_1 and M_2

Table 1. Initial matrix M_0.

	0	1	2	3	4	5	6
0	*X*	5	8	11	9,4	11,5	*X*
1	*X*	*X*	3	6	5,8	6,7	11
2	*X*	3	*X*	3	5	4,3	8
3	*X*	6	3	*X*	5,8	3	5
4	*X*	5,8	5	5,8	*X*	3,5	9,4
5	*X*	6,7	4,3	3	3,5	*X*	5,8
6	*X*	*X*	*X*	*X*	*X*	*X*	*X*

This matrix contains forbidden elements as it is accepted for the well-known branch-and-bound [4], namely:

– matrix diagonal elements, forbidding any point penetration once more right after its servicing;

* Corresponding author: kaf301@mai.ru

DOI: 10.1051/itmconf/20171001003

- elements in the first column forbidding return to the initial point for released routes;
- matrix low line elements forbidding any further movement after final point ($n + 1$) penetration;
- the element ($0,n+1$) forbidding the movement straightway form the initial point to the final.

1. Each point should be serviced once and by a single *AC*.
2. Formation of two flight paths so that their total length would be minimal is required.

3 Numerical solution of two-dimensional routing problem by branch-and-bound modified procedure

The solution of the problem is based on the well-known manipulations accepted for integer-valued branch-and-bound procedure for one-dimensional routing. New necessary operations have been added. As in the well-known procedure, the planning should consist of multiple steps of calculation (k=1,..., n+1). The difference is that instead of one matrix distance M_0, two matrices M_1 and M_2 are analyzed. One matrix per each route. The initial state of these matrices is equal to the state of the parent matrix (as shown below). However, attaching a new column to each of them to indicate coordinates x and z of the so-called "center of attraction" of both formed routes with numbers ($n + 2$) and ($n + 3$).

To explain the centers of attraction of the routes in the figure 2. the approximation of trajectories routes M_1 and M_2 is shown. It consists of two rectangular segments emanating from the origin and the end of the routes to the centers.

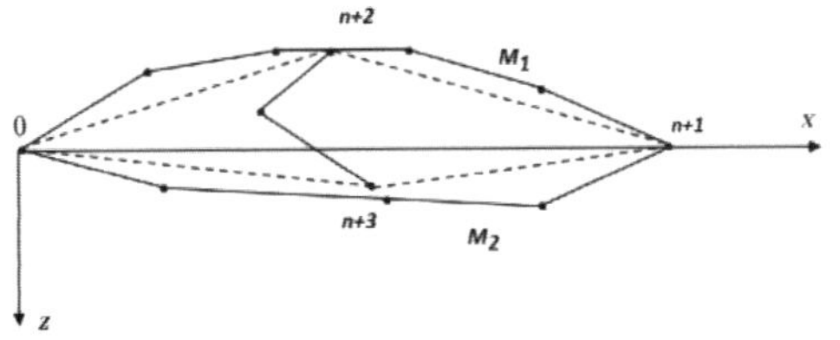

Fig. 2. Triangular approximation of the routes M_1 and M_2

We define this approximation as a triangular model. Its elements are dotted in rectangular segments.

At each computing step, we suggest to perform the following operations. Accentuating the new ones among them:

- alternately select one of the two matrices for the analysis. Find the element of the minimum length. This element should be included in the plan, as it is accepted for branch-and-bound;
- analyze the element obtained (i,j) in "nearness" to the first or the second route;
- in the selected one of the two matrices delete as usual the i row and the j row. Insert forbidding character into (j,i) element. After attachment of the element (i, j) you should additionally refine z and x coordinates of the corresponding route center of attraction. Insert them into the right column of the selected matrix.
- two rows (i, j) and two columns (i, j) should be deleted in the other matrix to exclude their servicing.

As a result, the dimension of both matrices can be reduced. After repetitions the number of updates of each matrix may be unequal. But the sum of these numbers at the end of calculation is equal to (n+1). In the end, the proposed approach found answers to two questions:

- which of the two matrices have to be analyzed for the elements of short length;
- which of the two matrices should contain it.

According to the principle of the equality the elements of both matrices are analyzed alternately. But then the joining element belongs to the route to which it is "nearer," no matter what matrix was selected.

At the first stage of calculating the proximity measure is determined by the difference between distances $m1$ and $m2$ from element (i,j) to the centers of attraction of (n+2) (n+3) of the two routes, as shown in figure 2. The result of these calculations makes it possible to reduce the order of both matrices. This process would be repeated until both matrices move to a single element after (n+1). In addition z and x coordinates of the centers of attraction would be separated from each other by the distance sufficient for the second stage of computations.

At the second stage of computations, additional criteria of proximity of each point to selected routes are implemented. They allow to form the joint list of two-dimensional routing algorithm operations.

4 Examples of the coordinated planning of the two routes close to each other

The first example shows the effect of disposal of jumpers and the usage of triangular model of the routes trajectories (figure 3).

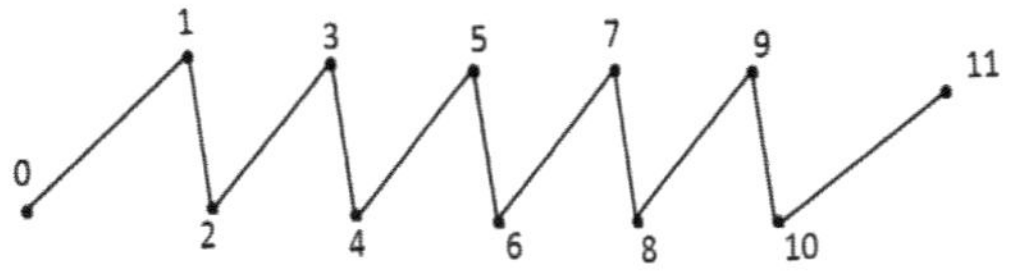

Fig. 3. An example of the trajectory in one-dimensional routing

Accordingly, a plan for a two-dimensional routing is shown in the figure 4. Flight time of one of the aircraft was reduced more than twice by eliminating "jumpers" between the two routes.

The figure 4 shows also the final allocation of the centers of attraction of the triangular flight trajectory approximation model (dashed lines № 12 and № 13).

The second example – environmental monitoring of 30 cities (a total length of 1,500 km) in the Moscow region using two aircraft. The task execution time was reduced by one and a half while during such flight.

 DOI: 10.1051/itmconf/20171001003

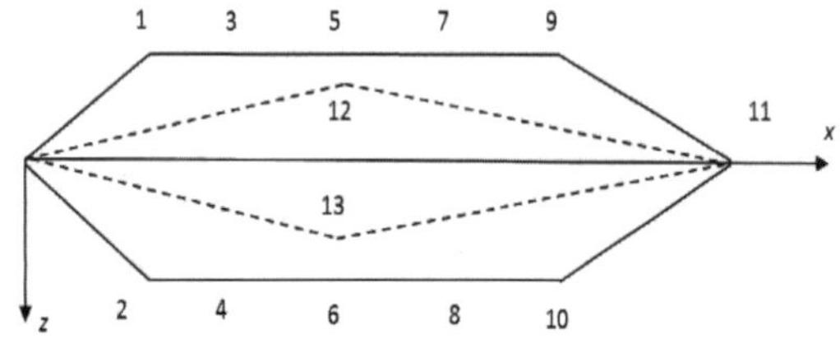

Fig. 4. The trajectories of two flight routes at the second calculation step

The two-stage calculation can be used for the task of coordinated selection of different flight route numbers (*N*). In that case, *N* matrices are replicated from the original matrix of distances. Then each of new matrices is to be analyzed alternately.

At each step of calculation a single element with minimum length is selected (*i,j*). It is assigned to one of the routes by the first criterion of proximity. Whereby new coordinates of its center of attraction are calculated, lines *i*, *j* and columns *i*, *j* in the other matrices are excluded. As a result, the trajectory centers of attraction will be uneven. It is sufficient to continue the solution of the problem.

5 Conclusions

As a tool for training the neural network, the method of solving the task of two-dimensional routing is proposed. This method is based on the initial matrix of distances between points of the few matrices for each open-loop route formation. The matrices are analyzed alternately with coordinated selection of the minimum length element in each of them.

It is shown that in comparison to one-dimensional routing, neural network two-dimensional route planning allows to reduce the overflight time in 1.5-2 times.

References

1. G.N. Lebedev etc., New technology. Mechatronics, automation, control, **11**, 60-65 (2009)
2. G.N. Lebedev, A.V. Efimov, Proceedings of Samara state aerospace University, **1**, 63-70 (2012)
3. G.N. Lebedev, L.A. Mirzoyan, New technologies. Mechatronics, automation, control, **12**, 24-28 (2011)
4. L.T. Kuzin, *Foundations of cybernetics* (Moscow, Energy, 1973)
5. G.N. Lebedev, Zaw Min Taik. New technologies. Mechatronics, automation, control, **5**, 61-68 (2014)
6. G.N. Lebedev, V.I. Goncharenko, A.V. Rumakina, New technologies. Mechatronics, automation, control, **17**(11), 783–791 (2016)

DOI: 10.1051/itmconf/20171001004

Methods of Computing Thrust Vector Coordinates for Aircrafts Equipped With Thrust Vector Control

Alexey V. Kanyshev[1], *Oleg N.* Korsun[2] and *Alexander V.* Stulovskii[2,*]

[1]Valery Chkalov State Flight Testing Center, Akhtubinsk, Russia
[2]FGUP "GosNIIAS", Moscow, Russia

Abstract. The paper proposes the formulas for simulation the forces and torques generated by thrust vectoring. The formulas are drawn using the polar coordinate system as well as the Rodrigues' vector rotation formula. The proposed results are confirmed by application to the processing of the aircraft flight test data.

1 Introduction

Nowadays thrust vectored aircrafts play an important role in aviation. Therefore, the precise mathematical models for simulation are necessary. The paper deals with the problem of simulation the forces and torques of the aircraft generated by the rotation of the thrust vector. The paper presents mathematical formulas for three-dimensional projections of forces and torques drawn through the evident geometrical considerations.

The most part of publications concerning this problem consider the approaches of numerical aerodynamics, which are not suitable for solving the dynamics of flight problems [1–3]. This paper proposes the relatively simple formulas, which meet the requirements of real-time simulation of the aircraft motion. The similar approach has been used in [4] to increase the accuracy of simulating the orientation angles of the aircraft.

Let us notice that in this paper we consider the thrust as a geometric sum of vectors of input and output impulses. The paper focuses on calculating the forces and torques created by the rotation of output impulse vector because the simulation of the effect of input impulse is similar for thrust vectoring aircrafts and other types of the aircraft.

2 The model of forces and torques generated by the thrust vector rotation

The methods for describing a direction toward a point in three-dimensional space are well known. Let us choose the polar coordinate system shown in figure 1. In this case φ is an angle between vector and horizontal plane, whereas ψ is an angle between projection of vector on horizontal plane and a coordinate axis. Using this method in regards to aircraft thrust vector we can determine thrust projections on aircraft principal axes as:

$$P_x = P\cos\varphi\cos\psi;$$
$$P_y = P\sin\varphi;$$
$$P_z = P\cos\varphi\sin\psi.$$

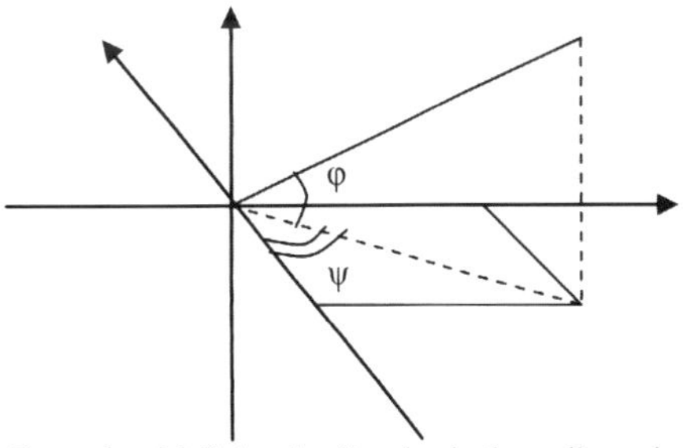

Fig. 1. Example of defining the direction in three-dimensional space by two orientation angles.

This simple model enables to describe engine thrust vector rotation assuming that nozzles are capable of turning in vertical and horizontal planes independently.

In practice, engine thrust nozzles are often capable of rotating only in single plane. This plane may be positioned at some angle to vertical plane, enabling generation of moments about all three axes simultaneously. Let us draw the mathematic expressions for torques and forces.

2.1 Vector rotating in a plane

Let us assume that plane of thrust vector rotation is positioned at known angle χ relative to vertical plane. At the same time η is the angle of rotation in this plane. The zero value of this angle $\eta = 0$ corresponds to vector lying in horizontal plane. It is also assumed that thrust vector crosses the center of nozzle's section. Let us draw axis parallel to aircraft's longitudinal axis, which comes through the center of nozzle's section in its zero position.

* Corresponding author: avstlv2@gmail.com

DOI: 10.1051/itmconf/20171001004

Let us choose two points A and O on this axis. Point O is a point of nozzle rotation, point A is positioned in the center of nozzle's section. Next, draw vertical plane, which includes line AO. Let us also draw rotation plane, which includes line AO and is positioned at angle χ to vertical plane (figure 2).

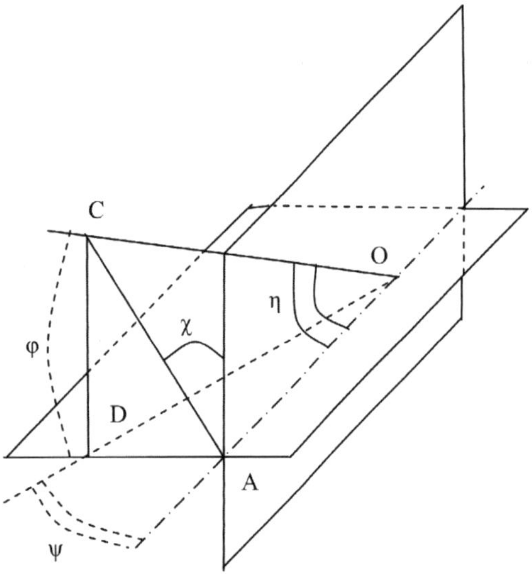

Fig. 2. Scheme connecting couples of angles χ , η и ψ , φ .

Let us assume that nozzle is turned by an angle η. Then the thrust vector would pass through the point C. From the point C let us draw perpendicular CD to horizontal plane.

Let us determine relations between couples of angles ψ, φ and η, χ. First, we would derive expression for angle ψ. Since the triangles AOD and AOC are the right triangles, the next expressions are true:

$$AC = AO tg\eta,$$
$$AD = AO tg\psi.$$

Triangle ADC is also a right triangle, therefore

$$\sin\chi = AD / AC.$$

The expression for the angle ψ could be derived from the following equation

$$tg\psi = tg\eta \sin\chi.$$

Second, we derive expression for the angle φ. Since the triangles CDO and AOC are the right triangles, the next formulas are true:

$$AC = OC \sin\eta,$$
$$CD = OC \sin\varphi.$$

The triangle ADC is also the right triangle, therefore

$$\cos\chi = CD / AC.$$

Value of φ can be obtained from following equation:

$$\sin\varphi = \sin\eta \cos\chi.$$

Finally, the formulas for values of angles ψ, φ in terms of angles χ, η are

$$\psi = arctg(tg\eta \sin\chi),$$
$$\varphi = \arcsin(\sin\eta \cos\chi).$$

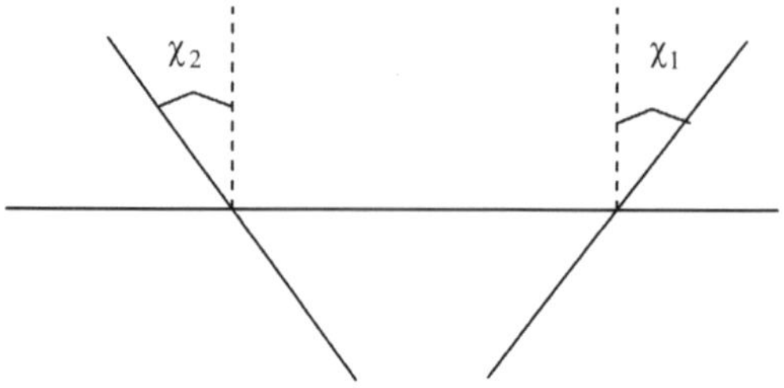

Fig. 3. Schematic picture of engine nozzle rotation planes viewed from the aircraft's tail.

Let us further consider projections of engine thrust vector on aircraft principal axes. Let us determine the signs for nozzles deviations in the same way as the signs of deviations of other control surfaces of the aircraft.

According to this rule, angle χ is positive for right engine ($\chi_1 > 0$) and negative for left engine ($\chi_2 > 0$) (figure 3). Angle η is positive when nozzle goes down and negative when nozzle goes up.

Let us assume that both nozzles are turned upwards. According to above formulas for angles ψ, φ we can easily determine the signs of thrust projections. Actually, in this case angle φ is negative for both engines while ψ is negative for right engine and positive for left one. Therefore, both engines will generate positive projections of engine thrust on longitudinal axis and negative projections on normal axis. Projections on lateral axis will have different signs, "+" for left engine and "-" for right engine.

Then let us assume that both nozzles are turned downward. In this case angle φ is positive for both engines, and angle ψ is positive for right engine and negative for left one. Both engines generate positive projections of engine thrust on longitudinal and normal axes. Right engine generates positive projection and left engine generates negative projection on lateral axis.

Results described above correspond to engineering common sense, and confirm correctness of proposed formulas.

2.2 Arbitrary rotating vector

Above mentioned way of computing thrust vector projections requires nozzles to be parallel to aircraft's longitudinal axis in their initial state. In case of arbitrary initial direction of thrust vector first method is inapplicable. Therefore, we should consider other methods for description of rotation. One such method is known as Rodrigues' rotation formula describing rotation of vector about arbitrary unit vector, when both vectors have common initial point.

Let **v** be vector of engine thrust in nozzle's initial state. Let **e** be a unit vector about which **v** rotates and η - angle of rotation. Coordinates of these vectors should be given in body axis coordinate system. Then Rodrigues' formula is:

$$\mathbf{v}_{\mathbf{rot}} = (\mathbf{e}\cdot\mathbf{v})\mathbf{e} + |\mathbf{e}\times\mathbf{v}|(\mathbf{e}_1\cos\eta + \mathbf{e}_2\sin\eta),$$

where $\mathbf{v}_{\mathbf{rot}}$ is result of vector $\mathbf{v}$ rotation, $\mathbf{e}_1$ and $\mathbf{e}_2$ with $\mathbf{e}=\mathbf{e}_3$ constitute right-handed basis and are defined by formulas

$$\mathbf{e}_1 = \frac{\mathbf{e}\times(\mathbf{v}\times\mathbf{e})}{|\mathbf{e}\times\mathbf{v}|},$$

$$\mathbf{e}_2 = \frac{\mathbf{e}\times\mathbf{v}}{|\mathbf{e}\times\mathbf{v}|}.$$

In Rodrigues' formula first expression corresponds to part of vector $\mathbf{v}$ collinear with $\mathbf{e}$, whereas second is orthogonal to it. Opening the brackets, we obtain

$$\mathbf{v}_{\mathbf{rot}} = (\mathbf{e}\cdot\mathbf{v})\mathbf{e} + \mathbf{e}\times(\mathbf{v}\times\mathbf{e})\cos\eta + \mathbf{e}\times\mathbf{v}\sin\eta.$$

After using vector triple product formula

$$\mathbf{a}\times(\mathbf{b}\times\mathbf{c}) = \mathbf{b}(\mathbf{a}\cdot\mathbf{c}) - \mathbf{c}(\mathbf{a}\cdot\mathbf{b}),$$

we derive formula describing rotated vector:

$$\mathbf{v}_{\mathbf{rot}} = (\cos\eta)\mathbf{v} + (\sin\eta)\mathbf{e}\times\mathbf{v} + (1-\cos\eta)(\mathbf{e}\cdot\mathbf{v})\mathbf{e}.$$

We can obtain projections of thrust vector by multiplying rotated vector by value of thrust:

$$\mathbf{P} = \begin{pmatrix} P_x \\ P_y \\ P_z \end{pmatrix} = |\mathbf{P}|\cdot\mathbf{v}_{\mathbf{rot}}.$$

Component-wise this formula can be written:

$$P_x = |\mathbf{P}|\left(v_x\cos\eta + (e_y v_z - e_z v_y)\sin\eta + (1-\cos\eta)(\mathbf{e}\cdot\mathbf{v})e_x\right),$$
$$P_y = |\mathbf{P}|\left(v_y\cos\eta + (e_z v_x - e_x v_z)\sin\eta + (1-\cos\eta)(\mathbf{e}\cdot\mathbf{v})e_y\right),$$
$$P_z = |\mathbf{P}|\left(v_z\cos\eta + (e_x v_y - e_y v_x)\sin\eta + (1-\cos\eta)(\mathbf{e}\cdot\mathbf{v})e_z\right).$$

The next step is to count torque using classical expression:

$$\mathbf{M} = \mathbf{r}\times\mathbf{P}.$$

Component-wise torque can be written as:

$$M_x = y(P_{z1}+P_{z2}) - z_1P_{y1} - z_2P_{y2};$$
$$M_y = z_1P_{x1} + z_2P_{x2} - x(P_{z1}+P_{z2});$$
$$M_z = x(P_{y1}+P_{y2}) - y(P_{x1}+P_{x2}).$$

3 Example of proposed model application

As an example of applications of a presented model let us consider the problem of aircraft parameter identification. The accuracy of the identification is usually associated with the condition number of Fisher information matrix. This number in its turn depends on correlation between the flight signals involved into identification process. So the introduction of additional parameters – angles of nozzle deviation can easily upset this balance because of the strong correlation between nozzle deviations and other control surfaces' signals.

Let us consider a set aircraft flight data obtained through flight test experiment. Let us calculate the torques generated by the engine nozzle's rotation using the above formulas and the value of thrust determined through the engine gas-dynamic model. Further, let us assume these torques as known functions and subtract them out of the flight signals. Thus, we exclude the influence of thrust vectoring. It enables to use the traditional identification methods [5] to obtain aerodynamic coefficient's estimates

As an example let us determine the efficiency coefficients of aircraft control surfaces in lateral channel and estimate the control torque produced by flaperons. Let us also compare these estimates obtained from flight data with corresponding torques calculated through known bank of this aircraft aerodynamic parameters. Results of this comparison in flaperon channel are shown in figure 4. In this case, happily, we obtain high degree of coincidence between two independent sources, that is the parameter flight data identification and the bank of aerodynamic parameters, drawn from wind tunnel tests. It confirms the validity of proposed engine thrust rotation model.

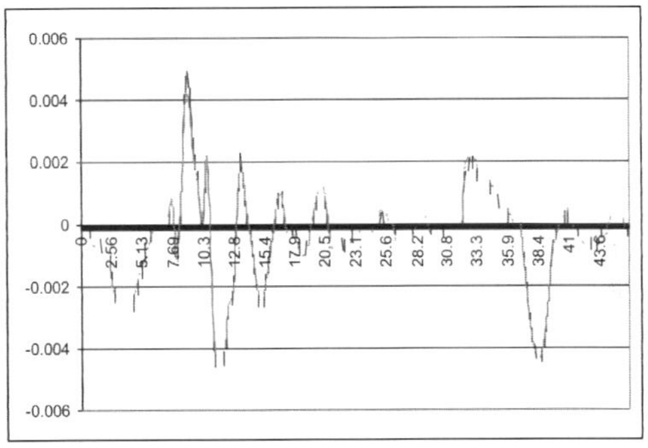

Fig. 4. Values of torque about normal axis generated by flaperons obtained from coefficients bank (blue line) and through parameter identification (violet line).

4 Conclusions

In this paper the algorithms to compute the forces and torques produced by engine thrust vector rotation are proposed. The paper also presents an example of testing this model validity using the results of aircraft parameter identification based on the flight data.

References

1. B. Gel-Or, Journal of thermal science, **7**, 1-6 (1998)
2. R. Deng, F. Kong, H.D. Kim, Journal of mechanical science and technology, **28**, 4979-4987 (2014)
3. L. Li, M. Hirota, K. Ouchi et al., Shock waves, **27**, 53-61 (2016)
4. Bulgakov, V.V., Korsun, O.N., Kulabukhov, V.S. et al., Journal of computer and systems sciences international, **55**, 150 (2016)
5. O.N. Korsun, B.K. Poplavsky, 29th Congress of the International Council of the Aeronautical Sciences, ICAS 2014; St. Petersburg, 2014-0210.

Development of a Computer Based Problem-Oriented Automated Remote Leakage Detection Control System

Alisa Kosach[1,*], and *Evgeny* Kovshov[1]

[1]JSC «NIKIMT-Atomstroy», Moscow, Russian Federation

Abstract. We explore the architecture and the concept of building an automation remote leakage detection system, in particular – a system for collection and processing of information. As practice shows, the development of those systems is a lengthy and time-consuming process involving management of heterogeneous hardware and analysis of large amounts of data. To implement the task, it is proposed to use the SCADA industry standard, universal communication protocols, and for data processing – open source database management systems and cluster analysis algorithms. A universal approach makes it possible to develop a scalable problem-oriented system. This approach takes into account the information received and processed during the leakage detection process.

1 Introduction

Leakage detection is a type of nondestructive testing performed to identify crosscutting defects. It is based on registration of passing of probe material through the defects. During the leakage detection process it is necessary to ensure safety of the staff, high sensitivity of the control process and integration of the control systems directly into the process line. Commonly instrumental leakage detection methods are used, they require complex equipment management and working with semi-structured data. Such remote leakage detection systems are unique, created especially to solve specific problems, and there is no single universal approach for their automation.

Today, there is a large number of tools and process automation systems, including the ones for non-destructive testing. The lack of a universal approach, diversity and often incompatibility of the equipment used, analysis of large amounts of unstructured data turn the development of an automated control system into a long and laborious task. As a result the systems of this kind often can be described as containing poorly aligned components, inefficient data processing algorithms and complex at maintaining performance. In addition, the requirements of a modern enterprise demand using of a single information space, so the measurement equipment and the remote leakage detection systems must be selected carefully according to the characteristics allowing being included in this space.

The target of the submitted work is to develop an automated computer based remote leakage detection control system.

To achieve this target the following research objectives should be addressed:

- development of the control system's architecture and the choice of the equipment for introduction it into a single information space;
- development of the data analysis system for processing the data obtained during the control process;
- development of a unified approach to the automation of remote leakage detection, including the one based on OPC servers and set of Modbus protocols.

2 Data Analysis Unit

Evaluation of the product is based on a comparison of the values of the flow test substance, penetrating through the defects, with the acceptance level, depending on the norm of tightness (Fig. 1). If the acceptance level is exceeded the product is considered to be leaking. Before the evaluation process it is necessary to "clean" the signal of noise and possible artefacts – distorted values resulting from the measurement and data transmission errors.

Also, any system has signal fluctuations that might be flattened using averaging. Such filters are used in processing of images to make changes of their sharpness [1]. In this case, each point on the graph is replaced by a weighted average of its neighborhood that provides smoothing of the signal. Filter kernel (i.e. each weight value when calculating the average) can be varied depending on the desired result.

Noise compensation can be performed in a static or a dynamic mode. The static mode involves subtraction of the noise part from the signal, the noise part is a constant value obtained when configuring the system. The dynamic compensation is based on monitoring of the slope angle of the signal curve and subtracting a straight line with a slope coefficient tgα.

* Corresponding author: kosachaa@atomrus.ru

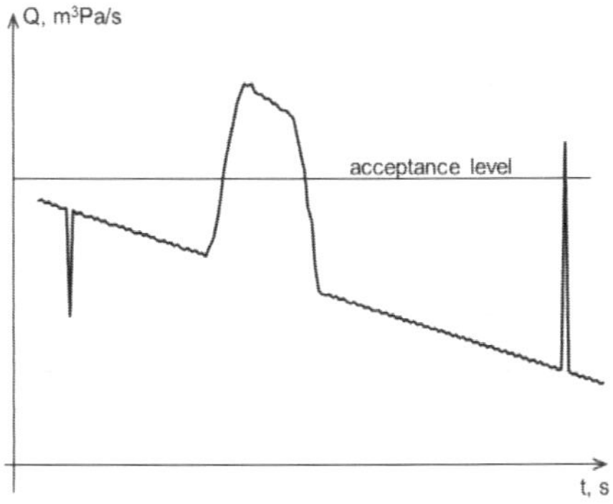

Fig. 1. Graph of the flow the test substance over time.

Removal of artifacts and the further search for the maximum value is based on the method of cluster analysis for pairwise weighted average [2]. As the criterion for connecting into clusters Euclidean distance is applied.

$$\rho_E(x;y) = \sqrt{(Q_x - Q_y)^2 + (t_x - t_y)^2} \qquad (1)$$

where ρ_E (x; y) is the distance between the values of x and y; Q_x, Q_y are the corresponding coordinates along the Y axis; t_x, t_y are the corresponding coordinates along the horizontal axis.

The algorithm distributing different values into clusters is used, in which the values are combined into groups based on general criteria. Gradually the scatter of the criteria in each cluster increases as the clusters themselves do. Because the curves representing the time dependency of the flow can be characterized as smoothly changing it can be assumed that the artifacts will appear in the clusters with a minimum number of members. To remove the corrupted values it is enough to remove the most numerically small clusters.

By using the method of cluster analysis the amount of the resources spent on the search for the maximum value is reduced. It uses the linear search algorithm, in which the first is the search for the cluster with a maximum average value of its members. After that, the maximum value is found in that cluster. When using this algorithm, one can be sure that the excess of the acceptance level is not caused by any noise fluctuations or random artifacts.

The possibility of modeling and documentation of data in an off-line mode is provided. This mode includes: creating a graph representing the time dependency of the flow of the test substance, data re-filtering and evaluation of the product shelf-life. According to the results of the monitoring process technological documents can be created in electronic format and printed on paper (protocols and reports) on demand.

3 Practical usage

This concept is applied to create the computer based automated system for remote mass-spectrometry leakage detection in canisters' closing welds after filling them with radioactive waste.

OPC servers and SCADA technology have been used to solve the problem. The SCADA technology [3] (Supervisory Control And Data Acquisition) is a hardware and software system designed for managing production processes in real time. The software that implements this technology allows communicating with the automated objects via the input-output drivers or servers. Thus, systems with any number of equipment included in the in-line production line can be simultaneously controlled.

OPC is a technology that uses the single interface to control devices [4]. Its use is especially important for remote leakage detection system. Usually, software developers have to include in the system the set of ready-made drivers and use different tools for developing original software for interacting with non-standard low-level devices. When replacing a device with the similar one made by another manufacturer it is necessary to change a part of the software for its management. OPC unified interface allows different software modules, manufactured by different companies successfully communicate with each other.

The control system for remote leakage detection is based on a distributed architecture (Fig. 2). This architecture consists of several control centers which are connected to a common control circuit. Because of this the distributed management architecture has no restrictions in the performance of the control center and the length of the communication channels. In addition, it is characterized by wide possibilities of modernization, changing and increasing capacity, component approach, easy commissioning and maintenance. The main software that implements the algorithm is located in the operator's computer, which receives data (with OPC-server and Modbus protocols) from the controller and the leak detector connected with the hub. The controller communicates with the digital and analog signals obtained from pressure sensors, valves, roughing pumps etc.

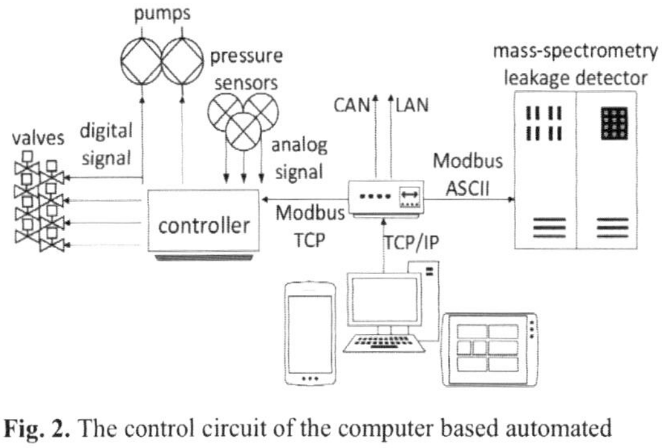

Fig. 2. The control circuit of the computer based automated remote leakage detection system.

For development of the applied software for the remote leakage detection system the open source and freeware public library Pascal SCADA and Lazarus IDE in Object Pascal for the compiler Free Pascal have been used. These software tools are cross-platform, they refer

DOI: 10.1051/itmconf/20171001005

to the concept of RAD (Rapid Application Development) and they are not proprietary, thereby constantly improving. For information exchange between the parts of the system the OPC-servers (OPC UA, OPC DA) and the data exchange protocols Modbus RTU and Modbus TCP are used. Communication is performed in CSV format [5] and PostgreSQL open source software is used as a relational DBMS (database management system) [6]. Choosing the DBMS PostgreSQL is caused by its compact data representation, a clear hierarchy of levels that determine the degree of data detail, low probability of obtaining errors and data inconsistencies.

4 Conclusion

During this work the hardware and software architecture of the control computer based remote leakage detection system, including the tools for integration of the equipment into a common information space, were defined and built, also the concept of the system analyzing data obtained as a result of a control process has been developed, and a unified approach to automation of remote leakage detection, (also taking into account the OPC-servers and Modbus protocols) has been designed.

With the SCADA and OPC technologies controlling of a system is implemented regardless of different communication protocols between physical devices and can be integrated into the technological line of the enterprise.

References

1. N.N. Mitropolsky, E.E. Kovshov, N.N. Hue, N.C. Minh, Control Systems and Information Technologies, **37**, 80 (2009)
2. P.A Jaskowiak., D. Moulavi, A.C.S. Furtado, Knowledge and Information Systems, **47**, 329 (2016)
3. C.P. Sandip, S. Pritimoy, Information Management & Computer Security Journal, **16**, 398 (2008)
4. A.A. Karataev, V.P. Palshin, Z.M. Yarmukhame-dova, Herald of KazNTU, **3**, 138 (2014)
5. CSV Files. URL: http://www.csvreader.com
6. E.E. Kovshov, A.E. Volkov, G.G. Charaev, Vestnik MSTU STANKIN, **27**, 136 (2013)

DOI: 10.1051/itmconf/20171001006

Speech Spectral Transfer Function

Oleg N. Korsun[1], *Evgeny.I.* Mikhaylov[2*] and *Magomed Z.* Nakhaev[2]

[1]FSUE "State Research Institute of Aviation Systems", Moscow, Russia
[2]Moscow Institute of Physics and Technologies (State University), Moscow, Russia

Abstract. The article discusses the problem of estimating the psychophysiological state of aircraft pilots by their speech. For this purpose, a new concept of an individual speaker's transfer function is proposed. This definition is based on the classical results of automatic control theory. The article presents the algorithms for calculating transfer function and the examples of using this feature for medical purposes.

1 Statement of the problem

Today man-machine interfaces based on various physical principles are intensively developed in aviation [1]. For example, the main trends of audio interfaces' development are the 3D-audio (surround sound effect) and automatic speech recognition [2], which are used for controlling onboard systems [3, 4].

It is known, that operator's speech characteristics depend on outer conditions and his own psychophysical state. Estimation of these changes is the key task for improving man-machine interface. There is a number of articles, where this problem has been investigated. For example, the impact of aircraft overload on operator's speech characteristics is presented in [3]. The connection between the degree of operator's fatigue and parameters of his speech is described in [4]. This relation is based on the A. M. Lyapunov's theory of stability [5,6]. The influence of the acoustic noises on the speech recognition performance score is analysed in papers [7,8]. The speech recognition algorithm, resistant to the noise, correlated with the voice signal, is proposed in [8]. The paper [9] discusses the speech characteristics of pilots with hearing loss diagnosis. This problem is particularly relevant to the helicopter aviation pilots. All the above mentioned researches are held in order to improve speech recognition algorithms. But on the other side, speech characteristics may be used to estimate operator's psychophysical state and the influence of various factors on it.

Evidently, the principal changes in the speech signal occur in the frequency and time domains [2, 3 , 4, 8]. The analysis of these changes in absolute values is coupled with the problem of representing the information because, for example, the power of speech signal in different frequency ranges varies by decades of decibels [2, 7]. So, the analysis of speech characteristics' changes should be carried out not in absolute, but in relative terms. It means, that the speech signal should be compared with a relevant one, for example, with the speech of another operator, considered as a reference, or standard.

To form a reference it is possible to use the mean value for the group of speakers. Another way is to choose a speaker, whose pronunciation is very close to the norms of the literature language. In this paper the concept of the speech transfer function is proposed in order to analyze the changes of operator's speech characteristics.

2 The algorithm for calculation transfer function of the operator

Let us introduce the speech transfer function of the operator, that is similar to transfer function $W(p)$, well-known in the theory of automatic control [6]. This function is defined as the ratio of the Laplace transform of the input and output signals for zero initial conditions [6].

We arrive at a transfer function $W(f)$, which depends on the frequency f, Hz, applying to the Laplace variable p [6] the substitution

$$p = j2\pi f,$$

where j – imaginary unit, that is $j^2 = -1$.

For an arbitrary value of argument f function $W(f)$ is a complex number containing information about the signal change in amplitude and phase on the frequency f. As it is known, an operator perceives the amplitude of a speech signal, while the phase information is ignored. So, we consider only the absolute value $|W(f)|$. Let us call it *the speech transfer function of the operator in frequency domain*. According to the Wiener–Khinchin theorem [6], the following ratio holds for the absolute value of the speech transfer function

$$|W(f)| = \sqrt{s_y(f)/s_x(f)}, \quad (1)$$

where $s_y(f)$, $s_x(f)$ – spectral densities of the input and output signals.

* Corresponding author: mihevkonig@mail.ru

DOI: 10.1051/itmconf/20171001006

To form a practical algorithm for calculating estimates (1) let us use a parametrization algorithm, widely known in automatic speech recognition [2, 8]. According to this algorithm, the speech fragment, for example, a recorded word, is divided into N_t time intervals (frames). The duration of each frame is 20 ... 40 ms. Then the Hann spectral window and fast Fourier transform are applied to each interval [2].

After that an absolute value of the Fourier transform is calculated for each frame. Then the whole frequency range, limited by Nyquist frequency [6], is divided into a predetermined number of bands $N_f = 20 \ldots 40$, and the average absolute value (the square root of the spectral density's estimation) is calculated for each band, as it is necessary for the formula (1). As a result, we obtain a matrix of the word's parametric portrait:

$$\mathbf{X} = \{x_{ij}\};\ i = 1, \ldots, N_f,\ \ j = 1, \ldots, N_t, \qquad (2)$$

which dimension is $N_f \times N_t$; each j-column describes the spectral content of the speech signal for the j- frame; each i-row describes a change in time of the mean absolute value of the signal components belonging to the i-frequency band.

It is known, that the error of the estimates, calculated by the formula (1), is considerable [2,6]. To improve the accuracy of estimation we will increase the amount of data. We take M = 10 ... 30 realizations for each word and determine the matrix of the mean parametric portrait

$$\overline{\mathbf{X}} = \frac{1}{M}\sum_{k=1}^{M}\{x_{ij}\}_k\,, \qquad (3)$$

where $\overline{\mathbf{X}}$ – matrix of dimension $N_f \times N_t$ of the operator's mean parametric portrait.

The above mentioned parametrization algorithm is a standard procedure of the speech recognition theory [2, 8]. When analyzing the general change in the spectral properties of speech, the time domain quantification is not necessary, because we do not need to take into account the features of sounds or syllables. So let us calculate the mean over all time intervals, i.e., over elements of the matrix's $\overline{\mathbf{X}}$ rows, and obtain the vector $\boldsymbol{a}$ of the mean amplitudes of the frequency components, belonging to the i-frequency band

$$\boldsymbol{a} = \frac{1}{N_t}\sum_{j=1}^{M}\{\overline{x}_{ij}\},\ \ i = 1, \ldots, N_f\,, \qquad (4)$$

where $\overline{x}_{ij}$ – the elements of the mean parametric portrait matrix (3).

In order to find estimates of the transfer function between two speakers it is necessary to calculate matrices $\overline{\mathbf{X}}_1$ and $\overline{\mathbf{X}}_2$, vectors $\boldsymbol{a}_1$ and $\boldsymbol{a}_2$ for each frequency band and for each speaker's speech data. Then the formula (1) is to be applied.

$$|W_{1,2}(f_i)| = \frac{a_{2i}}{a_{1i}} = \frac{1}{N_t}\sum_{j=1}^{N}\{\overline{x}_{2ij}\}\Big/\sum_{j=1}^{N}\{\overline{x}_{1ij}\},\ \ i = 1, \ldots, N_f\,, \qquad (5)$$

where f_i – frequency corresponding to the middle of the i-frequency band; a_{1i}, a_{2i} – elements of vectors $\boldsymbol{a}_1$ and $\boldsymbol{a}_2$, corresponding to the i-frequency band; $\overline{x}_{1ij}$, $\overline{x}_{2ij}$ – elements of matrices $\overline{\mathbf{X}}_1$ and $\overline{\mathbf{X}}_2$ of the mean paramatric portraits.

In (5) indices 1 and 2 denote respectively the first and second speakers.

The transfer function between the different states of the same speaker is determined by the same way.

The values of the transfer function (5) are expressed in dB as follows [6]:

$$|W_{1,2}(f_i)| = 20\lg\left(|W_{1,2}(f_i)|\right) = 20\lg\left(\frac{\boldsymbol{a}_2(i)}{\boldsymbol{a}_1(i)}\right),$$
$$i = 1, \ldots, N_f. \qquad (6)$$

The results of estimation will be improved, if the word is preliminarily divided into few parts in accordance with the algorithm [10].

3 Speakers in noisy conditions

Let us consider the applications of speech transfer functions in order to study the effects of noise on the speaker's speech. For this purpose the following experiment has been carried out. The noise recorded in the cockpit during the flight was fed only into the speaker's headphones, so as not to interfere with the record of the speaker's words. The registration frequency was 22 kHz. During the experiment audio data was recorded in three conditions: without noise; with noise in headphones 80 and 90 dB. Figure 1 shows plots of the speech transfer function for three speakers in noisy conditions (80 and 90 dB in the headphones). Transfer functions were calculated for the same speaker and the record without noise was taken as a reference.

The analysis of results shows that the impact of 80 dB noise causes a significant increase in the amplitude over the entire frequency range, with the largest rise in the range 1 ... 4 kHz, followed by decline in the range of high frequencies 4 ... 11 kHz. The maximum increase in amplitude is: for the first speaker 9 ... 10 dB with a decline to 3 ... 4 dB at high frequencies (figure 1a); second speaker 5.0 ... 6.5 dB with a decline to 3.5 ... 4.5 dB (figure 1b); third 4.5 ... 5.5 dB with a decline to 2.5 ... 3.5 dB (figure 1c). Noise augmentation from 80 to 90 dB increases the volume of speech by 1 ... 2 dB for all speakers. Thus, the proposed function allows to identify common and individual changes in the speech of speakers in noisy environment.

4 Speech transfer function in medical applications

Let us consider the use of the proposed function for investigating the speech of helicopter pilots with hearing loss diagnosis. A speaker without diseases of hearing and speech was chosen as a reference. Figure 2 shows plots of the speech transfer function for three speakers with a diagnosis of hearing loss with respect to the speaker without diseases of hearing and speech.

DOI: 10.1051/itmconf/20171001006

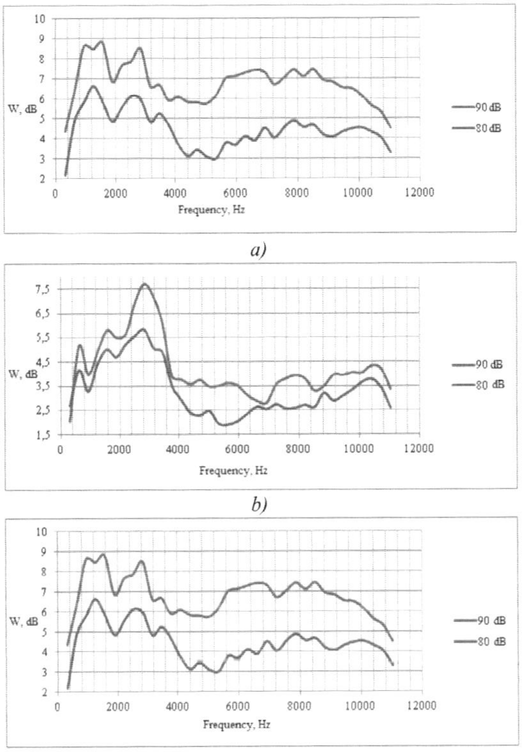

Fig. 1. Plots of speech transfer function for three speakers (*a*–c) with the noise in the headphone 80 (*1*) and 90 (*2*) dB.

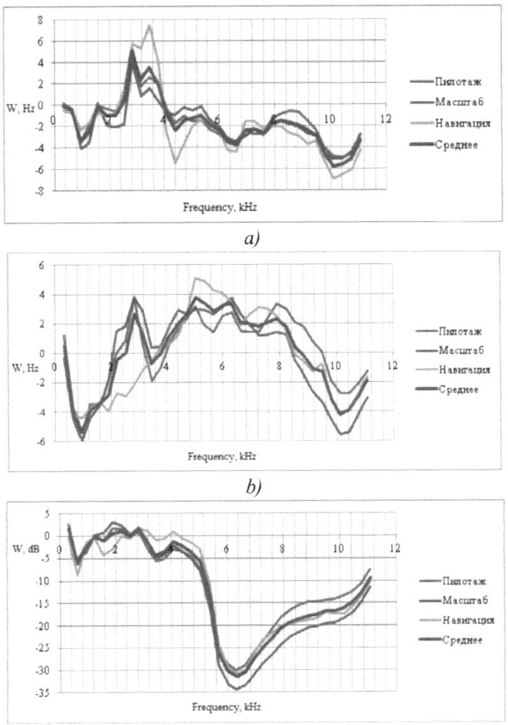

Fig. 2. Plots of speech transfer function for three speakers (*a*–*c*) with a diagnosis of hearing loss with respect to the speaker without diagnosed diseases of hearing and speech.

The plots show transfer function estimates calculated from records of the russian words "пилотаж", "масштаб", "навигация", corresponding to such english words as "pilotage", "scale", "navigation", and the mean ("среднее") between them.

Plots have obvious individual characteristics, but the common feature is the wide variation of values, which makes approximately ± 6 dB (figure 2a, b), and ± 20 dB (figure 2c).

The final experiment, which is to be discussed in this paper, is related to means for correcting teeth. Speech data of the speaker before installing corrective means was chosen as a reference. Then speech transfer function was calculated before and after installation of these means. Obtained results are presented in figure 3. This figure shows the significant changes in speech for the frequencies above 6 kHz.

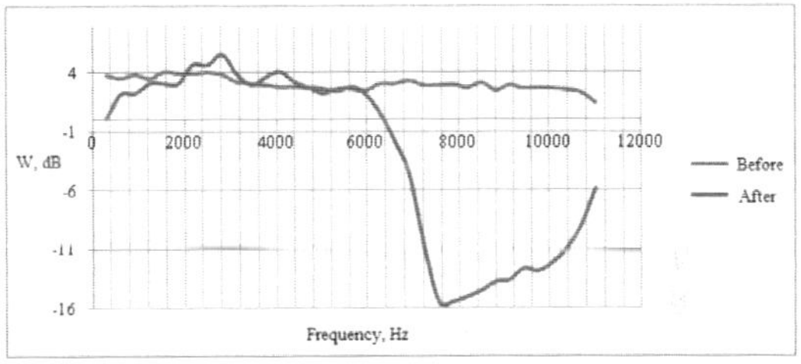

Fig. 3. Plot of speech transfer function for the same speaker before and after the installation of means for correcting the teeth.

5 Conclusion

In this paper we introduced the concept of speaker's speech transfer function in frequency domain in order to analyze the changes in speech characteristics and the influence of the outer conditions and psychophysical state of the speaker. The paper proposes the algorithm for calculating the estimates of speech transfer function, using experimental data. Some applications of the proposed function are also presented.

References

1. V.N. Evdokimenko., R.V. Kim, M.N. Krasil'shchikov, G.G. Sebryakov, Journal of Computer and Systems Sciences International, **54**(4), 609-620 (2015)
2. L. Rabiner, B.-H. Juang, *Fundamentals of Speech Recognition* (Prentice-Hall International, Inc., 1993)
3. A.I. Ivanov et al., Vestnik komp'iuternykh i informatsionnykh tekhnologii, **6**, pp. 3-7, (2012)
4. Iu.G. Bondaros, A.I. Ivanov, A.A. Tishchenko, Vestnik komp'iuternykh i informatsionnykh tekhnologii, **6**, 22-30, (2010)
5. K. Galkowski et al., Journal of Computer and Systems Sciences International, **55**(4), 503-514 (2016)

6. A.A. Erofeev, *Automatic control theory: textbook for universities*, (Moscow: Politekhnika, 2008)
7. A.S. Kolokolov, I.A. Liubinskii, Automation and Remote Control , **10**, 144-151, (2015)
8. O.N. Korsun, Vestnik komp'iuternykh i informatsionnykh tekhnologii, **4**, pp. 3-7, (2014).
9. A.I. Ivanov, Meditsina truda i promyshlennaia ekologiia, **11**, 40-45, (2014).
10. O.N. Korsun, A.V. Poliev, Journal of Computer and Systems Sciences International, **55**(4), 609-618 (2016)

DOI: 10.1051/itmconf/20171001007

Estimation of Aerodynamic Parameters in Conditions of Measurement

Moung Htang Om[1*], *Kyaw* Zin Latt[1], and *Tigran S.* Karapetyan[1]

[1]Russia Moscow Aviation Institute (National Research University), 125080 Moscow, Russia

Abstract. The paper discusses the problem of aircraft parameter identification in conditions of measurement noises. It is assumed that all the signals involved into the process of identification are subjects to measurement noises, that is measurement random errors normally distributed. The results of simulation are presented which show the relation between the noises standard deviations and the accuracy of identification.

1 Introduction

Identification of aerodynamic parameters could [1–3] be effective for estimating the technical state of the aircraft and the on-board systems [4, 5]. In this paper the aircraft motion model is formulated which includes the flight parameter sensors and pilot control inputs. For simulation of the measurement noises, the normally distributed discrete random variables with different standard deviations are used.

2 Simulation of the motion of the aircraft

The input signal (φ_t), generated by the pilot action, is shown in Fig. 1.

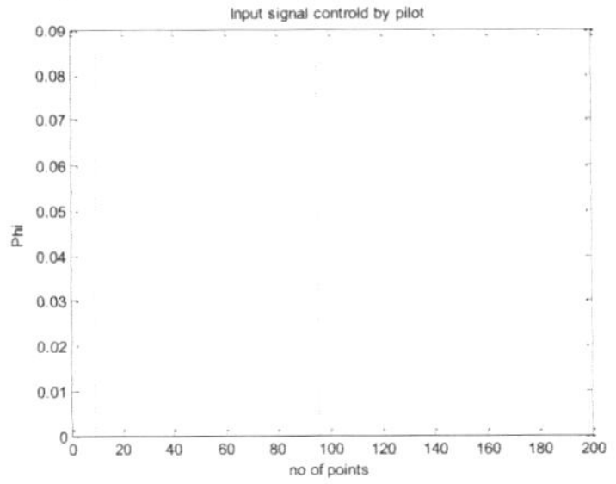

Fig.1. The input signal formed by the action of the pilot.

For simulation, it is necessary to form the object model and to know the output signals. For the formation of object model, the equations for angle of attack and angular velocity of pitch of the aircraft are used. The mathematical formulas in discrete form for the angle of attack (1) and angular velocity of pitch (2) are written as follow

$$\alpha(t_{i+1}) = \alpha(t_i) + \Delta t[-Y^{\alpha}\,\alpha(t_i) + \omega_z(t_i) - -Y^{\varphi}\varphi(t_i)] \quad (1)$$

$$\omega_z(t_{i+1}) = \omega_z(t_i) + \Delta t\big[M_z^{\alpha}\,\alpha(t_i) + M_z^{\omega z}\omega_z(t_i) - -M_z^{\varphi}\varphi(t_i)\big]. \quad (2)$$

Where, $\alpha(t_{i+1})$ – angle of attack for time instant $(t_{(i+1)})$ (radian); $\omega_z(t_{i+1})$ – angular velocity of pitch for time instant $(t_{(i+1)})$ (radian/s); $\alpha(t_i)$ – angle of attack for time instant(t_i); $\omega_z(t_i)$ – angular velocity of pitch for time instant(t_i); $\Delta t = t_{i+1} - t_i$ – time discretization interval, Y^{α}, Y^{φ}, M_z^{α}, $M_z^{\omega z}$, M_z^{φ} – aerodynamic parameters to be identified.

For simulation it was assumed that the registration frequency (*f*-registration) is 32 Hz. Therefore, the time sampling interval was $\Delta t = 1/32$ s. As a first step the input signal (φ_t), angle of attack (1), and the angular velocity of pitch (2) are simulated without any measurement noises. And the simulated signals without measurement noises are shown in Fig. 2.

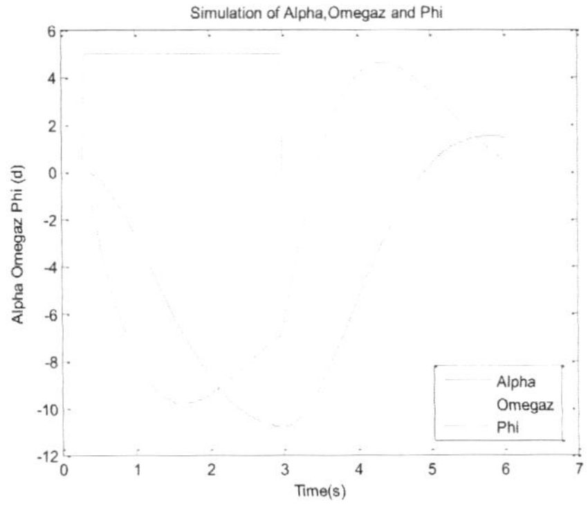

Fig.2. Simulation of the signals without any noises.

After simulation, the measurement of the input signal, angle attack (1) and angular velocity of pitch (2) with measurement noises is performed. The input signal, angle of attack and angular velocity of pitch after being measured with noises are shown in Fig 3.

* Corresponding author: mounghtangom50@gmail.com

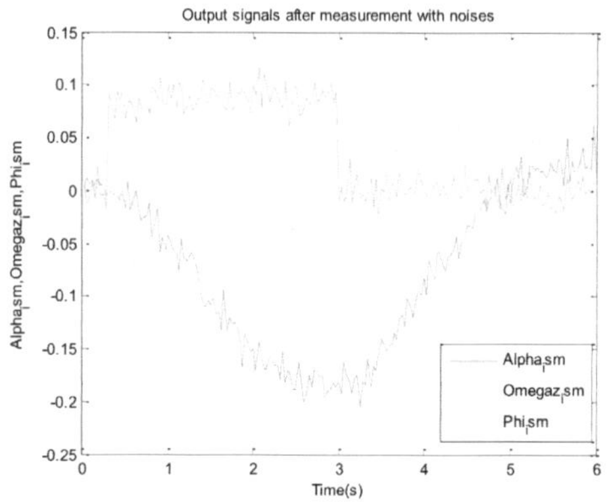

Fig.3. The input signal (φ_t), angle of attack and angular velocity after the measurement with noises

3 Identification of aerodynamic parameters

For the identification of parameters, it is necessary to form the object model. Let us consider every equation of the object model separately. In general form for an arbitrary instant t_i it may be expressed as follows

$$Y(t_i) = a_0 + a_1x_1(t_i) + a_2x_2(t_i) + a_3x_3\,(t_i),$$
$$i = \quad 1,2, \dots N.$$

Where a_0, a_1, a_2, a_3 - parameters to be identified;
N – number of samples.

The object model for identification can be used as a matrix X and a vector Y :

$$\boldsymbol{X} = \begin{bmatrix} 1 & x_{1t_{(1)}} & x_{2t_{(1)}} & x_{3t_{(1)}} \\ 1 & x_{1t_{(2)}} & x_{2t_{(2)}} & x_{3t_{(2)}} \\ & \dots & \dots & \dots \\ 1 & x_{1t_{(N)}} & x_{2t_{(N)}} & x_{3t_{(N)}} \end{bmatrix} \quad (3)$$

$$\boldsymbol{Y} = \begin{bmatrix} Y(t_1) \\ Y(t_2) \\ \dots \\ Y(t_N) \end{bmatrix}. \quad (4)$$

Where, X – matrix for object model, Y – vector for output signal.

In order to form the matrix X for the first equation, the input signals (φ_t), angle of attack (1), and angular velocity of pitch (2) are used. For the formation of output matrix Y (4) it is better to use the overload, which may be expressed as follow

$$n_y(t_i) = \left[\frac{V}{g}(Y^{\alpha}\alpha(t_i) + Y^{\varphi}\varphi(t_i))\right] + R(t_i) \quad (5)$$

Where, $n_y(t_i)$ – overload with specific noise for time instant (t_i), V – airspeed (ms^{-1}), g – gravitational acceleration (ms^{-2}), $R(t_i)$ – normally distributed random error.

For the purposes of identification it is better to present the second equation in the form

$$\frac{d\omega(t_i)}{dt} = M_z^{\alpha}\,\alpha(t_i) + M_z^{\omega_z}\omega_z(t_i) - M_z^{\varphi}\varphi(t_i) \quad (6)$$

In this case, the matrix X is the same as in the first equation, and the output vector Y consists of the estimates for angular velocity time derivative

$$\frac{d\omega(t_i)}{dt} = \frac{\omega(t_{i+1}) - \omega(t_{i-1})}{2\Delta t}$$

After forming all the required matrixes, the least square method (LSM) is used for parameter estimation. This least square method (LSM) is more effective for linear systems. The system which is used in this work is also linear. The least square method is given by

$$\hat{a} = (X^TX)^{-1}X^TY \quad (7)$$

Where, $\hat{a}$ – estimates of the parameters; X – matrix for object model; Y – vector for output signal.

In order to investigate statistically the accuracy of the parameter estimation and the influence of measurement noises, the simulation data and the processing of this data by least square method (LSM) were repeated many times. All the signals involved were distorted with simulated noises, normally distributed. In this work, the experiments were carried out for 6 different levels of the noises standard deviations, 20 independent tests for each level. For each test the LSM estimates of aerodynamic parameters were calculated. Then out of these 20 samples for each aerodynamic parameter the means and standard deviations of the estimates were determined.

It should be explained that a widely known formula [1] associated with the matrix $(X^TX)^{-1}$ for the LSM estimates errors dispersion, is valid in the case of output measurements noises only. In this paper we assume that all the signals used for identification are affected by measurements errors. For this reason we apply the statistical simulation in order to investigate the accuracy of the estimated parameters.

4 Analysis of the influence of error

The relative errors for all the estimated parameters are calculated by the following formula

$$e = \left(\frac{\hat{a} - a_{true}}{a_{true}}\right)100\% \quad (8)$$

Where, $\hat{a}$ – the identification estimate of a model parameter; a_{true} – the true value of the parameter used in the model while generating the test data.

For each test the means and standard deviations of the relative errors were determined. It is noticeable, that the standard deviation of the measurement noise, that is normally distributed random errors, can influence the accuracy of the estimated parameters. By varying the value of standard deviations of these random errors, we could easily notice the different values of the estimated parameters. The relative errors of the estimated parameters. The relative errors of the estimated parameters are shown in Fig. 4, where Sigma is the coefficient proportional to the standard deviation of the measurement noises.

The further analysis of the relative errors is performed for each of estimated parameters in order to know the identification accuracy and to see clearly the confidence boundaries for each estimated parameter. The confidence interval boundaries for the 95% confidence probability are calculated as follows:

$$Sig_m = M[e] + 1.96\sigma[e]$$
$$Sig_g = M[e] - 1.96\sigma[e] \quad (9)$$

Where, Sig_m, Sig_g – 95% confidence interval boundaries for an estimated parameter; $M[e]$– mean relative error of an estimated parameter, based on 20

DOI: 10.1051/itmconf/20171001007

independent tests for each level of the measurement noise; $\sigma[e]$ – standard deviation of a relative error, based on 20 independent tests for each level of the measurement noise.

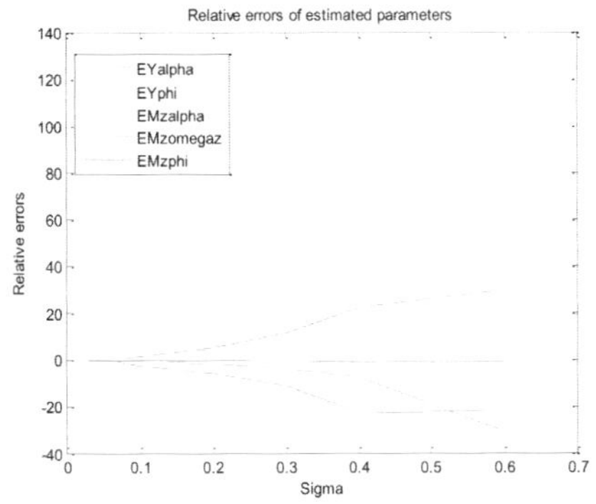

Fig.4. Relative errors of the estimated parameters

The results are presented in Fig. 5–9. The general trend is evident: epy larger is the value of Sigma, that is the level of measurement noises, the broader are the confidence boundaries.

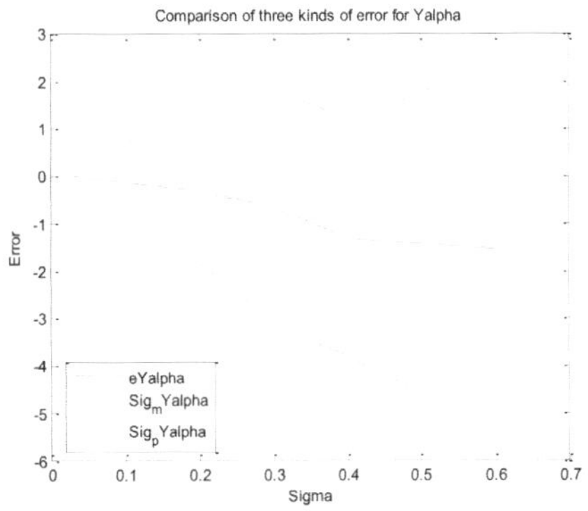

Fig.5. Mean relative error and 95% confidence interval boundaries for (Y^{α}).

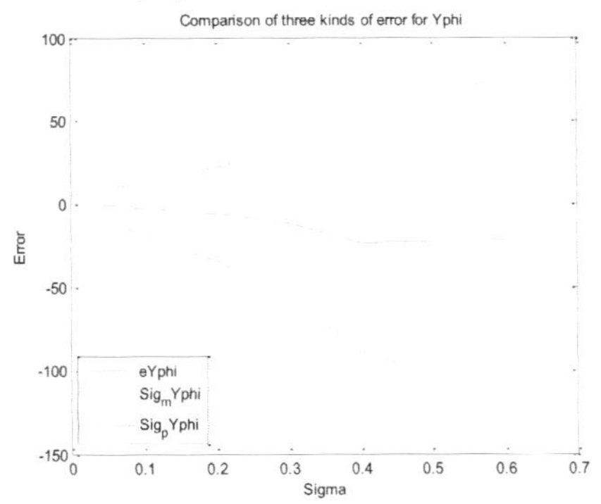

Fig.6. Mean relative error and 95% confidence interval boundaries for (Y^{φ}).

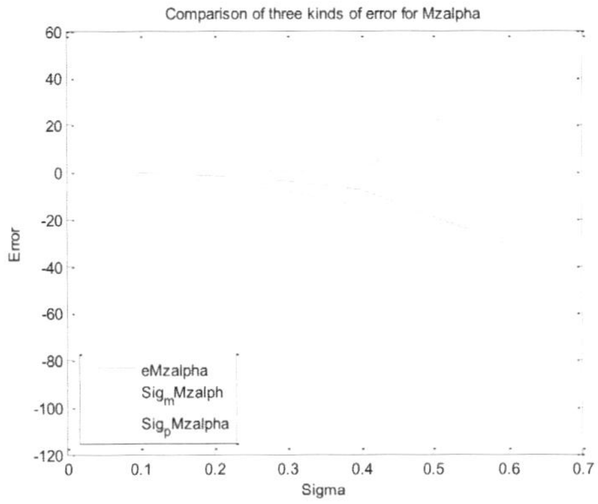

Fig.7. Mean relative error and 95% confidence interval boundaries for (M_z^{α}).

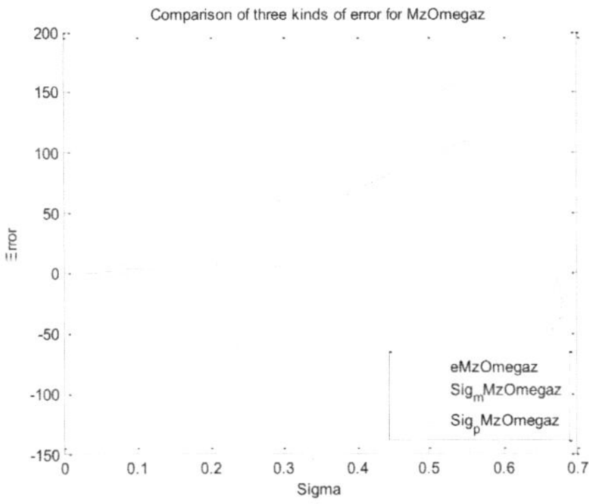

Fig.8. Mean relative error and 95% confidence interval boundaries for ($M_z^{\omega_z}$).

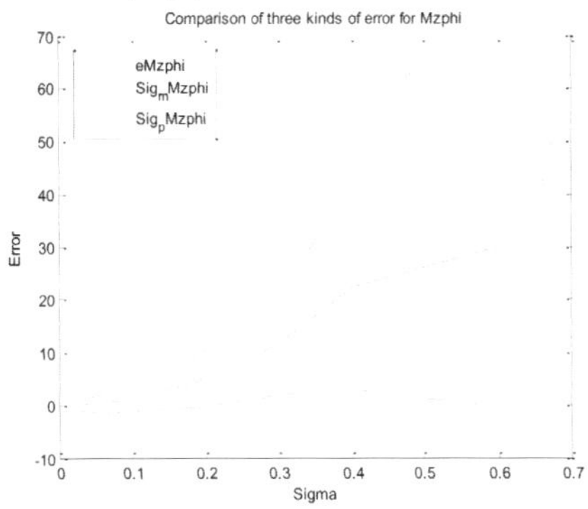

Fig.9. Mean relative error and 95% confidence interval boundaries for (M_z^{φ}).

The above figures present the influence of the average level of noises. In some cases it's better to investigate the influence of noise to signal relation. This relation can be express as

$$K = \left(\frac{\sigma_{noise}}{\sigma_{signal}}\right) \times 100\% \qquad (10)$$

Where, K – relation between noise and signal, σ_{noise} – standard deviation of noise, σ_{signal} – standard deviation of signal.

 DOI: 10.1051/itmconf/20171001007

The results are presented in Fig. 10–14, where in Fig. 10 and Fig. 12 we use noise to signal relation for angle of attack, in Fig. 13 – for angular velocity of pith, and in Fig. 11 and Fig. 14 for input signal (φ_t).

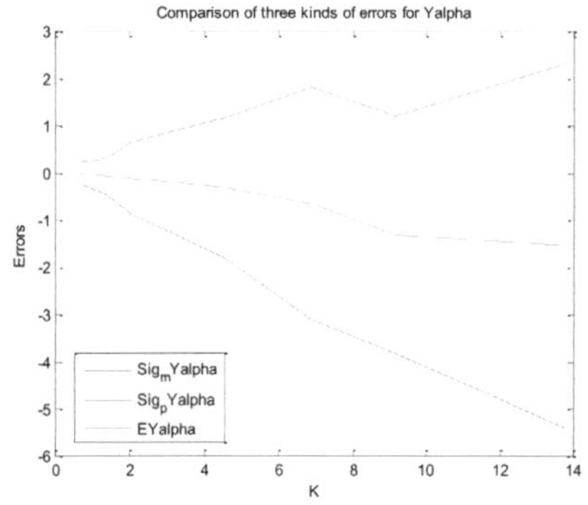

Fig.10. Mean relative error and 95% confidence interval boundaries depending on the relation between noise and signal (K) for (Y^{α}).

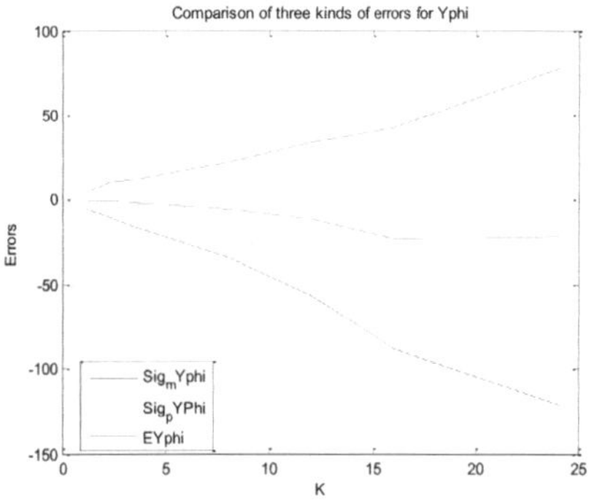

Fig.11. Mean relative error and 95% confidence interval boundaries depending on the relation between noise and signal (K) for (Y^{φ}).

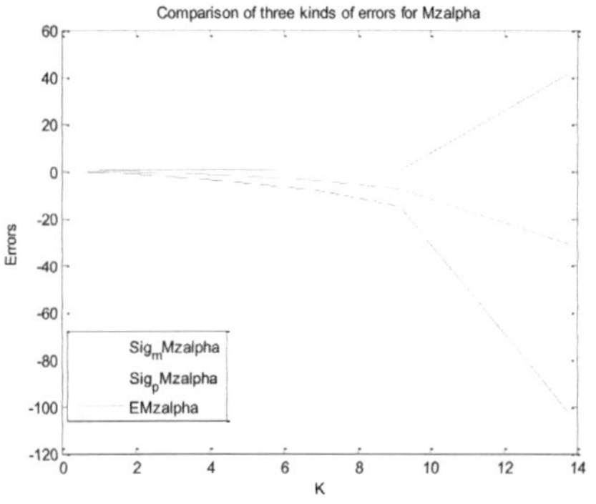

Fig.12 Mean relative error and 95% confidence interval boundaries depending on the relation between noise and signal (K) for (M_z^{α}).

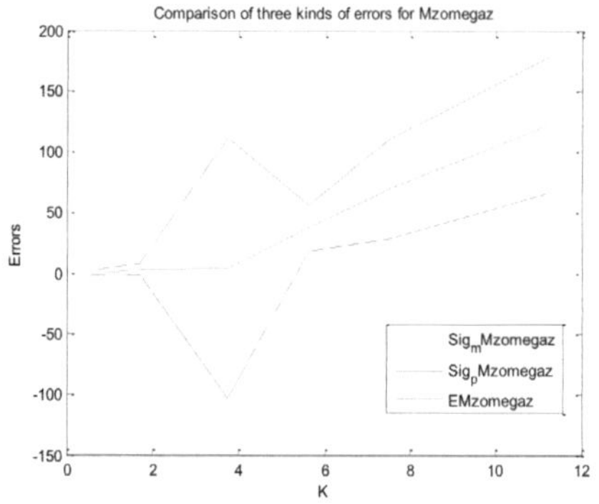

Fig.13. Mean relative error and 95% confidence interval boundaries depending on the relation between noise and signal (K) for ($M_z^{\omega_z}$).

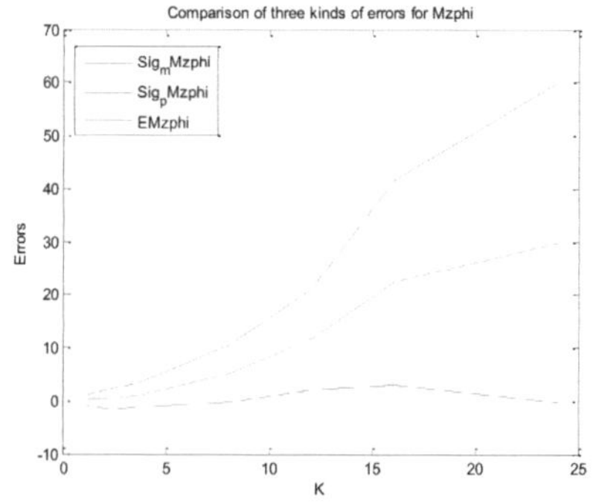

Fig.14. Mean relative error and 95% confidence interval boundaries depending on the relation between noise and signal (K) for (M_z^{φ}).

5 Conclusion

The obtained experimental results show that the proposed method of identification for estimating aerodynamic parameters can assure the high accuracy of estimation at considerable levels of noise to signal relation.

References

1. R.V. Jategaonkar, *Flight vehicle system identification: a time domain methodology* (American Institute of Aeronautics and Astronautics, Reston, 2006)
2. V. Klein, E.A. Morelli, *Aircraft system identification: theory and practice* (American Institute of Aeronautics and Astronautics, Reston, 2006)
3. O.N. Korsun, Automation and remote control, **64**, 772-781 (2003)
4. O.N. Korsun, B.K. Poplavskii, Journal of Computer and Systems Sciences International, **50**, 130-143 (2011)
5. O.N. Korsun, S.V. Nikolaev, S.G. Pushkov, Journal of Computer and Systems Sciences International, **55**, pp. 446-457 (2016)

DOI: 10.1051/itmconf/20171001008

Applying Simulation Method in Formulation of Gluten-Free Cookies

Marina Nikitina[1], *Igor* Nikitin[2,*], and *Vladimir* Kulakov[2]

[1]Gorbatov's All-Russian Meat Research Institute, 109316 Moscow, Russia
[2]Moscow State University of Technologies and Management named after K.G. Razumovskiy, 109004 Moscow, Russia

Abstract. At present time priority direction in the development of new food products its developing of technology products for special purposes. These types of products are gluten-free confectionery products, intended for people with celiac disease. Gluten-free products are in demand among consumers, it needs to expand assortment, and improvement of quality indicators. At this article results of studies on the development of pastry products based on amaranth flour does not contain gluten. Study based on method of simulation recipes gluten-free confectionery functional orientation to optimize their chemical composition. The resulting products will allow to diversify and supplement the necessary nutrients diet for people with gluten intolerance, as well as for those who follow a gluten-free diet.

1 Introduction

Celiac disease - an autoimmune enteropathy caused by eating gluten individuals with a genetic predisposition. This immune-mediated disease, wherein the deaminated peptides gliadin activate immune cells in the lamina propria of the small intestine, which stimulate T-lymphocytes, whereby runs an adaptive immune response, resulting in increased production of interferon-gamma (IFN-γ) and Interleukin IL-15. All this leads to a pronounced infiltration intraepithelial lymphocytes and correspondingly to change and damage to the intestinal epithelium [1].

Celiac disease - a disease in which pathogenesis plays intake of foods containing gluten. Autoimmune process stops when the withdrawal of gluten from the ration, so there is the cessation of development of autoimmune enteropathy, followed by normalization of serum markers of disease.

One of the first advocates the philosophy of "Gluten - Poison" became a cardiologist William Davis [2]. Based on his own research, he says, that gluten causes serious diseases, including arthritis and hypertension.

In 2011, there was another study: scientists from Monash University (www.monash.edu) came to the conclusion that the gastrointestinal diseases caused by consumption of gluten can occur even in those who do not have celiac disease. Especially true this statement is for people over 40 years, who have gluten entering the body in large amounts, causes inflammation of the intestinal wall. The implication of this - digestive disorders, the emergence of weight loss, decreased muscle activity.

These findings are confirmed by the experts of University of Maryland Baltimore Washington Medical Center (www.mybwmc.org), which found that gluten intolerance develops with age. It is manifested by flatulence, feeling of heaviness, digestive disorders that occur after the use of flour products.

The problem of intolerance to gluten is not confined to only one of celiac disease, often it causes food allergy in infants, manifestations of which may be quite varied: from skin rashes to chronic diarrhea. Currently, for example, school feeding organization provides for the development and implementation of diets mainly to healthy children, but there is the problem of catering to children with hereditary diseases, such as phenylketonuria, cystic fibrosis, celiac disease. Therefore, the development of gluten-free products and their inclusion in the diet of a particular category of patients in organized groups is relevant and requires further consideration.

In accordance with the international standards governing the quality of the food, gluten-free products can have it on label if level does not exceed 20 mg / kg.

According to a survey Innova Market Insights, in 2014 the growth of production of gluten-free products amounted to 9% of total food and beverage products sold in the world. It is noteworthy that this figure was 17% in the US.

In April 2015 every 10th launched new product in the world was gluten free. The largest number of new products indicated in the bakery and confectionery industries (bread - 9% of the total, cookies - 8% of the total volume of similar products). In other areas of the grocery market is also a growing interest in gluten-free products. More and more companies are joining the trend of exclusion of gluten from the products [3].

The main types of gluten-free vegetable raw materials in most gluten-free confectionery using amaranth, soy, peanut, pea, buckwheat flours, as well as various types of starches. The greatest interest in terms

* Corresponding author: nikito.igor@gmail.com

DOI: 10.1051/itmconf/20171001008

of enrichment of final product additional nutrients is amaranth flour. An analysis of the literature [4, 5] devoted to the study of complex processing of amaranth seeds, their chemical structure and pharmacological properties, characterizes them as a promising plant sources of protein, dietary lipids, dietary fiber and minerals, which shows the feasibility studies aimed at exploring the possibility of their use in the bakery and confectionery industry.

The content of essential amino acids and biological value of amaranth flour in comparison with wheat flour of the first grade is shown in Table 1.

Table 1. The content of essential amino acids and biological value of amaranth and wheat flour

Name of aminoacids	Protein FAO/WHO, % to protein	Wheat flour 1st grade, gr / 100gr of protein	Protein Amaranth flour semi-skimmed, gr / 100gr of protein
Isoleucine	4.0	0.530	1.659
leucine	7.0	0.813	2.279
Lysine	5.5	0.265	3.692
Methionine + Cystine	3.5	0.400	1.522
Phenylalanine + Tyrosine	6.0	0.880	3.319
Threonine	4.0	0.318	1.917
Tryptophan	1.0	0.120	1.082
Valine	5.0	0.510	2.186
Biological value, %		94.08	77.58

For development of gluten-free confectionery recipes with improved composition, increased bioavailability, optimized by ratio of protein/fat, as well as content of unsaturated (UFA), monounsaturated (MUFA), polyunsaturated (PUFA) fatty acids UFA/MUFA/PUFA apply the principles of food combinatorics.

2 Food combinatorics

Simulation of combined products is based on the principles of food combinatorics and aims to create recipes of new types of food products on basis of methods of mathematical optimization by reasonable selection of the basic raw materials, ingredients, food additives and dietary supplements, totality of which ensures formation desired organoleptic, physical and chemical properties product as well as a predetermined level of food, biological and energy value.

Modeling process of combined products recipes includes the following three stages: preparation of input data for the design, formalization requirements for the composition and properties of raw ingredients and quality final product, process modeling; product design with desired structural properties [6].

Application mathematical methods in design of multicomponent products allows you to:
- optimize recipe composition;
- expand range of industrial food products;
- in conditions of deficiency protein-containing raw materials optimize and engage in consumption sphere - non-traditional sources raw materials and dietary supplements [7].

2.1 Mathematical model gluten-free confectionery product with improved composition

When modeling gluten-free confectionery recipes goal was to optimize chemical composition of finished product, so as align them in ratio of protein to fat, as well as optimize ratio of essential amino acids and fatty acids.

Thus, the goal was in selection prescription weight of recipe components so that product meets following conditions:
- ratio protein weight fraction to fat weight fraction shall be 1,27

$$\sum_{j=1}^{m} b_j^a x_j \Big/ \sum_{j=1}^{m} b_j^f x_j = 1.27 \qquad (1)$$

where b_j^a, b_j^f – weight fraction respectively for protein and for fat in the j-th component; x_j – weight fraction of j-th component; m – number of components in the recipe.

- ratio weight fraction amino acid lysine to weight fraction amino acids methionine + cystine should trends to one

$$\sum_{j=1}^{m} \left[a_{lys} - \left(a_{meth} + a_{cys} \right) \right] \cdot b_j^a x_j \leq eps \qquad (2)$$

where $a_{lys}, a_{meth}, a_{cys}$ – weight fractions aminoacids lysine, methionine and cystine, gr /100 gr of protein.

- weight fraction aminoacid tryptophan should be less than 1 gr/100 gr of protein

$$\sum_{j=1}^{m} a_{mpn} b_j^a x_j \geq 1 \qquad (3)$$

where a_{mpn} – weight fraction aminoacid tryptophan, gr/100 gr of protein.

- ratio weight fractions UFA:MUFA:PUFA = 3: 6: 1

$$\begin{gathered} 6\sum_{k=1}^{7}\sum_{j=1}^{m} q_{kj} b_j^f x_j = 3\sum_{k=8}^{10}\sum_{j=1}^{m} q_{kj} b_j^f x_j; \\ \sum_{k=1}^{7}\sum_{j=1}^{m} q_{kj} b_j^f x_j + \sum_{k=8}^{10}\sum_{j=1}^{m} q_{kj} b_j^f x_j = \sum_{k=11}^{13}\sum_{j=1}^{m} q_{kj} b_j^f x_j \end{gathered} \qquad (4)$$

where k =1, ..., 7 – corresponds UFA; k = 8, 9, 10 – MUFA; k = 11, 12, 13 – PUFA; q_{kj} – weight fraction k-th fatty acid at j-th component of the formulation, gr/100 gr of fat.

DOI: 10.1051/itmconf/20171001008

As objective function was taken criterion of amino acid correspondence

$$P(A)=\sum_{k=1}^{n}\left(A_k^0-\sum_{j=1}^{m}a_{ki}b_{ij}x_j\Big/\sum_{j=1}^{m}b_{ij}x_j\right)^2\rightarrow\min \quad (5)$$

where a_{ki} – specific content of k-th monostructural ingredient in i-th element of chemical composition; b_{ij} – specific content of i-th element of chemical composition at j-th component designed product.

2.2 Recipe, food and biological value of modeled food product

As a result of structural-parametric optimization confectionery product composition by simulation modeling has been obtained gluten-free cookies with the following distribution weight fractions of components in recipe (Table 2) and corresponding chemical composition and biological value (Table 3).

Table 2. Recipe of cookie for 100 gr of product

Raw materials	Amount, gr
Amaranth flour	30
Corn starch	24
Butter	30
Sugar powder	8
Walnut	2
Eggs	5
Salt	0,5
Vanillin	0,5

Table 3. The indicators chemical composition and biological value of cookie

Indicator name	**Data**
Moisture, %	16.29
Protein, %	4.28
Fat, %	24.88
UFA/MUFA/PUFA	4:8:1
Carbohydrates, %	45.18
Energy value, kcal	340
Essental aminoacids, gr / 100 gr of protein	
Isoleucine	2.38
Leucine	3.65
Lysine	3.80
Methionine + Cystine	2.66
Phenylalanine + Tyrosine	4.61
Threonine	2.56
Tryptophan	1.12
Valine	2.98
Biological value, %	80.99

Selected ratio components of the recipe allowed us to obtain a product with high biological value (80.99%) and biological efficiency (ratio UFA/MUFA/PUFA = 4:8:1).

Determination organoleptic (color, taste, smell, shape, surface condition, view of the fracture) and physicochemical (mass fraction of moisture, water absorption) quality indicators developed cookie confirmed its compliance with the requirements of GOST 24901-2014.

3 Conclusions

Based on simulation of prescription composition gluten-free biscuits with amaranth flour obtained confectionery recipe having high biological value, as well as optimal ratio protein/fat and UFA/MUFA/PUFA.

Obtained cookies on quality indicators in line with requirements of normative and technical documentation. Thus, developed products will enable to diversify and supplement necessary nutrients diet for people with gluten intolerance, as well as for those who follow a gluten-free diet.

References

1. G. Serena, S. Camhi, C. Sturgeon, S. Yan, A. Fasano, Nutrients **7**(9), 7143-7162 (2015)
2. W. Davis. *Wheat Belly: Lose the Wheat, Lose the Weight, and Find Your Path to Health* (Rodale Books, 2011)
3. I.A. Nikitin, V.G. Kulakov, E.S. Korovina, A.I. Pisereva. Bread products **11**, 29-31 (2016)
4. L.P. Pacshenko, I.A. Nikitin. The success of modern science, **10** (2003)
5. R.U. Uazhanova, U.F. Roslyakov, I.M. Zharkova, N.A. Shmalko. *Amaranth - food culture (origin, taxonomy, morphology, physiology, introduction, cultivation, chemical composition, storage, processing, use)* (KSTU, 2016)
6. A.I. Zharinov, U.A. Ivashkin. All about meat, **3**, 6-15 (2004)
7. M.E. Titova, M.A. Nikitina, N.A. Tihomirova. Storage and processing of agricultural **7**, 41-45 (2013)

Automated Determination of the Type of Genre and Stylistic Coloring of Russian Texts

Vladimir Barakhnin[1,2,*], *Olga* Kozhemyakina[2], and *Ilya* Pastushkov[1]

[1]Institute of Computational Technologies of SB RAS, Lavrentiev av., 6, 630090, Novosibirsk, Russia
[2]Novosibirsk State University, Pirogova st., 1, 630090, Novosibirsk, Russia

Abstract. In this paper we propose the algorithm of automated definition of the genre type and semantic characteristics of poetic texts in Russian. We formulated the approaches to the construction of a joint ("two-dimensional") classifier of genre types and stylistic colouring of poetic texts, based on the definition of interdependence of the type of genre and stylistic colouring of the text. On the basis of these approaches the principles of formation of the training samples for the algorithms for the definition of styles and genre types were analyzed. The computational experiments with a corpus of texts of the Lyceum lyrics of A.S.Pushkin were implemented, which showed good results in determining the stylistic colouring of poetic texts and sufficient results in determining the genres. The proposed algorithms can be used for automation of the complex analysis of Russian poetic texts, significantly facilitating the work of the expert in determining their styles and genres by providing appropriate recommendations.

1 Introduction

In the tasks of automated text analysis in natural language, the problem of determination of their genre and stylistic characteristics is determined. The researcher can get this problem in a wide range of situations: from the problems of automation of the complex analysis of poetic texts, for which the type of genre and stylistic characteristics are the important attributes used in determining of the impact of lower levels on higher levels of the verse (see for example [1]), to the tracking of messages in social networks to identify the terrorist threats, the determination of marketing preferences of buyers, etc.

The researches in the field of automated determination of the genre type of texts were started recently – in early 2010-ies. So, in work [2] the algorithms of determination of genre types of odes, songs, epistles, elegies and epitaphs are based on the works of English poets-sentimentalists of the XVIII century. The time period in this study was not chosen by chance: in the poetry of the XVIII century the classicism with its strict genre rules dominated, and this greatly facilitated the development of algorithms.

The paper [3] describes the method of text classification (for certain genres and authors) based on the analysis of statistical regularities of letter distributions, i.e. the probabilities of occurrence of letters and letter combinations, along with this a solution is found without the "invasion in the sphere of literature, i.e., without the analysys of syntax, literary techniques and patterns of character interactions". However, in [4], the authors build an original counterexample to the statistical method of identification that shows the necessity of using, at least, the methods of morphological analysis.

As for the automation of determination of stylistic characteristics of the texts, we don't know the researches in this area, at least for the texts in Russian. Thus, our researches on computer joint definition of the type of genre and stylistic coloring of Russian texts are of a pioneer nature. In the present work we implement to develop the approaches to the construction of a joint classifier of the types of genre and stylistic colouring of poetic texts as well as we made the comparative analysis of algorithms of determination of these characteristics.

We underline that our purpose is not the creation of new theories of genre and stylistic relationships within literary works but the development of the analyzer that allows to correlate correctly the stylistic coloring of the text with its genre identity what has relevance for researches in the field of Informatics, because we are talking about the tools used not in the strictly linguistic space.

2 The building of the joint classifier of genre types and stylistic colouring of poetic texts

While we built the joint ("two-dimensional") classifier of genre types and stylistic colouring of texts, we took into account that the classifier itself is a multidimensional structure, based on the totality of parameters, which define the object of study. The multidimensionality of the structure itself implies some

* Corresponding author: bar@ict.nsc.ru

error in the final result of the analysis, because the more we put into the system than the more potential probability of the occurrence of many variants at each stage of the analysis is possible. So, when we construct the multidimensional classifiers associated with such difficult (for unequivocal definition) categories like genre and style, the phased development of each analysis parameter is required in order to exclude possible errors and the variability of results, what is crucial in the case of unstructured text analysis.

We are working on the joint classifier of genre types and stylistic colouring of poetic texts. Such classifier is created for the first time (at least for texts in Russian).

The creation of a "universal" classifier of literary texts according to their genre and stylistic characteristics requires the synthesis of a vast empirical material, so we decided to stay on the classification of lyrics of A.S.Pushkin of Lyceum period. The rationale of this choice is given below.

The most efficient approach to automatic determination of the genre types is the usage of algorithms with learning. However, the formation of the training sample is not a trivial task. Our attempt to use as a training sample the lyrics of Pushkin's of mature period (1828-1831), was failed at an early stage, since the variety of genres of Pushkin's work of this period is very subjective, in correlation with the stylistic features of the works of Pushkin in a special manner, herewith it does not follow the generally accepted laws. This feature is formulated by V.A.Grekhnev: "The genres and style does not confront each other as hostile, dening fundamentals, but there is always internal tension between them. This tension is increasing, where the power and scope of the writer's personality are increasing" [5. P. 234]. This fact causes the genre and stylistic varieties and variants, the "internal tension" between style and genre originate the non-canonical genres, and for training samples this becomes critical, as there are features that do not fit into the system and, therefore, are contrary in essence to the material for the construction of the system. As a result, we decided to stay at the Lyceum lyrics (1814 – 1817), as it has the most strict genre forms, stylistic unity, and adherence to the rules of grammar of that period: "Almost all the Lyceum lyrics belongs to the sublime style, except a few poems. Even many of the satirical poems are written entirely in the sublime style. It can be argued that in the early poems of Pushkin, there is the influence of the rigid rules of "Grammar" of his Lyceum teacher N.F.Koshanskiy" [6. P. 24].

In turn, the usage of the Lyceum lyrics as material for the creation of training samples, is justified by stylistic dimension, since the stylistic differentiation of lexemes is the development stage of the classifier. For texts in the Russian language there is the upward to the works of M.V.Lomonosov [7] the division of the texts (primarily literary) for the relevant to high, neutral and low styles. Historically, each of them is characterized by the ratio of the usage of the old Slavonic (Church Slavonic) and the Russian words (a group of words common to the Slavonic and Russian languages is separately considered), a share of archaisms, and the usage of certain syntactic constructions. In the classic theory the genre strictly dictates the choice of a particular style. So, with regard to the poetic texts this dependence is discussed in detail in the monograph by D.M.Magomedova [8].

So, for implementation of given task, we are going from practice, making a selection of the works of Pushkin Lyceum period, from 1813 to 1817, as material, on which we can build the most accurate system, what certainly makes the end result of analysis the most accurate and allows to develop the most appropriate classifier relating to the stylistic aspect. We exclude the poems, the tales, the translations, Dubia, and we do the list, statistically including the poems, as relevant to the genre system given in [8] and also not included in this system. So this system includes the canonical and non-canonical genres, the latter, however, occur after the considered period, and therefore they are not described in the list.

As the result of analysis of this list of works, we distinguish the following groups of genres.

Canonical: ode – 4 poems, elegy – 27 poems (including one historical elegy – "Napoleon on Elba", idyll – 2 poems, epistle – 55 poems, ballad – 3 poems, non-canonical (a fragment, a story in verse) – no.

Also, we're adding the genres, which are not in the system of canonical and non-canonical: epigram - 18 poems, madrigal – 4 poems, sonnet – 1 poem, romance – 1 poem, anecdote –1 poem, Parable – 2 poems.

In addition, the poem "Unbelief" (1817) is defined as philosophical ode and elegy [9]. But for the analysis we defined it as philosophical ode.

Genre types of these works formed the basis of the classifier: along one axis we have placed the genre types in order of ascending "the sublimity": an ode, the elegy, the idyll, the epistle, etc., and along another axis - the traditional styles (see Table 1). On this empirical material an obvious correlation between genre and stylistic characteristics of texts can be seen: an ode, the elegy, the idyll are usually written in high style, they do not use lexical content corresponding to the low style, but the epigrams, on the contrary, are characterized by the usage of elements of the vocabulary of the low style. In general, the style of a text is determined by the most "low" of its lexemes, what is especially typical for epigrams: the presence of high vocabulary, which is often used in an ironic way, must not mislead, because the usage of one or two words of spoken or obscene vocabulary characterize immediately the author's intention. However, for the genres that traditionally imply the sublime form, especially, a madrigal, we do not consider to refer the poems of these genres to reduced style if the several "reduced" (but not obscene!) words are used in them with ironic purposes.

It should be noted that a style is characterized by the lexemes much more than a genre, although, in our experiment, in particular, and to the global literary categories processes and, in general, the number of genres is much more than a number of styles. This complicates the choice, as because of direct factors, and also because of given training sample of works. The features of training sample include works written in the genre of the parable, one of them ("Riders") belongs to high style, the second ("Truth") – to the neutral, although, as we know, the parable, being the closest to the genre of the fable, suggests the possibility of writing it in different styles, as evidenced, in particular, by the parable "The Cobbler", which can be attributed rather to the low ("colloquial") style.

Table 1. The statistics on the genre and stylistic compliance.

	High	Neutral	Low
Ode	4	-	-
Parable	1	1	-
Madrigal	4	-	-
Epistle	-	55	5
Idyll	-	2	-
Elegy	-	37	-
Romance	-	1	-
Ballad	-	3	-
Epigram	-	-	18
Anecdote	-	-	1

3 About the creation of the dictionary of stylistically differentiated lexemes

Before the choice of algorithms of determination of stylistic and genre characteristics of poetic texts, it is necessary to answer the question: is it possible to use a priori compiled dictionaries of lexemes with a particular stylistic or genre painting?

Great attention is paid on the stylistic differentiation of words in the monograph of O.S.Akhmanova "Essays on General and Russian lexicology" [10]. The list of "spoken" words, with "reduced" stylistic characteristics and with "increased" stylistic characteristics. However, these lists are not complete and rather more illustrative, moreover, the author concedes that "not all included words are equally convincing (many of them, undoubtedly, will seem disputable)", and finally, the stylistic colouring of some of the lexemes have changed over time, i.e. this feature, taken from the monograph [10], could be other for the language of the XIX century, as for the modern language. Therefore, in the same monograph, for relation of the words with a particular style it is proposed to use the analysis of their structural-semantic forms. So, nouns with the suffix -к-а in a variety of structural-semantic variants, and also the various suffixes meaning "a person" refer to "conversational" or "reduced" vocabulary; for "spoken" in contrast to "reduced", the vocabulary is characterized by a large number of dialects; for "book" vocabulary the borrowed words are typical, and for the "sublime" – Slavic words with a complex structure, as well as archaisms, etc.

However, all these observations are of a rather private nature. So, the words with the suffix *-к-а*: *пытка*, *речка*, *шутка*, etc., are found in Pushkin's verses which are not related to "low" or "conversational" style, the same applies to the words *бочка*, *кружка*, *пушка*, etc., in which *-к* is a part of the root, but the establishment of this fact requires a non-trivial etymological analysis, which is difficult to automation. Similarly, the borrowed words over time have become available to all styles, and it's not only about "ancient" borrowings like *лошадь* or *собака*, but also about new: *велосипед*, *танк*, etc.. The slavonicisms, including the words with complex structure, could be used, in particular, to give the poem an ironic tone (e.g., Pushkin's "Ode to his Excellency Graf D.I.Khvostov" and numerous satirical verses by A.K.Tolstoy).

The situation is complicated as by the fact that often not all the word's variants are belong to "conversational" or "reduced" style, but only one of its lexical-semantic variants, as well as because of the gaining the word of a particular stylistic colouring only at the entry to the idiom. Thus, the occurrence in the text of certain lexemes cannot serve as a sufficiently reliable criterion for attribution of the text to a particular stylistic type because most of the words are of polysemantic colouring.

Moreover, a strict definition of genre colouring of separate words seems quite a unpromising task to us and we don't know any satisfactory attempt at its resolution at least on a theoretical level. That is why it seems to us that the most appropriate way is to define the stylistic and genre characteristics of poetic texts on the basis of the occurrence in them of a set of lexemes defined by the training samples.

4 Description of the numerical experiment

For the experiment we used the above-described massive of the texts of Pushkin's lyrics of Lyceum period, comprising 121 poems, marked by an expert on genres and styles.

We used the standard method of support vectors machine (support vector machine) [11] with a linear core and the RBF nonlinear core, in addition, for comparison, the results of calculations were carried out with the use of neural network based on multilayer perceptron [13]. When training the dictionary of all used words was created, except service words, and each text was coded by sequence of the symbols 0 and 1 corresponding to the dictionary in word order: 0 was set if a word is not in the text, 1 – if the word is in the text. Also we used the linear regression to determine the styles, our hypothesis was that as styles can be unambiguously ranked: low – 1, neutral – 2, high – 3, the regression can give a numeric value which will be close to the value of the style, and a divergence with the value will be a mistake. The experimental results are following (see Table 2): we calculated the average, the minimum, and the maximum of the proportion of correct predictions of the method with 100 runs, the sample is divided into 80% training and 20% test, the division into which is random every time, each run is independent from the previous ones (algorithm was implemented in the language python using the library scikit-learn). As it is difficult to rank a neutral along with the others, than in each method there is the experiment with it and without it.

As can be seen from the obtained data, the high style is not practically recognized – probably because of its insufficient representation in the sample. The method of support vector machines is the best in this case. It is worth to note that in the case of non-linear core the high style was recognized, but by the common parameters, the case of linear core is better than the multilayer perceptron and logistic regression.

Table 2. The statistics on the genre and stylistic compliance.

	Average value	Max	Min
SVM, neutral is ignored	0.76	0.92	0.58
SVM	0.80	0.96	0.57
SVM, rbf core	0.62	0.85	0.11
Multilayer neural network	0.77	0.96	0.46
Logistic regression	0.76	0.96	0.46
Linear regression, neutral is ignored	0.70	0.82	0.45
Linear regression	0.70	0.45	0.58

	High	Neutral	Low
SVM, neutral is ignored	0.0	0.86	0.72
SVM	0.0	0.86	0.70
SVM, rbf core	0.10	0.75	0.13
Multilayer neural network	0.0	0.96	0.33
Logistic regression	0.0	0.85	0.72
Linear regression, neutral is ignored	-	-	-
Linear regression	-	-	-

Similarly, we carried out the experiment on definition of the genre (one series of experiments was carried out under the simplified scheme, when the historical elegy and philosophical ode was not seen as separate genres). From Table 3 it is seen that the definition of genre has fared worse than the definition of styles as each genre is represented by a relatively small number of samples. The lexical signs are not enough for genres, we need poetic features (rhyme, size, number of accented syllables) which should strengthened, for example, with the help of the AdaBoost algorithm [13].

Table 3. Experiment with the definition of the genre.

	Average value	Max	Min
SVM. simplified types	0.45	0.65	0.22
SVM	0.45	0.65	0.27

5 Conclusion

The paper proposes the approaches to the construction of a joint ("two-dimensional") classifier of genre types and stylistic colouring of poetic texts, based on the definition of interdependence of the type of genre and stylistic colouring of the text. On the basis of these approaches we analyse the principles of formation of the training samples for the algorithms to define styles and genre types. We implement the computational experiments with a corpus of texts of the Lyceum lyrics of A.S.Pushkin, which showed good results in determining the stylistic colouring of poetic texts and sufficient results in determining the genres. Thus, the proposed algorithms showed their efficiency and can be used for automation of the complex analysis of Russian poetic texts, significantly facilitating the work of the expert in determining their styles and genres by providing appropriate recommendations.

Work is executed with partial support of the Presidium of RAS (project 2016-PRAS-0015) and of the Presidential programme "Leading scientific schools of RF" (grant 7214.2016.9).

References

1. V.B. Barakhnin, O.Yu. Kozhemyakina, CEUR Workshop Proceedings, 934 (2012) (in Russian)
2. M.A. Lestsova, Bulletin of the Chelyabinsk State Pedagogical University, 4 (2014) (in Russian)
3. Yu.N. Orlov, K.P. Osminin, Applied Informatics, **26,** 2 (2010) (in Russian)
4. Yu.N. Orlov, K.P. Osminin, *Methods of statistical analysis of literary texts* (Editorial URSS, Moscow, 2012) (in Russian)
5. V.A. Grehnev, *Lyrics of Pushkin. About the poetics of genres* (Gorkiy, 1985) (in Russian)
6. M.V. Lomonosov, The preface about the advantages of Church books in Russian language, In: M.V.Lomonosov, Complete Collection, **7** (Moscow, Leningrad, 1952) (in Russian)
7. V.B. Barakhnin, O.Yu. Kozhemyakina, Vestnik of Tomsk State University. Philology, **13**, 2 (2016) (in Russian)
8. D.M. Magomedova, *Linguistic analysis of a lyric poem*. (Moscow, 2004) (in Russian)
9. S.F. Svobodina, Pushkin Museum: an almanac, **6** (2014) (in Russian)
10. O.S. Akhmanova, *Essays on General and Russian lexicology* (Moscow, 1957) (in Russian)
11. N. Cristianini, J. Shawe-Taylor, *An Introduction to Support Vector Machines and Other Kernel-based Learning Methods* (Cambridge University Press, 2000)
12. S. Haykin, *Neural Networks: A Comprehensive Foundation* (Prentice-Hall, 1999)
13. Y. Freund, R.E. Schapire, Journal of Japanese Society for Artificial Intelligence, **14**, 5 (1999)

Improving the Classification Quality of the SVM Classifier for the Imbalanced Datasets on the Base of Ideas the SMOTE Algorithm

Liliya Demidova [1,2,*], and *Irina* Klyueva[2]

[1]Moscow Technological Institute, 119334 Moscow, Russia
[2]State Radio Engineering University, 390005 Ryazan, Russia

Abstract. The approach to the classification problem of the imbalanced datasets has been considered. The aim of this research is to determine the effectiveness of the SMOTE algorithm, when it is necessary to improve the classification quality of the SVM classifier, which is applied for classification of the imbalanced datasets. The experimental results which demonstrate the improvement of the SVM classifier quality with application of ideas the SMOTE algorithm for the imbalanced datasets in the sphere of medical diagnostics have been given.

1 Introduction

The problem of imbalanced data is one of the main problems which must be solved before the application of some machine learning classification algorithm if we want to receive the high quality classification results.

Dataset is called imbalanced if the samples size from one class is very much smaller or larger than the other classes.

Training the classifiers for the imbalanced datasets compromises the performance of most well-known machine learning algorithms. It is fair, in particular, for the support vector machine algorithm (SVM, Support Vector Machine) [1 – 9].

The incorrect classification of objects of the minority class usually costs significantly more than the incorrect classification of the object of the majority class since the minority class instances are rare, but the most important data used in real data sets.

As shown by experimental studies, the training of the classifiers on the imbalanced datasets leads to the fact that the constructed classifier tend to classify all objects as objects of the majority class, completely ignoring the underrepresented minority class, which generally does not correspond to the actual purpose of the research [3 – 6].

There are a significant number of real-world applications that are suffering from the class imbalance problem (for example, medical and fault diagnostics, anomaly detection, face recognition, telecommunication, the web and email classification, ecology, biology and financial services. For example, in medical diagnostics the number of sick patients is usually significantly less then the number of healthy people.

Currently, the different strategies of sampling are applied to solve the problem of the imbalance datasets. In this paper the study of the aspects of the applicability of the sampling strategies to restore the balance between the classes in the problem of binary classification has been performed. In particular, the capabilities of the synthetic sampling algorithm called as the SMOTE (Synthetic Minority Oversampling Technique) [3] have been investigated.

2 The basic principles of the SVM classifier development

The SVM algorithm proposed by Vapnik [1, 4] is a modern approach for solving the pattern recognition problems. The SVM algorithm maps the sample points into a highdimensional feature space to seek for an optimal separating hyperplane through maximizing the margin between two classes.

The Support Vector Machine (SVM) algorithm is the supervised machine learning algorithm [1 – 9]. The SVM algorithm is successfully used for the different classification problems in various applications [8]. The SVM classifiers on the base of the SVM algorithm have been applied for credit risk analysis, medical diagnostics, text categorization, information extraction, etc [8].

To develop the best SVM classifier it is necessary to find correctly the kernel function type, values of the kernel function parameters and value of the regularization parameter [8]. The solution of this problem can be achieved by the grid search of the kernel function types, values of the kernel function parameters and value of the regularization parameter that demands significant computational expenses. Quality of the SVM classifier can be measured by different classification quality indicators. There are the cross validation data indicator, the accuracy indicator, the classification completeness indicator and the ROC curve analysis based indicator, etc [8].

* Corresponding author: liliya.demidova@rambler.ru

The SVM classifier with satisfactory training and testing results can be used to classify new objects.

The separating hyperplane for the objects from the training set can be represented by equation $\langle w, z \rangle + b = 0$, where w is a vector-perpendicular to the separating hyperplane; b is a parameter which corresponds to the shortest distance from the origin of coordinates to the hyperplane; $\langle w, z \rangle$ is a scalar product of vectors w and z.

The condition $-1 < \langle w, z \rangle + b < 1$ specifies a strip that separates the classes. The wider the strip, the more confidently we can classify objects. The objects closest to the separating hyperplane, are exactly on the bounders of the strip.

Finding the separating hyperplane is basically the dual problem of searching a saddle point of the Lagrange function, which reduces to the problem of quadratic programming, containing only dual variables [8].

In training of the SVM classifier it is necessary to determine the kernel function type $\kappa(z_i, z_\tau)$, values of the kernel parameters and value of the regularization parameter C, which allows finding a compromise between maximizing of the gap separating the classes and minimizing of the total error [8].

One of the approaches using for the search of the optimal values of the parameters of the SVM classifier is based on the application of the Particle Swarm Optimization algorithm (PSO algorithm) [7 – 9].

Search space in the PSO algorithm is filled with a population of particles each of which has some location and velocity in the space of the problem parameters at the concrete moment of time.

Corresponding value of the objective function is calculated for each particle location. Particle location and velocity is changed after calculation of a new value of the objective function.

After every iteration under determination of the following particle location, information on the best particle from a number of neighboring particles (particles can share information) and also information on this particle location during that iteration when the best value of the objective function corresponds to this particle (particles have "memory"), are taken into account [7].

In this research we used the canonical version of the PSO algorithm [8].

3 The basic ideas of the SMOTE algorithm

A dataset is imbalanced if the classes are not approximately equally represented.

The SMOTE algorithm [3] creates the artificial objects of the minority class based on the similarities in the feature space between the existing objects using the k-nearest neighbor algorithm (kNN alrorithm) (Fig. 1) [10].

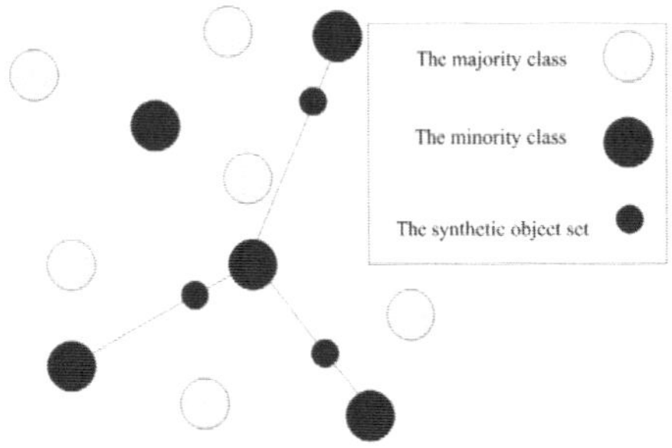

Fig. 1. The diagram of SMOTE algorithm.

Herewith, the number of the artificial objects which are "similar" to the objects of the existing minority class, but do not duplicate them is generated.

The SMOTE technique is an important approach by oversampling the minority class.

4 The experimental study

In this research, we implemented the following approach to application of the SMOTE to improve the classification quality of the SVM classifier for imbalanced datasets.

Step 1. The initial dataset is splited into the train and test datasets.

Step 2. The new synthetic objects are generated by the SMOTE algorithm for each dataset obtained in step 1.

Step 3. The SVM algorithm is implemented for the new received datasets. Herewith, the search for the optimum parameters values of the SVM classifier is implemented by the PSO algorithm (in particular, the PSO algorithm is used for the search of two optimal parameters values of the SVM classifier for the radial basis kernel function: the values of the parameter regularization C and the kernel function parameter σ) [8].

Python 2.7 was used for software implementation of the SMOTE and SVM algorithms. Herewith, the default settings were applied for the SMOTE algorithm.

We use the real medical datasets from the UCI repository of the machine learning database [4] to demonstrate the classification performance of the approach proposed in this paper.

Table 1. The characteristics of the datasets.

Dataset	Total number of the positive data	Total number of the negative data	Imbalance ratio
Heart (270 × 13)	120	150	0.2
Hepatitis (155 × 19)	123	32	0.74
Pima diabetes (768 × 8)	268	500	0.46

Table 2. The classification results on the "Heart" dataset.

Type of algorithm	The size of the training/testing set	Errors						Accuracy, (%)	Sensitivity, (%)	Specificity, (%)
		At the training			At the testing					
		positive	negative	total	positive	negative	total			
1	216/ 54	4	2	**6**	4	3	**7**	95.18	93.33	96.67
2	252/ 60	2	2	**4**	4	5	**9**	95.83	96.15	95.51
1	216/ 54	6	4	**10**	5	4	**9**	92.96	94.67	90.83
2	252/ 60	1	1	**2**	0	8	**8**	96.67	94.00	99.33

Table 3. The classification results on the "Hepatitis" dataset.

Type of algorithm	The size of the training/testing set	Errors						Accuracy, (%)	Sensitivity, (%)	Specificity, (%)
		At the training			At the testing					
		positive	negative	total	positive	negative	total			
1	124/ 31	0	17	**17**	0	11	**11**	81.94	100	12.50
2	208/ 38	0	0	**0**	2	8	**10**	95.93	98.37	93.50

Table 4. Classification results on the "Pima diabetes" dataset.

Type of algorithm	The size of the training/testing set	Errors						Accuracy, (%)	Sensitivity, (%)	Specificity, (%)
		At the training			At the testing					
		positive	negative	total	positive	negative	total			
1	614/ 154	63	20	**83**	22	15	**37**	84.38	68.28	93.00
2	800/ 200	15	34	**49**	17	19	**36**	91.50	93.60	89.40

These free medical datasets are "Heart", "Hepatitis" and "Pima diabetes". In each of them, the positive class consists of the data corresponding to the healthy, normal, or benign cases, while the negative class contains the data for the diseased, abnormal, or malignant cases. Further details of these datasets are provided in Tabl. 1.

In Tabl. 1 the value of imbalance ratio (Ratio) was calculated by the following formula:

$$Ratio = 1 - \frac{a_1}{a_2},$$

where a_1 is the number of objects in the minority class; a_2 is the number of objects in the majority class.

The results of application of the SVM-PSO algorithm and the Smote-SVM-PSO algorithm are shown in Tabl. 2, Tabl. 3, and Tabl. 4 (with the following type of algorithms: 1 is the SVM-PSO algorithm, 2 is the Smote-SVM-PSO algorithm).

For the "Heart" dataset the class imbalance is not obviously shaped, therefore, the results of the SVM-PSO algorithm is not very different from the Smote-SVMPSO algorithm. Herewith, Tabl. 1 shows the results for the "Heart" dataset for two cases depending on the choice of datasets for training and testing.

We can say that the effectiveness of the SVM classifier can be improved indeed when the structure of the data is taken into consideration.

For the other datasets the class imbalance is considerable, therefore the SVM-PSO algorithm concedes to the Smote-SVM-PSO algorithm, as the results of the SVM-PSO algorithm are characterized by the low values of accuracy, specificity and sensitivity. These results justify the fact that standard SVM algorithm are sensitive to the class imbalance problem.

The obtained results correspond to the implementation of the SMOTE algorithm with the default parameters values used in the Python library.

Also, we suggested the searching algorithm for the optimum parameters values of the SMOTE algorithm. In particular, we considered two parameters: the number k of nearest neighbours to used to construct synthetic samples; the number m of nearest neighbours to use to determine if a minority sample is in danger.

The suggested searching algorithm can be described by the following sequence of steps.

Step 1. To generate the pairs (k_i, m_j) on the base of the integer parameters values from the ranges $[k_{min}, k_{max}]$ and $[m_{min}, m_{max}]$ ($i = \overline{1, k_{max} - k_{min} + 1}$; $j = \overline{1, m_{max} - m_{min} + 1}$).

Step 2. To build for each pair (k_i, m_j) n SVM classifiers using the SMOTE algorithm for the imbalanced data (that is to apply the SMOTE algorithm for each pair (k_i, m_j) with equal probability).

Step 3. To evaluate the classification quality of the developed SVM classifiers and save the obtained SVM classifiers. To find the best SVM classifier, if the maximum value of iteration is achieved, and finish the algorithm. Otherwise, to go to step 4.

Step 4. To estimate the average classification quality of the SVM classifiers using, for example, the F-measure indicator for each pair (k_i, m_j). To change the probabilities of application for each pair (k_i, m_j): to increase the probability for the best pair (k_i, m_j) (with the maximum value of the average classification quality), and to decrease the probabilities for the other pairs (k_i, m_j). To build for each pair (k_i, m_j) the SVM classifiers using the SMOTE algorithm for the imbalanced data according to the new probabilities. Go to step 3.

It is proposed to use the following ideas at the step 4 to estimate the average classification quality of the SVM classifiers for each pair (k_i, m_j):

• to find the total number N_{ij}^g of the SVM classifiers for each pair (k_i, m_j), obtained to the current number g of iteration of the suggested algorithm;

• to find the total sum S_{ij}^g of the classification quality of the SVM classifiers for each pair (k_i, m_j), obtained to the current number g of iteration of the suggested algorithm;

• to find the ratio S_{ij}^g / N_{ij}^g for each pair (k_i, m_j), and use it as the average classification quality of the SVM classifiers for pair (k_i, m_j).

It is necessary to say, that we generate the different balanced datasets, using the random number generator for each pair (k_i, m_j), therefore, the developed SVM classifiers will be differ from each other.

The offered algorithm allows minimizing the time expenditures for the search of the optimal parameters values of the SMOTE algorithm, and, hence, for development of the SVM classifier.

5 Conclusion

The experimental results show that the SMOTE algorithm improves the classification quality of the SVM classifiers for the imbalanced data. Herewith, for the datasets with the high imbalance, the effectiveness of the SMOTE algorithm is very high.

The offered algorithm allows minimizing the time expenditures for the search of the optimal parameters values of the SMOTE algorithm.

Further, we plan to consider the values of several classification quality indicators simultaneously at the choice of the optimal parameters values of the SMOTE algorithm.

References

1. V.N. Vapnik, *Statistical Learning Theory*, (Wiley, 1998)
2. L. Yu, S. Wang, K. K. Lai, L. Zhou, *Bio-Inspired Credit Risk Analysis. Computational Intelligence with Support Vector Machines* (Springer, 2008)
3. N. Chawla, K. Bowyer, L.Hall, W. Kegelmeyer, JIAR, **16**, 341-378 (2002)
4. X. Gu, T. Ni, H. Wang, Scientific World Journal, **2014**, 102-113 (2014)
5. S. Zafeiriou, A. Tefas, I. Pitas, IEEE Transactions on Image Processing, **16**(10), 2551-2564 (2007)
6. R. Batuwita, V. Palade, IEEE Transactions on Fuzzy Systems, **18**(3), 558-571 (2010)
7. L. Demidova, I. Klyueva, A. Pylkin, 5-th Mediterranean Conference on Embedded Computing (MECO'2016), 322-325 (2016)
8. L. Demidova, I. Klyueva, Y. Sokolova, N. Stepanov, N. Tyart, *Procedia Computer Science*, **103**, 222-230 (2017)
9. L. Demidova, E. Nikulchev, Y. Sokolova, International Journal of Advanced Computer Science and Applications, **7**(5), 294 (2017)
10. H. Wang, D. Bell, Computer Journal, **47**(6), 662-672 (2004)

SVM Classifiers: The Objects Identification on the Base of Their Hyperspectral Features

Liliya Demidova[1, 2, *], *Yulia* Sokolova[2], and *Sergey* Trukhanov[3]

[1]Moscow Technological Institute, 119334 Moscow, Russia
[2]State Radio Engineering University, 390005 Ryazan, Russia
[3]Branch of JSC „SRC „Progress" – Special Design Bureau „Spectr", 390005 Ryazan, Russia

Abstract. The problem of the objects identification on the base of their hyperspectral features has been considered. It is offered to use the SVM classifiers on the base of the modified PSO algorithm, adapted to specifics of the problem of the objects identification on the base of their hyperspectral features. The results of the objects identification on the base of their hyperspectral features with using of the SVM classifiers have been presented.

1 Page layout

The problem of analysis of the hyperspectral information formed on the base of the hyperspectral images of the Earth's surface is one of the actual problems solved by the remote sensing systems. The russian „Resource-P" spacecrafts No. 1 – 3 with the hyperspectral equipment on the board give out the hyperspectral image (HSI) in the form of pictures in 130 narrow adjoining ranges of visible area of spectrum. During the HSI processing much attention is paid to the questions of the objects identification on the base of their hyperspectral features (HSF).

The object's HSF in a graphic form can be presented as the relationship mapping between the wavelength and the values of the spectral brightness coefficient (SBC), or the spectral reflection coefficient (SRC) of the analyzed object. However, at the solution of the problem of the objects identification on the base of their HSF the use of the SRC dependence on wavelength is more preferable because the brightness feature doesn't depend on the shooting conditions in such degree as the SBC. Besides, unlike the SBC, for obtaining the SRC values the standard reflecting surface in sight of the analyzed object isn't necessary.

In this paper we suggest to use the SVM classifiers on the base of the modified PSO algorithm, adapted to specifics of the problem of the objects identification on the base of their hyperspectral features. Herewith, we test the different approaches to application of the SVM algorithm to development of the SVM classifier: the basic SVM classifier, the two-level classifier, the SVM ensemble. All of them apply the modified PSO algorithm to find the type of the kernel function, the values of the parameters of the kernel function and the value of the regularization parameter of the SVM classifier. Also, the SVM ensemble uses the principle of maximum decorrelation to choose the individual SVM classifier, which will be included into the SVM ensemble.

The SVM algorithm (Support Vector Machines, SVM) is successfully used for development of the SVM classifiers for a wide range of the classification problems [1]. The SVM classifier uses the special kernel function to construct a hyperplane separating the classes of data. The SVM classifier is used for training and testing. The satisfactory quality of training and testing allows using the resulting SVM classifier in the classification of new objects.

Choosing the optimal parameters values for the SMV classifier is a significant problem at the moment. It is necessary to find the kernel function type, values of the kernel function parameters and the value of the regularization parameter [1, 2]. It is impossible to provide implementing of high-accuracy data classification with the use of the SVM classifier without adequate solution to this problem. In the simplest case solution to this problem can be found by a search of the kernel function types, the values of the kernel function parameters and the value of the regularization parameter that demands significant computational expenses. The gradient methods are not suitable for search of the optimum of this objective function, but search algorithms of stochastic optimization, such as the genetic algorithm, the artificial bee colony algorithm, the particle swarm algorithm, etc., have been used. Each of the optimal decision is carried out at once in all space of possible decisions.

The PSO algorithm, which is based on an idea of possibility to solve the optimization problems using modelling of animals' groups' behaviour is the simplest algorithm of evolutionary programming because for its implementation it is necessary to be able to determine only value of the optimized function.

* Corresponding author: liliya.demidova@rambler.ru

The traditional approach to application of the PSO algorithm consists of the repeated applications of the PSO algorithm for the fixed type of the kernel function to choose the optimal values of the kernel function parameters and the value of the regularization parameter with the subsequent choice of the best type of the kernel function and the values of the kernel function parameters and the value of the regularization parameter corresponding to this kernel function type.

Here, we suggest to use the modified PSO algorithm to find the type of the kernel function, the values of the parameters of the kernel function and the value of the regularization parameter of the SVM classifier simultaneously.

2 Theoretical part

Let the experimental data set be a set in the form of $\{(z_1,y_1),\ldots,(z_s,y_s)\}$, in which each object $z_i \in Z$ ($i=\overline{1,s}$; s is the number of objects) is assigned to a number $y_i \in Y=\{+1;\ -1\}$ having a value of +1 or −1 depending on the class of the object z_i. It is assumed that every object z_i is mapped to q-dimensional vector of numerical values of features $z_i=(z_i^1,z_i^2,\ldots,z_i^q)$ (typically normalized by values from the interval [0, 1]) where z_i^l is the numeric value of the l-th feature for the i-th object ($i=\overline{1,s}$, $l=\overline{1,q}$) [1–3]. It is necessary to use the kernel function $\kappa(z_i,z_\tau)$ to build the classifier $F:Z\to Y$, which compares the class to the number from the set $Y=\{+1;\ -1\}$ or some object from the set Z. In training of the SVM classifier it is necessary to determine the kernel function type $\kappa(z_i,z_\tau)$, values of the kernel parameters and value of the regularization parameter C, which allows finding a compromise between maximizing of the gap separating the classes and minimizing of the total error [1–4]. A herewith typically one of the following functions is used as the kernel function $\kappa(z_i,z_\tau)$: linear function; polynomial function; radial basis function; sigmoid function [5, 6].

To build "the best" SVM classifier it is necessary to implement the numerous repeated training (for the training data set with S elements) and testing (for the test data set $s-S$ elements, $S<s$) on the different randomly generated training and test sets with following determination of the best SVM classifier in terms of the highest possible classification quality provision. The SVM classifier with satisfactory training and testing results can be used to classify new objects [6].

As a result of the training, the classification function is determined in the following form [1–3]:

$$f(z)=\sum_{i=1}^{S}\lambda_i\cdot y_i\cdot\kappa(z_i,z)+b\,. \qquad (1)$$

The classification decision, associating the object z to the class −1 or +1, is adopted in accordance with the rule [1–3]:

$$F(z)=sign(f(z))=sign\left(\sum_{i=1}^{S}\lambda_i\cdot y_i\cdot\kappa(z_i,z)+b\right). \qquad (2)$$

The training of the SVM classifier results in determining the support vectors [1–4]. Using the modified PSO algorithm provides the better classification accuracy by choosing the kernel function type, the values of the kernel function parameters and the value of the regularization parameter. Also, the modified PSO algorithm allows reducing the time expenditures for development of the SVM classifier [5]. The quality of the SVM classifier can be measured by different classification quality indicators.

In the traditional PSO algorithm the n-dimensional search space (n is the number of parameters which are subject to optimization) is inhabited by a swarm of m agents-particles. The position of the i-th particle is determined by vector $x_i=(x_i^1,x_i^2,\ldots,x_i^n)$, which defines a set of values of optimization parameters. These parameters can be presented in an explicit form or even absent in the analytical record of the objective function $u(x)$ of the optimization algorithm Each i-th particle ($i=\overline{1,m}$) has its own vector of speed $v_i\in R^n$ which influence i-th particle ($i=1,m$) coordinates' values in every single moment of time corresponding to some iteration of the PSO algorithm.

The coordinates of the i-th particle ($i=\overline{1,m}$) in the n-dimensional search space uniquely determine the value of the objective function $u(x)$ which is a certain solution of the optimization problem. For each position of the n-dimensional search space where the i-th particle ($i=\overline{1,m}$) was placed, the calculation of value of the objective function $u(x_i)$ is performed. Each i-th particle remembers the best value of the objective function found personally as well as the coordinates of the position in the n-dimensional space corresponding to the value of the objective function. Moreover each i-th particle ($i=\overline{1,m}$) "knows" the best position among all positions that had been "explored" by particles. At each iteration particles correct their velocity to, on the one hand, move closer to the best position which was found by the particle independently and, on the other hand, to get closer to the position which is the best globally at the current moment. After a number of iterations particles must come close to the best position (globally the best for all iterations). However, it is possible that some particles will stay somewhere in the relatively good local optimum.

There are different approaches to implementation of velocity vector v_i correction for the i-th particle ($i=\overline{1,m}$). In the classical version of the PSO algorithm correction of each j-th coordinate of velocity vector ($j=\overline{1,n}$) of the i-th particle ($i=\overline{1,m}$) is made in accordance with formula [6]:

$$v_i^j=v_i^j+\hat{\varphi}\cdot\hat{r}\cdot(\hat{x}_i^j-x_i^j)+\tilde{\varphi}\cdot\tilde{r}\cdot(\tilde{x}^j-x_i^j), \qquad (3)$$

where v_i^j is the j-th coordinate of velocity vector of the i-th particle; x_i^j is the j-th coordinate of vector x_i, defining the position of the i-th particle; $\hat{x}_i^j$ is the j-th coordinate of the best position vector found by the i-th particle during its existence; $\tilde{x}^j$ is the j-th coordinate of the globally best position within the particles swarm in which the objective function has the optimal value; $\hat{r}$ and $\tilde{r}$ are random numbers in interval (0, 1); $\hat{\varphi}$ and $\tilde{\varphi}$ are personal and global coefficients for particle acceleration.

With personal and global acceleration coefficients in (3) random numbers $\hat{r}$ and $\tilde{r}$ must be scaled; the global acceleration coefficient $\tilde{\varphi}$ operates by the impact of the global best position on the speeds of all particles and the personal acceleration coefficient $\hat{\varphi}$ operates by the impact of the personal best position on the velocity of some particle.

Currently different versions of the traditional PSO algorithm are known. In one of the most known canonical version it is supposed to undertake the normalization of the acceleration coefficients $\hat{\varphi}$ and $\tilde{\varphi}$ to make the convergence of the algorithm not so much dependent on the choice of their values [6].

The correction of each j-th coordinate of the velocity vector ($j = \overline{1,n}$) of the i-th particle ($i = \overline{1,m}$) is performed in accordance with formula [6]:

$$v_i^j = \chi \cdot [v_i^j + \hat{\varphi} \cdot \hat{r} \cdot (\hat{x}_i^j - x_i^j) + \tilde{\varphi} \cdot \tilde{r} \cdot (\tilde{x}^j - x_i^j)], \quad (4)$$

where χ is a compression ratio;

$$\chi = 2 \cdot K / \left| 2 - \varphi - \sqrt{\varphi^2 - 4 \cdot \varphi} \right|; \quad (5)$$

$$\varphi = \hat{\varphi} + \tilde{\varphi} \ (\varphi > 4); \quad (6)$$

K is some scaling coefficient, which takes values from the interval (0, 1).

Let the correction of velocity vector of the i-th particle ($i = \overline{1,m}$) is executed in accordance with one of the formulas (3) or (4). The correction of the j-th coordinate of the i-th particle ($i = \overline{1,m}$) can be executed in accordance with the formula:

$$x_i^j = x_i^j + v_i^j. \quad (7)$$

Then for each i-th particle ($i = \overline{1,m}$) the new value of the objective function $u(x_i)$ can be calculated and the following check must be performed: whether a new position with coordinates vector x_i became the best among all positions in which the i-th particle has previously been placed. If new position of the i-th particle is recognized to be the best at the current moment the information about it must be stored in a vector $\hat{x}_i$.

The value of the objective function $u(x_i)$ for this position must be remembered. Then among all new positions of the swarm particles the check of the globally best position must be carried out. If some new position is recognized as the best globally at the current moment, the information about it must be stored in vector $\tilde{x}$. Value of the objective function $u(x_i)$ for this position must be remembered. In the case of the SVM classifier development with the use of the PSO algorithm the swarm particles can be defined by vectors declaring their position in the search space and corded by the kernel function parameters and the regularization parameter: (x_i^1, x_i^2, C_i), where i is a number of particle ($i = \overline{1,m}$); x_i^1, x_i^2 are the kernel function parameters of the i-th particle, (parameter x_i^1 is equal to the kernel function parameters d, σ or k_2; parameter x_i^2 is equal to the kernel function parameter k_1, if the swamp particle corresponds to the sigmoid type of the kernel function, otherwise this parameter is assumed to be zero); C_i is the regularization parameter [5, 6].

As a result, for each type T of the kernel function, participating in the search, the particle with the optimal combination of the parameters values $(\tilde{x}^1, \tilde{x}^2, \tilde{C})$ providing high quality of classification will be defined [6]. The best type and the best values of the required parameters are found using the results of the comparative analysis of the best particles received at realization of the PSO algorithm with the fixed kernel function type.

Along with the traditional approach to the application of the PSO algorithm in the development of the SVM classifier there is a new approach that implements a simultaneous search for the best kernel function type $\tilde{T}$, parameters' values $\tilde{x}^1$ and $\tilde{x}^2$ of the kernel function and value of the regularization parameter $\tilde{C}$ [6]. At such approach each i-th particle in a swamp ($i = \overline{1,m}$) defined by a vector which describes particle's position in the search space: (T_i, x_i^1, x_i^2, C_i), where T_i is the number of the kernel function type (for example, 1, 2, 3 – for polynomial, radial basis and sigmoid functions accordingly); parameters x_i^1, x_i^2, C_i are defined as in the previous case. It is possible to "regenerate" particle through changing its coordinate T_i on number of that kernel function type, for which particles show the highest quality of classification. In the case of particles' "regeneration" the parameters' values change so that they corresponded to new type of the kernel function. Particles which didn't undergo "regeneration", carry out the movement in own space of search of some dimension. The number of particles taking part in "regeneration" must be determined before start of algorithm. This number must be equal to 15% – 25% of the initial number of particles.

The offered modified PSO algorithm can be presented by the following consequence of steps [5, 6].

Step 1. To determine parameters of the PSO algorithm: number m of particles in a swamp, velocity coefficient K, personal and global velocity coefficients $\hat{\varphi}$ and $\tilde{\varphi}$, maximum iterations number $N_{\max}$ of the PSO algorithm. To determine types T of kernel functions, which take part in the search and ranges boundaries of the kernel function parameters and the regularization parameter C for the chosen kernel functions' types T: $x^{1T}_{\min}$, $x^{1T}_{\max}$, $x^{2T}_{\min}$, $x^{2T}_{\max}$, $C^{T}_{\min}$, $C^{T}_{\max}$ ($x^{2T}_{\min}=0$ and $x^{2T}_{\max}=0$ for $T=1$ and $T=2$). To determine the particles' "regeneration" percentage p.

Step 2. To define equal number of particles for each kernel type function T, included in search, to initialize coordinate T_i for each i-th particle ($i=\overline{1,m}$), other coordinates of the i-th particle ($i=\overline{1,m}$) must be generated randomly from the corresponding ranges: $x^1_i \in [x^{1T}_{\min}, x^{1T}_{\max}]$, $x^2_i \in [x^{2T}_{\min}, x^{2T}_{\max}]$ ($x^2_i=0$ under $T=1$ and $T=2$), $C_i \in [C^T_{\min}, C^T_{\max}]$. To initialize random velocity vector $v_i(v^1_i, v^2_i, v^3_i)$ of the i-th particle ($i=\overline{1,m}$) ($v^2_i=0$ under $T=1$ and $T=2$). To establish initial position of the i-th particle ($i=\overline{1,m}$) as its best known position ($\hat{T}_i, \hat{x}^1_i, \hat{x}^2_i, \hat{C}_i$), to determine the best particle with coordinates' vector ($\tilde{T}, \tilde{x}^1, \tilde{x}^2, \tilde{C}$) from all the m particles, and to determine the best particle for each kernel function type T, including in a search, with coordinates' vector ($\overline{T}, \overline{x}^{1T}, \overline{x}^{2T}, \overline{C}^T$). Number of executed iterations must be considered as 1.

Step 3. To execute while the number of iterations is less than the fixed number $N_{\max}$:

• "regeneration" of particles: to choose p% of particles which represent the lowest quality of classification from particles with coordinate $T_i \neq \tilde{T}$ ($i=\overline{1,m}$); to change coordinate on $\tilde{T}$; to change values of the parameters x^1_i, x^2_i, C_i of "regenerated" particles to let them correspond to a new kernel function type $\tilde{T}$;

• correction of velocity vector $v_i(v^1_i, v^2_i, v^3_i)$ and position (x^1_i, x^2_i, C_i) of the i-th particle ($i=\overline{1,m}$) using formulas:

$$v^j_i = \begin{cases} \chi\cdot[v^j_i + \hat{\varphi}\cdot\hat{r}\cdot(\hat{x}^j_i - x^j_i) + \tilde{\varphi}\cdot\tilde{r}\cdot(\overline{x}^{jT} - x^j_i)], & j=1,\ 2, \\ \chi\cdot[v^j_i + \hat{\varphi}\cdot\hat{r}\cdot(\hat{C}_i - C_i) + \tilde{\varphi}\cdot\tilde{r}\cdot(\overline{C}^T - C_i)], & j=3, \end{cases} \quad (8)$$

$$x^j_i = x^j_i + v^j_i \text{ for } j=1,\ 2, \quad (9)$$

$$C_i = C_i + v^3_i, \quad (10)$$

where $\hat{r}$ and $\tilde{r}$ are random numbers in interval (0, 1), χ is a compression ratio calculated using the formula (5); formula (8) is the modification of formula (4): the coordinates' values $\overline{x}^{1T}, \overline{x}^{2T}, \overline{C}^T$ are used instead of the coordinates' values $\tilde{x}^1, \tilde{x}^2, \tilde{C}$ of the globally best particle;

• accuracy calculation of the SVM classifier with parameters' values (T_i, x^1_i, x^2_i, C_i) ($i=\overline{1,m}$) with aim to find the optimal combination ($\tilde{T}, \tilde{x}^1, \tilde{x}^2, \tilde{C}$), which will provide high quality of classification;

• increase the number of iterations on 1.

The particle with the optimal combination of the parameters' values ($\tilde{T}, \tilde{x}^1, \tilde{x}^2, \tilde{C}$) which provides the highest quality of classification on chosen the function types will be defined after execution of the offered algorithm.

3 Experimental studies

The SVM classifiers were applied for classification of the objects of the Earth's surface. Herewith, we considered the identification problem of the water objects and the identification problem of the anthropogenous objects.

The datasets have been created on the base of 127 hyperspectral features of 220 standard objects. Information on these objects has been obtained according to the hyperspectral shooting from the „Resource-P" spacecraft No. 1. This information forms the spectral library of the HSFs. The HSF of the analyzable object represents a vector of the coefficients dependence of the spectral reflection on the wavelength of the registered radiation.

At the development of the SVM classifier we used the several train and test sets, formed randomly on the base of the dataset with the HSFs of the standard objects. Herewith, we applied the several kernel function types with the values of parameters set by default. The size of the test set was equal to 20% of the size of the initial dataset with the HSFs of the standard objects.

For evaluation of the classification quality of the developed SVM classifier we used the well-known classification quality indicators, such as the F-measure indicator, the sensitivity indicator (Se), the specificity indicator (Sp), the accuracy indicator, the number of errors of I and II type, the AUC indicator, calculated on the test set, etc. The results of the SVM classifier development are given in Table 1.

The SVM classifiers developed with the values of the parameters set by default for the water objects have the high ability to generalization: the values of all quality indicators are high (Table 1), and the SVM classifiers developed with the values of the parameters set by default for the anthropogenous objects are inferior in the classification quality to the SVM classifiers for the water objects (Table 1). Therefore, there is a need for finding of the values of the parameters of the SVM classifiers allowing to identify the anthropogenous objects with the more high classification quality.

The search of the optimum values of the SVM classifier parameters for the anthropogenous objects was performed using the traditional and modified PSO algorithms (with the identical ranges of change of the parameters values and with the identical parameters values of the PSO algorithm). We used the swarm of 300 particles and carried out 15 iterations of the PSO algorithms. Hence, we analyzed 4500 SVM classifiers and have chosen from them the best.

Table 1. The results of the SVM classifier development with the values of the kernel function parameters set by default.

Objects of classify-cation	The experiment number	The kernel function type	Value of the kernel function parameter	C	The SV number	The errors number				AUC_{test}	Se, %	Sp, %	F-measure, %	Accuracy, %
						At the training	At the testing	1-st type	2-st type					
Water objects	1	polynom.	3	1	34	0 of 176	1 of 44	1	0	1.0000	98.11	100	99.05	99.55
	2	polynom.	3	1	32	0 of 176	1 of 44	0	1	1.0000	100.00	99.40	99.07	99.55
	3	rbf	1	1	149	0 of 176	4 of 44	3	1	0.9746	94.34	99.40	96.15	98.18
	4	rbf	1	1	152	1 of 176	3 of 44	1	3	0.9818	98.11	98.20	96.30	98.18
Anthro-pogenous objects	5	rbf	1	1	155	9 of 176	9 of 44	7	11	0.8190	91.25	92.14	89.02	91.82
	6	rbf	1	1	156	8 of 176	8 of 44	3	13	0.8437	96.25	90.71	90.59	92.73
	7	rbf	1	1	154	11 of 176	8 of 44	5	14	0.8506	93.75	90.00	88.76	91.36

Table 2. The results of the SVM classifier development with the values of the kernel function parameters which are found the modified PSO algorithm for the anthropogenous objects.

The experiment number	The found parameters		First iteration	Search first time (sec.)	Search time (sec.)	The SV number	The errors number				AUC_{test}	Se, %	Sp, %	F-measure, %	Accuracy, (%)
	C	σ					At the training	At the testing	1-st type	2-st type					
8	9.4510	1.9650	0	84	400	123	6 of 176	7 of 44	4	9	0.8594	95.00	93.57	92.12	94.09
9	4.1483	1.2558	2	165	296	143	6 of 176	6 of 44	3	9	0.8301	96.25	93.57	92.77	94.55
10	8.6251	1.7315	15	341	341	132	5 of 176	5 of 44	3	7	0.9107	96.25	95.00	93.90	95.45
11	5.1753	1.1390	12	262	294	142	3 of 176	7 of 44	4	6	0.8388	95.00	95.71	93.83	95.45

As a result, both PSO algorithms determined the radial kernel function as the optimum kernel function type, the similar values of the parameter of kernel function and the value of the regularization parameter, and also the similar values of the accuracy indicator on the train and test sets for the SVM classifier developed taking into account the found parameter values. However, the modified PSO algorithm was more effective on the search time: the search time of the required decision spent by it appeared less (by 2 – 3 times) than the search time using by the traditional PSO algorithm. Table 2 shows the results of the SVM classifier development with the values of the kernel function parameters which are found the modified PSO algorithm for the anthropogenous objects.

4 Conclusions

The use of the SVM classifier to the objects identification on the base of their HSF allows providing the high classification accuracy. The results of experimental studies confirm the expediency of further development of the offered approach to the solution of the objects identification on the base of their HSF.

The use of the offered approach will allow to solve the objects identification's problem of the Earth's surface on allocated from the processed space images of the „Resource-P" spacecraft HSF with the subsequent accumulation of the standard HSFs in the database that, in turn, will provide creation of actual domestic spectral library of standards HSFs which can be applied when monitoring a condition of agricultural grounds, forests, water resources, an ecological condition of soils, etc. [7]. Herewith, it is necessary to create the representative dataset of the HSFs and use it to learn the SVM-classifiers. Then, we can identify the new HSF as the HSF of the known class.

References

1. O. Chapelle, V. Vapnik, O. Bousquet, S. Mukherjee, Machine Learning, **46**, 131 (2002)
2. L. Yu, S. Wang, K. K. Lai, L. Zhou, *Bio-Inspired Credit Risk Analysis. Computational Intelligence with Support Vector Machines* (Springer, 2008)
3. L. Demidova, Yu. Sokolova, E. Nikulchev, International Review on Modelling and Simulations, **8**, 446 (2015)
4. L. Demidova, Y. Sokolova, International Conference "Stability and Control Processes" in Memory of V.I. Zubov, 619-622 (2015)
5. L. Demidova, E. Nikulchev, Y. Sokolova, International Journal of Advanced Computer Science and Applications, **7**(2), 16 (2016)
6. L. Demidova, E. Nikulchev, Y. Sokolova, International Journal of Advanced Computer Science and Applications, **7**(5), 294 (2016)
7. O. Grigorieva, O. Brovkina, V. Mochalov, Y. Akhtman, V. Zelentsov, S. Potryasaev, I. Kozyr, N. Belova, The 4th International Workshop on Simulation for Energy, Sustainable Development and Environment (2016)

ITM Web of Conferences **10**, 02004 (2017) DOI: 10.1051/itmconf/20171002004
2017 Seminar on Systems Analysis

Complete Binary Variational Analytic Programming for Synthesis of Control at Dynamic Constraints

Askhat Diveev[1,2], and *Elizaveta* Shmalko[1,2,*]

[1]Federal Research Centre "Computer Science and Control" of Russia Academy of Sciences, 119333Moscow, Russia
[2]RUDN University, Engineering Academy, 117198 Moscow, Russia

Abstract. Dynamic constraints arise at control of the robot moving in the neighborhood of other robots. In this case, together with ensuring stability of the robot in a goal point it is necessary to provide instability for the robot in the area of state space where is some other robot. For the solution of this task, we use a new method of symbolic regression - a method of binary variational analytical programming. The new method has advantages in comparison with genetic or analytical programming in case of performing crossover, and it uses the principle of small variations of the basic solution to increase the efficiency of an algorithm of search of the optimal solution.

1 Introduction

Solution of control tasks for robot movement originally involves providing stability of the robot concerning the set of points in state space, then building trajectories of robots movements. The trajectories consist of points of state space. To design trajectories, engineer must consider various constraints including the dynamic constraints arising because of presence of other robots in the neighbourhood of the trajectory. The problem of control of movement of stable robot concerning some set of points in a state space does not cause big difficulties. It is enough to set a point in the state space, and the robot because of property of stability itself will be going to it. Difficulties in control arise when the constraints in the neighbourhood of the robot appear. The most complex problem arises when some other moving robot creates the constraints. If we know the paths of the other robot, then to avoid collisions we can construct such trajectories of stable points in the state space that both robots can move without collisions among them. The most complex problem arises when in the neighbourhood of the robot there appears another robot with unknown direction of the movement. In this case, creation of trajectories of stable points in the state space is impossible because of difficulty to predict real position of other robot. In practice in these cases a control system turns on a special mode which has the main objective to avoid collision with the disturbing object.

In this work for the solution of the stated problem, we use a method of synthesis of "stable-unstable" control. The synthesized control system in the form of feedback function depending on a state of the object has to provide stability of the object concerning one given point of state space and instability concerning other point of the state space. We deliver two types of points of state space to an input of a control system. The points of the first type define the goal of the movement of the robot. The points of the second type determine space coordinates of the disturbing robot. For the second type points, we determine also the area of instability. The synthesized function of control together with the set of two-type points in the state space defines mathematical model of the control object in the form of system of ordinary differential equations with special points of two types, a stable point of the goal of the movement and an unstable point to avoid a collision with the disturbing robot. For the second point we set the limited area of instability. To solve the problem of synthesis of stable-unstable control, we use a method of symbolic regression [1-3].

Application of numerical methods of symbolic regression for the solution of the problem of synthesis is already known [3-9]. Unlike the known numerical solutions of the synthesis problem, in the present work we use a new approach of synthesis of stable-unstable control of a plant. Moreover, the known methods of symbolic regression have an essential shortcoming for an algorithm of evolutionary search. In these methods [1-9] at search of the optimal solution by a genetic algorithm, it is necessary to carry out the main crossover operation in certain points, or it is essential to adjust the new solution after accomplishment of the crossover. Use of the principle of small variations [10] of the basic solution, as in variational methods of genetic and analytical programming [11-13], does not significantly change the situation. It is possible to obtain an incorrect code after some variations, and this requires a correction of the code. It leads to consumption of computing time and breaks the principle of small variations.

* Corresponding author: e.shmalko@gmail.com

To search for a solution, we use a method of binary variation analytic programming [14] in its complete form. The method codes mathematical expressions in the form of a copmlete binary computing tree and in the computer memory in the form of the ordered limited set of integers. Nodes of the tree-graph are connected with functions with two arguments. Edges of the graph are connected with functions with one argument. Leaves of the tree or source-nodes of the graph are connected with arguments of mathematical expression or with unit elements of functions with two arguments. Functions with one argument includes the identity function. To expand a class of required functions, we add constant parameters to arguments of mathematical expression. The proposed method of complete binary variation analytic programming allows carry out crossover operation in any point and does not demand correction of a code at any variations. We look for values of parameters together with structure of mathematical expression.

2 Problem Statement

Consider formal problem statement of synthesis of stable-unstable control.

Set a model of control object

$$\dot{\mathbf{x}} = \mathbf{f}(\mathbf{x},\mathbf{u}), \quad (1)$$

where $\mathbf{x}$ is a vector of state, $\mathbf{x} \in \mathbf{R}^n$, $\mathbf{x} = [x_1 \ldots x_n]^T$, $\mathbf{u}$ is a vector of control, $\mathbf{u} \in \mathbf{R}^m$, $\mathbf{u} = [u_1 \ldots u_m]^T$, $m \le n$.

Set constraints on the control

$$\mathbf{u} \in \mathrm{U} \subseteq \mathbf{R}^m, \quad (2)$$

where U is a compact set.

Set a terminal point

$$\mathbf{x}^* \in \mathbf{R}^n. \quad (3)$$

Set a limited unstable area

$$\tilde{\mathrm{X}} \subseteq \mathbf{R}^n \quad (4)$$

and an unstable point

$$\tilde{\mathbf{x}} \in \tilde{\mathrm{X}} \subseteq \mathbf{R}^n. \quad (5)$$

It is necessary to find a control in the form of function of space coordinates

$$\mathbf{u} = \mathbf{h}(\mathbf{x}),$$

$$\mathbf{h}(\mathbf{x}): \mathbf{R}^n \to \mathbf{R}^m,\ \forall \mathbf{x} \in \mathbf{R}^n,\ \mathbf{h}(\mathbf{x}) \in \mathrm{U} \subseteq \mathbf{R}^m. \quad (6)$$

The closed system of the differential equations $\dot{\mathbf{x}} = \mathbf{f}(\mathbf{x},\mathbf{h}(\mathbf{x}))$ is locally unstable concerning $\tilde{\mathbf{x}}$ in unstable area $\tilde{\mathrm{X}} \subseteq \mathbf{R}^n$ and is stable concerning the terminal point $\mathbf{x}^* \in \mathbf{R}^n$.

For the solution of the task, we use a numerical method of symbolic regression which by means of an evolutionary algorithm will find the function meeting the specified requirements. For numerical assessment of the selected function we use the following criterion:

$$J(\mathbf{x}^0) = \int_0^{t^+} f_0(\mathbf{x}(t), \mathbf{x}^*, \tilde{\mathbf{x}})dt, \quad (7)$$

where t^+ is a defined time of control process, $\mathbf{x}^0$ is initial conditions $\mathbf{x}^0 = \mathbf{x}(0)$,

$$f_0(\mathbf{x}(t),\mathbf{x}^*,\tilde{\mathbf{x}}) = \begin{cases} \|\mathbf{x}(t)-\mathbf{x}^*\|, \text{ if } \|\mathbf{x}(t)-\tilde{\mathbf{x}}\|_2 > r \\ \|\mathbf{x}(t)-\mathbf{x}^*\| + r - \|\mathbf{x}(t)-\tilde{\mathbf{x}}\|_2, \text{otherwise} \end{cases},$$

r is a given size of unstable area,

$$\|\mathbf{x}-\tilde{\mathbf{x}}\|_2 = \sqrt{\sum_{i=1}^{n}(x_i - \tilde{x}_i)^2}$$

$$\|\mathbf{x}-\mathbf{x}^*\| = \max\{|x_i - x_i^*| : i = 1,\ldots,n\}.$$

For ensuring properties of stability and instability, calculate the functional (7) for a given set of initial conditions

$$J = \sum_{i=1}^{M} J(\mathbf{x}^{0,i}) \to \min, \quad (8)$$

where $\mathbf{x}^{0,i}$ is given initial conditions, $i = 1,\ldots,M$.

3 Complete Binary Variational Analytic Programming

To build a code of binary analytic programming we use the following basic sets:

- a set of arguments of mathematical expression

$$\mathrm{F}_0 = (q_1,\ldots,q_P,x_1,\ldots,x_N); \quad (9)$$

- a set of functions with one argument

$$\mathrm{F}_1 = (f_{1,1}(z) = z, f_{1,2}(z),\ldots,f_{1,R}(z)); \quad (10)$$

- a set of functions with two arguments

$$\mathrm{F}_2 = (f_{2,1}(z_1,z_2),\ldots,f_{2,S}(z_1,z_2)); \quad (11)$$

- a set of unit elements for functions with two arguments

$$\mathrm{E}_2 = (e_1,\ldots,e_M). \quad (12)$$

A set of function with one argument must include the identity function

DOI: 10.1051/itmconf/20171002004

$$f_{1,1}(z)=z\,. \qquad (13)$$

Every function with two arguments of the set (11) has unit element from the set (12), $\forall f_{2,i}(z_1,z_2)\in \mathrm{F}_2$ $\exists e_j \in \mathrm{E}_2$

$$f_{2,i}(e_j,z_2)=z_2\,,\ f_{2,i}(z_1,e_j)=z_1\,, \qquad (14)$$

where $i\in\{1,\ldots,S\}$, $j\in\{1,\ldots,M\}$.

To generate a code of the binary analytic programming we combine into one ordered set a set of arguments (9) of mathematical expression, a set of unit elements (12)

$$\mathrm{F}=(f_1=q_1,\ldots,f_P=q_P,f_{P+1}=x_1,\ldots,f_{P+N}=x_N,$$

$$f_{P+N+1}=e_1,\ldots f_{P+N+M}=e_M) \qquad (15)$$

We write down mathematical expression in the form of composition of nested functions and arguments of mathematical expression

$$y=f_{\alpha_1}(f_{\alpha_2}(\ldots f_{\alpha_K})\ldots)=f_{\alpha_1}\circ f_{\alpha_2}\circ\ldots\circ f_{\alpha_K}\,, \qquad (16)$$

where $f_{\alpha_i}\in \mathrm{F}\cup\mathrm{F}_1\cup\mathrm{F}_2$, $i=1,\ldots,K$.

We define the most nesting depth of an element by the composition. Let the most depth is equal L. It means that we have binary computing tree with level L. It has 2^L leaves. We write down mathematical expression in the form of a complete binary computing tree (see Fig.1)

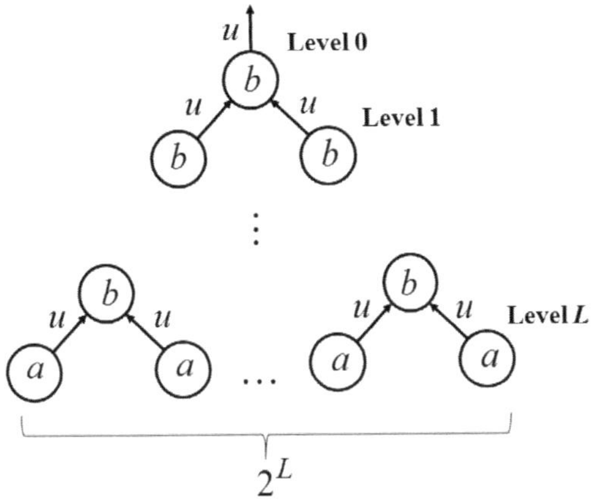

Fig. 1. A comlete binary computing tree

In the Fig.1 a is number of an element of set F (15), b is number of an element of set F_2 (11), u is number of an element of set F_1 (10). Each level includes numbers of elements from the set F_1 and the sane numbers of elements from the set F_2, and the last level includes numbers from the set F. If the tree has redundant nodes or edges, then we use number of any function with two arguments for nodes/ number the identity function for edges and number of unit element for this function with two arguments on the last level.

Code of binary variational analytic programming for mathematical expression is an ordered set of numbers of elements from first, second and others levels of the tree

$$\mathrm{C}=(u_1,b_1,u_{2,1},u_{2,2},b_{2,1},b_{2,2},\ldots$$

$$\ldots,u_{L,1},u_{L,2},\ldots,u_{L,2^L},a_{L,1},a_{L,2},\ldots,a_{L,2^L}) \qquad (17)$$

4 Variational Genetic Algorithm

To search for optimal solution, we use a variational genetic algorithm. Define a small variation of a code of binary analytic programming as an integer vector of two components

$$\mathbf{w}=[w_1\ w_2]^T\,, \qquad (18)$$

where w_1 is a position in a code, w_2 is a new value of element of the code.
Let

$$\mathrm{C}=(c_1,\ldots,\ c_K) \qquad (19)$$

be a code of mathematical expression for level L. Then

$$K=2^{L+2}-2\,, \qquad (20)$$

and we obtain after variation (18) a new code

$$\mathbf{w}\circ\mathrm{C}=(c_1,\ldots,\overbrace{w_2}^{w_1},\ldots,c_K)\,. \qquad (21)$$

The small variation (18) satisfies the following conditions

$$w_1\in\{1,\ldots,2^{L+2}-2\}\,, \qquad (22)$$

$$w_1\in\begin{cases}\{1,\ldots,|\,\mathrm{F}_1\,|\},\ \text{if}\ 2^i-1\le w_1\le 3\cdot 2^{i-1}-2\\ \{1,\ldots,|\,\mathrm{F}_2\,|\},\ \text{if}\ 3\cdot 2^{i-1}-1\le w_1\le 2^{i+1}\text{-}2\\ \{1,\ldots,|\,\mathrm{F}\,|\},\ \text{if}\ 3\cdot 2^L-1\le w_1\le 2^{L+2}-2\end{cases}, \qquad (23)$$

where $i=1,\ldots,L$.

A variational genetic algorithm consists of the following stages:

1) Set a code of basic solution

$$\mathrm{C}_0=(c_1^0,\ldots,\ c_K^0)\,;$$

2) Generate a set of ordered sets of small variations

$$\Omega=\{\mathrm{W}_1,\ldots,\mathrm{W}_H\}\,,$$

where W_1 is an ordered set of variations $\mathrm{W}_i=(\mathbf{w}^{i,1},\ldots,\mathbf{w}^{i,l})$, $\mathbf{w}^{i,j}=[w_1^{i,j}\ w_2^{i,j}]^T$, $i=1,\ldots,H$, $j=1,\ldots,l$, l is a set of numbers of variations.

We carry out crossover and mutation on the sets of variations. Select two parents $W_i = (\mathbf{w}^{i,1}, \ldots, \mathbf{w}^{i,l})$ and $W_j = (\mathbf{w}^{j,1}, \ldots, \mathbf{w}^{j,l})$, and randomly define a point of crossover $k \in \{1, \ldots, l\}$ and exchange tails of the parents

$$\tilde{W}_i = (\mathbf{w}^{i,1}, \ldots, \mathbf{w}^{i,k-1}, \mathbf{w}^{j,k}, \ldots, \mathbf{w}^{j,l}),$$

$$\tilde{W}_j = (\mathbf{w}^{j,1}, \ldots, \mathbf{w}^{j,k-1}, \mathbf{w}^{i,k}, \ldots, \mathbf{w}^{i,l}).$$

Define randomly a mutation point $\mu \in \{1, \ldots, l\}$ and generate new variation in the point μ $\mathbf{w}^{i,\mu} = [w_1^{i,\mu} \; w_2^{i,\mu}]^T$ for one and other new solutions.

5 Computational example

Consider a mobile robot as a control object

$$\dot{x} = u_1 \cos(\theta),$$

$$\dot{y} = u_1 \sin(\theta),$$

$$\dot{\theta} = u_2,$$

where $-1 \le u_{1,2} \le 1$.

It is necessary from some initial conditions

$$X_0 = \{\mathbf{x}^{0,1} = [-1 \; -2 \; 0]^T, \mathbf{x}^{0,2} = [-1 \; -1.6 \; 0]^T, \ldots$$

$$\ldots, \mathbf{x}^{0,11} = [-1 \; 2 \; 0]^T, \mathbf{x}^{0,12} = [2 \; -2 \; 0]^T, \ldots$$

$$\ldots, \mathbf{x}^{0,22} = [2 \; 2 \; 0]^T\}$$

to find such a control to rich the terminal condition

$$\mathbf{x}^f = [0 \; 0 \; 0]^T$$

with minimal time.

Functionals have the following forms

$$J_1 = \sum_{j=1}^{22} (t_f(\mathbf{x}^{0,j}) + s(\mathbf{x}^{0,j})),$$

where

$$s(\mathbf{x}^{0,j}) = \int_0^{t_j} f_0(\mathbf{x}(t))dt,$$

$$t_j = t(\mathbf{x}^{0,j}),$$

$t(\mathbf{x}^{0,j})$ is a time of control process,

$$t(\mathbf{x}^{0,j}) = \begin{cases} t, \text{ if } \|\mathbf{x}(t) - \mathbf{x}^f\| < \varepsilon \\ t^+ \text{ - otherwise} \end{cases},$$

$$f_0(\mathbf{x}(t)) = \begin{cases} r = \sqrt{(x(t) - \tilde{x}(t))^2 + (y(t) - \tilde{y}(t))^2}, \text{ if } r < r^+ \\ 0 \text{ - otherwise} \end{cases},$$

$(\tilde{x}, \tilde{y})$ are coordinates of unstable point, ε, t^+, r^+ are given positive values, $\varepsilon = 0.01$, $t^+ = 4$. $r^+ = 0.5$.

For calculation, we used the following functions with one argument:

$$F_1 = (f_1(z) = z, f_2(z) = z^2, f_3(z) = -z,$$

$$f_4(z) = \text{sgn}(z)\sqrt{|z|}, f_5(z) = \frac{1}{z}, f_6(z) = e^z,$$

$$f_7(z) = \ln(|z|), f_8(z) = \frac{1 - e^{-z}}{1 + e^{-z}}, f_9(z) = \begin{cases} 1, \text{ if } z \ge 0 \\ 0 \text{ - otherwise} \end{cases},$$

$$f_{10}(z) = \text{sgn}(z), f_{14}(z) = z^3, f_{15}(z) = \sqrt[3]{z},$$

$$f_{16}(z) = \begin{cases} z, \text{ if } |z| \le 1 \\ \text{sgn}(z)\text{- otherwise} \end{cases}, f_{17}(z) = \text{sgn}(z)\ln(|z| + 1),$$

$$f_{18}(z) = \text{sgn}(z)\exp(|z| - 1), f_{23}(z) = z - z^3).$$

The set of functions with two arguments were

$$F_2 = (f_1(z_1, z_2) = z_1 + z_2, f_2(z_1, z_2) = z_1 z_2).$$

A basic solution was

$$u_{1,2} = q_1(x^f - x) + q_2(y^f - y) + q_3(\theta^f - \vartheta) +$$

$$q_4(\tilde{x} - x) + q_5(\tilde{y} - y).$$

where $q_i = 1$, $i = 1, \ldots, 5$.

A genetic algorithm had the following parameters: number of possible solutions in initial set – 1024, number of generations among exchange of the basic solution – 256, number of crossovers in one generation – 256, number of variations for one solution – 8.

We have obtained the following control

$$u_{1,2} = \begin{cases} \text{sgn}(u_{1,2}), \text{if } |u_{1,2}| > 1 \\ \tilde{u}_{1,2} \text{ - otherwise} \end{cases},$$

where

$$\tilde{u}_1 = \text{sgn}(AB)\sqrt{|AB|},$$

$$\tilde{u}_2 = \text{sgn}(\text{sgn}(C + D)\ln(|C + D| + 1) +,$$

$$(G + H)^2)\sqrt{|\text{sgn}(C + D)\ln(|C + D| + 1) + (G + H)^2|},$$

$$A = \text{sgn}(-\Delta_y q_2 q_3 \Delta_\theta)\exp(|-\Delta_y q_2 q_3 \Delta_\theta| - 1),$$

$$B = (\mu(q_4) + q_5 + q_1),$$

DOI: 10.1051/itmconf/20171002004

$$C = \frac{1 - \exp(-(\tilde{\Delta}_x - \tilde{\Delta}_y)\mu(q_5 \tilde{\Delta}_y^3))}{1 + \exp(-(\tilde{\Delta}_x - \tilde{\Delta}_y)\mu(q_5 \tilde{\Delta}_y^3))},$$

$$D = \mathrm{sgn}\left(\mathrm{sgn}(\Delta_x) q_3 + q_2 \frac{1 - \exp(-\Delta_x)}{1 + \exp(-\Delta_x)} \right) \times$$

$$\exp\left(\left| \mathrm{sgn}(\Delta_x) q_3 + q_2 \frac{1 - \exp(-\Delta_x)}{1 + \exp(-\Delta_x)} \right| - 1 \right),$$

$$G = \sqrt[6]{\Delta_\theta \ln(|q_3| + 1)^3 \sqrt{-\tilde{\Delta}_x^2}},$$

$$H = \sqrt[3]{\mathrm{sgn}(q_5^3 - q_5) \sqrt{|q_5^3 - q_5|} \ln(|q_2 \Delta_y| + 1)},$$

$$\mu(z) = \begin{cases} \mathrm{z}, \text{ if } |z| \le 1 \\ \mathrm{sgn(z)} \text{ - otherwise} \end{cases},$$

$$\Delta_x = x^f - x, \ \Delta_y = y^f - y, \ \Delta_\theta = \theta^f - \theta,$$

$$\tilde{\Delta}_x = \tilde{x} - x, \ \tilde{\Delta}_y = \tilde{y} - y,$$

$q_1 = 2.28516$, $q_2 = 1.47559$, $q_3 = 2.87891$, 0,07324 $q_4 = 0.07324$, $q_5 = 3.95410$.

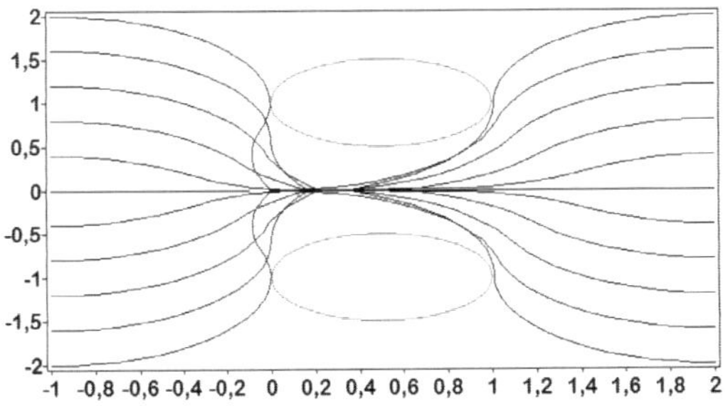

Fig. 2. Movement of robot from 22 intial positions

The fig 2 shows results of simulation of robot movement from twenty two initial positions. There red areas are dynamic phase constraints.

6 Conclusion

The paper presents new method of symbolic regression binary variational analytic programming. A new method codes a mathematical expression in the form of binary computing tree. We have solved the problem of synthesis of control for mobile robot with disturbing phase constraints by the new method. The method has obtained control as a nonlinear complex function depending on the space state coordinates of object and disturbing dynamical phase constraints.

This research was supported by Russian Foundation for Basic Research according to the research project №. 14-08-00008-a and №. 16-29-04224-ofi_m.

References

1. M. O'Neill and C. Ryan, IEEE Trans. Evol. Comp. **5**, 349 – 358 (2001)
2. I. Zelinka, Proc. of 1st Int. Conf. on New Trends in Physics'01, 210–214 (2001)
3. A. Diveev, J. of Comp. and Syst. Sci. Int. **51**(2), 228–243 (2012)
4. K. Cpałka, K. Łapa, A. Przybył, G. Eason, Inf. Tech. And Contr., **44**(4), 433-442 (2015)
5. J. Imae, Y. Kikuchi, N. Ohtsuki, T. Kobayashi, G. Zhai, Proc. of 43rd IEEE Conf. on Decision and Contr., 2734-2739 (2004)
6. R.A. Maher, M.J. Mohamed, Intel. Contr. and Autom., **4**, 94-101 (2013)
7. A. Diveev, E. Sofronova, Proc. 17th IFAC World Congr., 6106 – 6113 (2008)
8. J. Yu, M.A. Keane, J.R. Koza, Proc. of 2000 IEEE Int. Symp. on Comp.-Aided Contr. Syst. Design, 234 – 242 (2000)
9. A.I. Diveev, E.Yu. Shmalko, Proc. of 3rd Int. Conf. on Contr., Decision and Inf. Tech. (CoDIT'16), 077-082 (2016)
10. A.I. Diveev, Proc. of 16th IFAC Workshop on Contr. App. of Optimization, 28-33 (2015)
11. S.I. Ibadulla, E.Yu. Shmalko, K.K. Daurenbekov, Procedia Comp. Sci., **103**, 155-161 (2017)
12. A. Diveev, S. Ibadulla, N. Konyrbaev, E. Shmalko, IFAC-PapersOnLine, **48**(19), 106-111 (2015)
13. A. Diveev, S. Ibadulla, N. Konyrbaev, E. Shmalko, IFAC-PapersOnLine, **48**(19), 113-118 (2015)
14. A.I. Diveev, N.B. Konyrbaev, E.A. Sofronova, Procedia Comp. Sci., **103**, 597-604 (2017)

Evaluation of Filtering Methods Applied to the Unstructured Datasets in the Predictive Learning Services

Dmitry Ilin[1,2], *Egor* Mateshuk[3,*], *Rustam* Gilaztdinov[2], and *Gregory* Bubnov[1,3]

[1]Moscow Technological Institute, 119334, Moscow, Russia
[2]Moscow Technological University MIREA, 107996, Moscow, Russia
[3]Moscow Institute of Physics and Technology, 141700, Dolgoprudny, Moscow Region, Russia

Abstract. Predictive learning services perform aggregation and homogenization of open data from public sources, in particular from the online recruitment agencies. However, the sample of vacancies may contain various percentage of noise due to the frequent occurrence of homonyms. This article will consider two approaches of noise reduction: the first one is based on the cosine similarity and the second one is based on the contextual words.

1 Introduction

Many of the major online services provide application programming interface (API) for integration of third-party applications, particularly adhering to the REST principles [1]. Some of the online recruitment agencies (e.g. Indeed.com [2], HeadHunter [3]) provide an API for fetching a vacancy list matching the specified search criteria.

During the development of the predictive learning service [4], the vacancy data of the IT sector were obtained from the mentioned agencies in order to analyze which skills are the most demanded and which are the fastest-growing in demand. However, in the course of experiments it was found that the data from the Indeed.com may comprise a significant percentage of noise. One of the reasons is unstructured vacancy descriptions. For example, a sample of vacancies with the Haskell programming language requirement had noise percentage about 54%, which means the unsuitability of data to assess the real needs of the market in regard of the corresponding skills.

Table 1. Online recruitment agencies' API limitations

	Indeed	**HeadHunter**
Maximal number of documents in the sample	1025	2000
Maximal document size	~200 characters	~400 characters
Historical data	No	No

The binary text classification is well studied [5, 6], but it hasn't been applied to the analysis of the demand for skills yet. In addition, the integration of the filtering into the predictive learning service, with regard to the existing constraints (Table 1), is a relevant issue.

2 Materials and Methods

2.1. Materials

Samples of vacancies taken from the Indeed and HeadHunter (Tables 2 and 3 respectively) were processed manually and classified according to the following rule: job title or description must clearly specify requirement of the skill. In other words, the vacancies containing the text of a technical orientation, but not containing an explicit reference to skill/technology, are considered noise. The use of keywords within the meaning other than the skill is considered to be noise as well.

Possible error in the table values – 5 vacancies which does not affect the result. Haskell, Boo and Clarion skills were excluded from Russian online recruitment agency data, due to the fact that the number of the results was lower than the possible error.

Figures 1 and 2 show visualisation of the vacancy to noise ratio.

Significantly lower noise percentage in the second sample due to the fact that in the HeadHunter service, where the main language is Russian, the probability of the use of professional English terms with varying semantics is lower than in the Indeed, where the main language is English.

* Corresponding author: e.mateshuk@gmail.com

Table 2. Vacancy to noise ratio in the data sample from the Indeed service.

Skill	Total vacancies	Relevant vacancies	Noise vacancies
Java	1025	945	80
PHP	1025	897	128
Objective-C	1025	379	646
Haskell	373	171	202
Boo	88	2	86
Pascal	67	37	30
MySQL	1025	784	241
Microsoft Access	1025	433	592
SQLite	471	320	151
Clarion	412	24	388

Table 3. Vacancy to noise ratio in the data sample from the HeadHunter service.

Skill	Total vacancies	Relevant vacancies	Noise vacancies
Java	484	448	36
PHP	416	386	30
Objective-C	53	50	3
Pascal	8	8	0
MySQL	346	298	48
Microsoft Access	20	18	2
SQLite	14	14	0

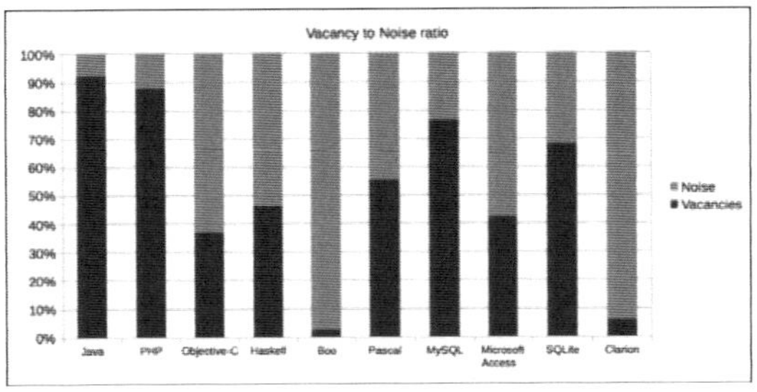

Fig. 1. Vacancy to noise ratio in the data sample from the Indeed service.

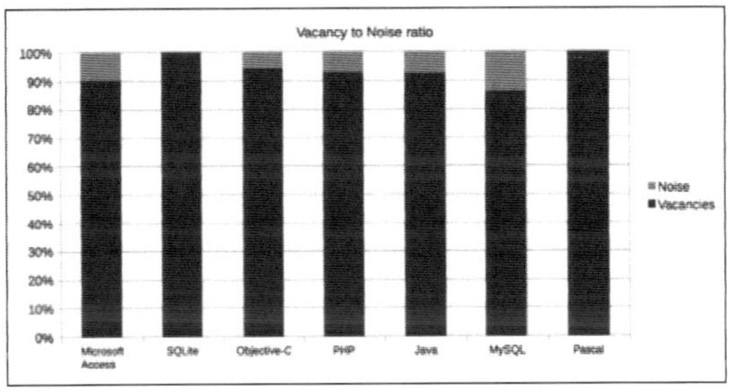

Fig. 2. Vacancy to noise ratio in the data sample from the HeadHunter service.

2.2 Methods

Due to the sample limitations, word2vec [7] and doc2vec [8] models perform with low efficiency. Therefore two different approaches have been chosen as the possible filtration method:

1. Unsupervised, based on the use of cosine similarity.
2. Supervised, based on the use of contextual words.

The first approach is based on the calculation of the cosine similarity between the vector representations of the vacancy texts. The algorithm consists of the following steps:

1. Tokenization.
2. Stemming.
3. Removal of the stop-words.
4. Calculation of the cosine similarity matrix between all the vacancies.
5. Calculation of an ordered list of factors.
6. Selection of the reference factor.
7. Filtering based on the reference factor and standard deviation.

The algorithm is shown in the form of a pseudocode in Figure 3.

```
CosineSimilarityFilter(vacancyTextList)

 tokenOccurencesList = []
 for vacancyText in vacancyTextList
  rawTokenList <- Tokenize(vacancyText)
  stemmedTokenList <- PorterStemming(rawTokenList)
  tokenList <- RemoveStopWords(stemmedTokenList)
  tokenOccurencesMap <- CountWordOccurences(tokenList)
  tokenOccurencesList += tokenOccurencesMap

 csMatrix = [][]
 for to1, i in tokenOccurencesList
  for to2, j in tokenOccurencesList
   csMatrix[i][j] <- CosineSimilarity(to1, to2)

 similarityList = []
 for csList in csMatrix
  similarityList += Mean(csList) + 0.75 * Std(csList)
 similarityList <- Sort(similarityList, 'desc')

 referenceValue <- First(similarityList)
 lBound <- referenceValue - 3 * Std(similarityList)
 uBound <- referenceValue + 3 * Std(similarityList)

 filteredVacancyList = []
 for similarity in similarityList
  if (similarity > lBound AND similarity < uBound)
   filteredVacancyList += similarity

 return count(filteredVacancyList)
```

Fig. 3. Filtering algorithm written in pseudocode

The second approach is to use a keyword search including keywords from the contextual domain. Procedure for this approach can be described as follows:

1. Preparation of a list of keywords for the contextual domain.
2. Indexation of unfiltered vacancies. The index includes both vacancy description and its title.
3. Next step is the search for vacancies matching the following condition: the text should contain the keyword and at least one of the contextual keywords.

List of contextual keywords can be prepared once for each category and can be reused. The list itself was formed of the keywords with significantly higher frequency of appearance in the domain compared to the frequency of their occurrence in a common text. An additional manual selection of contextual keywords was performed after the initial automated selection to eliminate the ambiguous words, such as "basic", which is both a commonly used adjective and the name of the programming language.

3 Results

The experiment shows that a filter based on the cosine similarity reduces the percentage of noise in the vacancy list (fig. 4). The values in the chart represent the difference between the raw number of vacancies and the number of vacancies after application of the filtering algorithm. Mean decrease of the noise is about 15.34%. However, in some cases, the filter result shows lower number of vacancies than the actual one. It may affect the representativeness of the skill assessment.

As is evident from fig. 5, the approach based on contextual keywords shows higher accuracy. The amount of noise vacancies decreased by 91.7%. Miscalculation on keywords "MySQL" and "Microsoft Access" might be related to their wide distribution outside software development sector. Therefore, contextual keywords in the software development sector do not always occur in the vacancies containing mentioned keywords, which leads to an underestimation of the number of results.

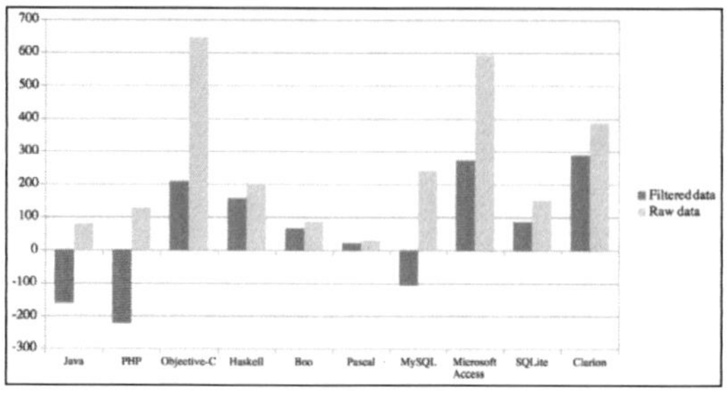

Fig. 4. Results of the algorithm based on the cosine similarity

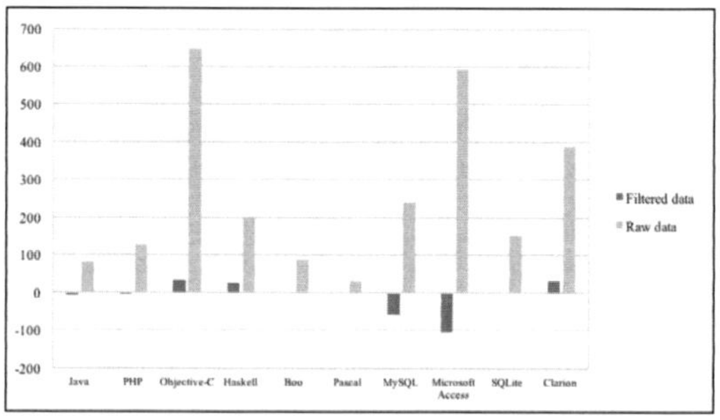

Fig. 5. Results of the algorithm based on the contextual keywords

4 Discussion

Both solutions have their advantages and disadvantages.

The performance of the filter based on the cosine similarity is acceptable to solve problems with a limited set of data, as the complexity of calculating the cosine similarity between all the texts is $O(n^2)$. Due to the fact that the algorithm can underestimate the actual number of vacancies, it is reasonable to carry out further studies in order to improve the accuracy of the algorithm.

Filter based on the contextual keywords has a lower computation complexity $O(n \log(n))$ and shows higher accuracy. But it requires manual preparation of a list of contextual keywords prior to the filtering. As a result, filtering can be performed on a limited number of professional scopes. An algorithm for automatic selection of contextual keywords can be implemented to expand a given set of professional scopes, that would eliminate the manual stage of preparation and will provide an opportunity to apply the method to any area of job search.

5 Conclusion

It is reasonable to integrate both solutions into the predictive learning service and to monitor the sustainability of both approaches to changes in the labor market.

The method based on the contextual keywords provides an ability to carry out studies to identify the most demanded skills in the labor market with high accuracy [9].

References

1. R. T. Fielding, R. N. Taylor, ACM Trans. Internet Technol., **2**, 407-416 (2002)
2. Indeed Publisher Program, https://www.indeed.com/publisher (Accessed: 01/12/2017)
3. HeadHunter API, https://dev.hh.ru/ (Accessed: 01/12/2017)
4. E. Nikulchev, D. Ilin, E. Matishuk, Procedia Computer Science, **103**, 44-51 (2017)
5. T. Joachims, ECML, 137-142 (1998)
6. K. Nigam, A. McCallum, S. Thrun, T. Mitchell, Mach. Learn., **39**, 103-134 (2000)
7. T. Mikolov, I. Sutskever, K. Chen, G. S. Corrado, J. Dean, Adv. Neural Inf. Process. Syst., 3111-3119 (2013)
8. Q. Le, T. Mikolov, ICML, **32**, 1188-1196 (2014)
9. D. Ilin, D. Strunitsyn et al., ITM Web of Conference, **29**, 02017 (2016)

DOI: 10.1051/itmconf/20171002006

Real-time Evolutionary Computation in the Control of Mobile Cyber-Physics System

Gennady Rogachev[1,*], *Mikhail* Patkin[1] and *Nikolai* Rogachev[1]

[1]Samara State Technical University, 443100, Samara, Russia

Abstract. The procedure of the time-optimal controller synthesis in the mobile cyber-physical system control problems in the form of the Dubins car is considered. In the decision quality assessment, the total time spent on executing the task of transferring an object to a given point is taken into account, including the time for the control program calculation and the time of the object movement to the target. Both online and offline variants of the production model numerical determination of the controller as a system of rules "condition" – "action" are considered. As an online variant, it is suggested to use an anytime genetic algorithm. A comparison between online and offline methods of calculating a rule system for the regulator performance is made. The advantages of the online method in solving the problem of transferring the mobile cyber physical system in a homogeneous environment and the advantages of an offline method in a heterogeneous environment are demonstrated.

1 Cyber-physical systems as special kind of systems

The world now is at the beginning of a new technological revolution. Its essence is in the iniquitousness of cyber-physical systems (CPS - cyber-physical systems) [1-3]. The essential feature of CPS is an inextricable connection between physical elements they include and elements implementing the calculation. The important category of cyber-physical systems is mobile CPS, the physical part of which has its own mobility. When developing cyber-physical systems one must take into account that they are a single set of interactive computing, communication and physical processes.

Built-in (in the real physical world) computers immediately affect physical processes and, in turn, are influenced by them. The calculations and the physical process are becoming the integral whole; it is impossible to predict and understand the behavior of any of these two parts separately. When parts of such a system (sensors, controllers, actuation devices) exchange information, a third component is added to the specified integral whole: the process of network communication. The robust relationship between discrete computational processes and information transfer with continuous processes in the control objects requires a fundamentally new technology of description, analysis and synthesis of cyber-physical systems.

A certain step in this direction is to use a production model of the controller when modeling a cyber-physical system as a digital control system of continuous object [4]. The dynamic part of the system, which determines the performance of the control object, is described by differential equations, and the control part (controller, sensors, actuation devices and data transmission network from the object to the control part and back) – by the algorithm of its work (a productions system, a system of rules "condition" - "action"). The production (algorithmic) form of controllers description allows unifying the problem of their synthesis. Indeed, the number of elements of the production systems (the pairs of the type "condition" –"action") and its contents are to be specified regardless of the specific problem. At the same time the multi-step synthesis, comprising the controller structure selection, the definition of its parameters, the development of algorithm and program code implementing the controller, is replaced by a direct synthesis of controller action program – the system of rules, i.e. the algorithm of its performance in the form of pseudo-code.

2 Cyber-physical systems controller synthesis problem

At present, a general formalized method of solving the problem of controllers synthesis in the production form is absent. One can only indicate some particular methods, which are based on the optimization procedure [5]. One of

* Corresponding author: grogachev@mail.ru

DOI: 10.1051/itmconf/20171002006

them is the automation of the production systems synthesis procedure through evolutionary computation as a stochastic method of global optimization. This approach will eventually allow to create technical devices that would be able to generate their own software for their control systems and upgrade them if necessary. Evolutionary algorithms are traditionally divided into genetic algorithms (GA) and genetic programming. GA are generally intended to find a solution for optimization problems in the form of a set of parameters.

On the base of this approach, software tools that automate the entire development process of control systems from setting objectives to modeling their work, including software testing, can be created. This approach is especially effective under conditions of extremum no uniqueness of the objective function J(x). However, since GA are required to analyze a large number of alternative solutions, the calculation time would be long, which is a significant disadvantage of this method and can be an obstacle for its usage in the controllers performance algorithms synthesis in cyber-physical systems in real-time mode.

In order to overcome this disadvantage, it is suggested to combine the control actions calculating procedure with the control process. In such an application of GA before the calculations are completed every few epochs one should choose the solution that provides the greatest movement of control object towards the target compared to the other available control options and use it at a time interval as a controlling action. In artificial intelligence, this approach corresponds to the online variant of the intelligent agent performance, whereas the previous version of the single computation of controlling action before the beginning of the controlling process is the offline variant. The term "operating in the online mode" is used in relation to the algorithms that are to process data inputs as they become available, rather than waiting until the entire set of data inputs becomes available. Such an intelligent agent performs in accordance with the calculations and actions shift method: firstly, it takes action, and then monitors the environment and computes the next action. In the theory of algorithms, this variant of solving a problem is known as an anytime algorithm - iterative computational algorithm, which is able to produce the best solution for a given moment at any time. When applying the anytime algorithm and the evolutionary method together one should choose the best solution every few epochs before the calculations are completed. This solution is used for some time as the current controlling action.

3 Example of program controller for mobile cyber-physical system

As an example of the suggested approach, we consider the problem of synthesis by evolutionary computation of the real time of the rule of mobile cyber-physical system control. Mobility is achieved with the help of a wheeled robot in the form of the Dubins car. A kinematic model of the wheeled robot is a system of nonlinear ordinary differential equations of the form

$$[\dot{x}, \dot{y}, \dot{\varphi}]^T = [v \cdot \cos(\varphi), v \cdot \sin(\varphi), u]^T \quad (1)$$

where the state variables are two location coordinates x and y of the object on the plane and φ the angle of the velocity vector direction. Velocity vector magnitude $v = 1$. Scalar control u is limited in magnitude $|u| \leq 1$ and determines the instantaneous rotation velocity of the velocity vector. Solve the problem of the quickest transfer of the Dubins car from a point $[-4,0,-\pi]$ to a small neighborhood of the point with coordinates x=0, y=0. Since the third coordinate (the angle φ) at the end point is not set, this is the problem with a movable end of the trajectory. In addition, not only will we take into account the time the control object needs move from the initial point to the final, but also the time during which the computation of the control law is being made. Since the known exact analytical solution for the time-optimal problem [6] involves fixation of the trajectory end and does not take into account the control computation time, we will solve the problem numerically. We will use GA as a method of computing the control law. The software is Global Optimization Toolbox, CPU Intel® CoreTM 2 Duo 2.2 GHz. Limit the controlling action calculation time by a preselected value. In the first case, firstly, we will fully define a production system of a software controller and then we will use it for controlling purposes. We assume that if the controlling strategy is chosen correctly, the Dubins car will reach the desired point in eight seconds and that the allowable frequency of the controlling action change equals 1 s^{-1}. Then the controller production system takes the form: "if $t \in [i-1, i)$ then $u(t) = u_i$ ", $i = 1,2,\ldots 8$.

When carrying out the first series of 15 computational experiments controlling action computation time was limited by 16 sec, which corresponds to 3 working epochs of GA in the specified computing environment. After 16 sec the object motion is under control of the best of the found controller work programs. Thus, the total time from receiving the problem to the end of the movement is 24 sec. As it is shown in Figure 1, in none of the 15 experiments the neighborhood of the point with coordinates $x = 0$, $y = 0$ was not reached in 40 sec in consequence of the poor quality of the derived solutions.

The second series of experiments was carried out with controlling action computation time limited by 64 sec (12 GA working epochs). In this case (Figure 2) one third of the trajectory ended in neighborhood of the given point, but the total time for solving the problem was 72 seconds.

Change the tactic. Initially, under the limit computation time of 1 to define the parameter using the GA so that the rule "if $t \in [0,1)$ then $u(t) = u_1$ " provides the object (1) at a minimum compared to all alternatives resulting deviation from the specified conditions$x$=0, y=0 the desired final

DOI: 10.1051/itmconf/20171002006

position. Then, using this rule to control for the first second, we seek out the same arguments parameter u_2 simultaneously. Repeat these steps for the first 7 sec of movement. The total time from the receipt of the task before the end of the movement will be only 9 sec. As in Figure 3, in this embodiment, the search failed to achieve guaranteed a small neighbourhood of a point x=0, y=0.

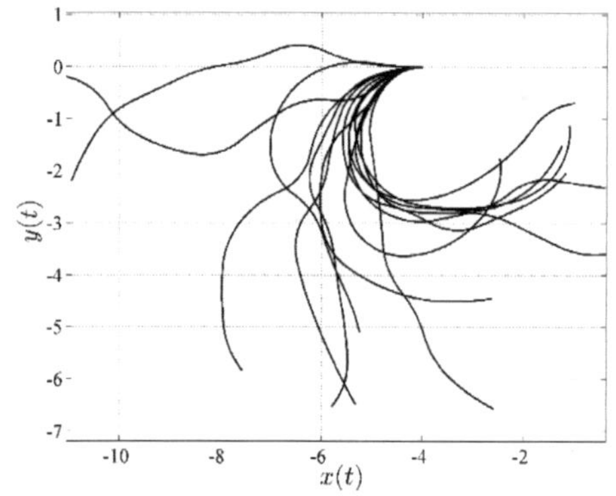

Fig. 1. Dubins car trajectories (computational time 16 sec)

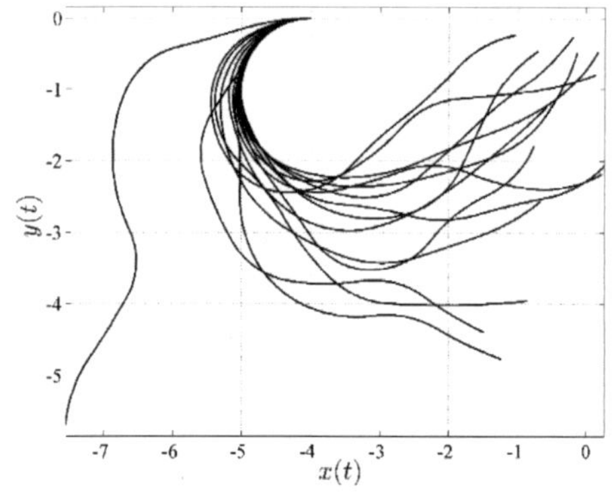

Fig. 2. Dubins car trajectories (computational time 64 sec)

The achieved effect of improving the solution quality while significantly reducing the total solution time can be explained not only by combining in time the processes of determining the control law and movement under the control, but also by decreasing the computational complexity of the problem. Indeed, at each $i$step only one parameter u_i instead of eight is to be determined. Thus a major disadvantage of evolutionary computing, which is the excessive computation time necessary for the analysis of a large number of alternative variants, can be overcome. Therefore, the synthesis problem can be successfully solved in real-time scale by using evolutionary computation and genetic algorithm in particular. Moreover, in a homogeneous environment online variant is undoubtedly more advantageous than the offline variant.

In a heterogeneous environment, the situation is different. Let us assume that on the way of Dubins Car there is an area where movement is not desirable due to any reason (in the following figures this area is indicated as a grey hexagon). Now the online variant of computations on the basis of the plenitude of the knowledge about the environment in which the movement will occur demonstrates the advantage, because it allows the Dubins car to pass the restricted area quite successfully (Figures 4, 5). In contrast, the offline control of the Dubins car copes with simple obstacles, but fails to overcome more difficult ones. (Figures 6, 7).

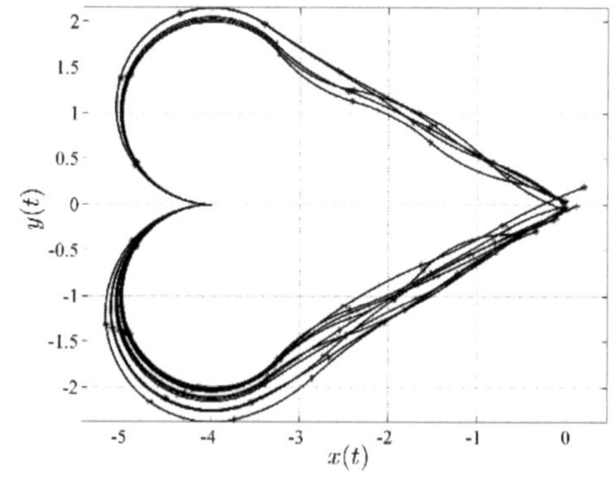

Fig. 3. Dubins car trajectories (anytime algorithm of controlling, full time 9 sec), marks are put through 1 sec

This fact has a rational explanation. Indeed, in the offline variant the rule system of controller performance is fully determined before the movement starts. Plenitude of the information both about the environment and about how all the movement stages impact on the final result is used, long-term planning is carried out. On the contrary, in the online variant of computations there is a short-term planning, each step is determined by the local target to minimize the remaining distance to the desired point. The available information is not about all the environment, but only about its nearest part. In this case, it is difficult to map a route of movement outside the restricted area.

4 Conclusions and recommendations

The examples considered demonstrate the possibility of using evolutionary computing in problems of the synthesis of real-time control systems for wheel mobile devices moving in homogeneous and in heterogeneous environments.

It was found that there is a possibility of improving the quality of solving the control problem with both a significant reduction in the total time by accomplishing essential computational procedures for determining the control law while implementing and a reduction of the problem computational complexity due to the use of successive operations of sequential search for each of the

DOI: 10.1051/itmconf/20171002006

production system instead of the multivariable search algorithm.

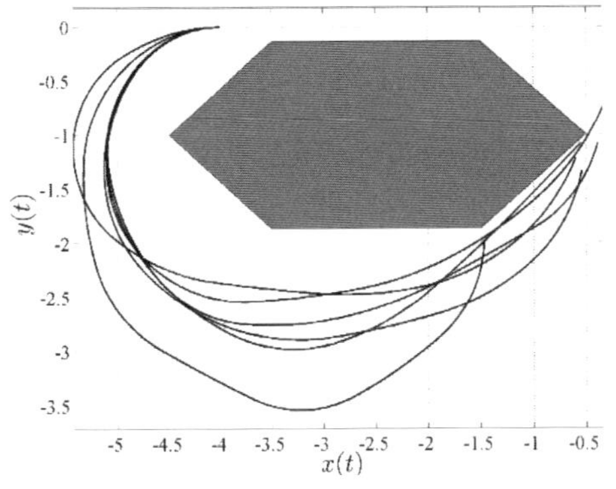

Fig. 4. Dubins car trajectories in a heterogeneous environment (offline variant, computational time 64 sec, full time 72 sec)

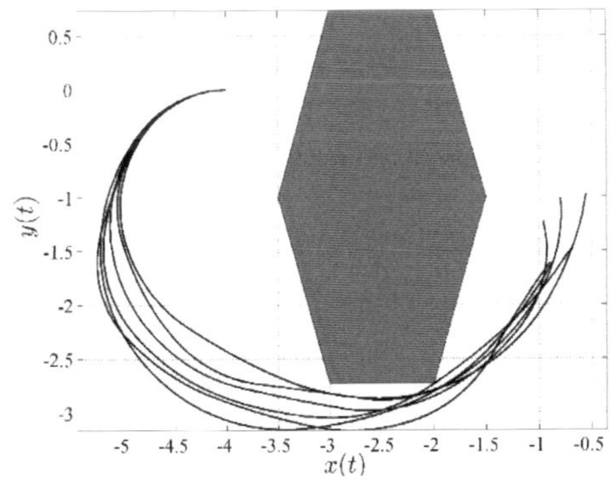

Fig. 5. Dubins car trajectories in a heterogeneous environment (offline variant, computational time 64 sec, full time 72 sec)

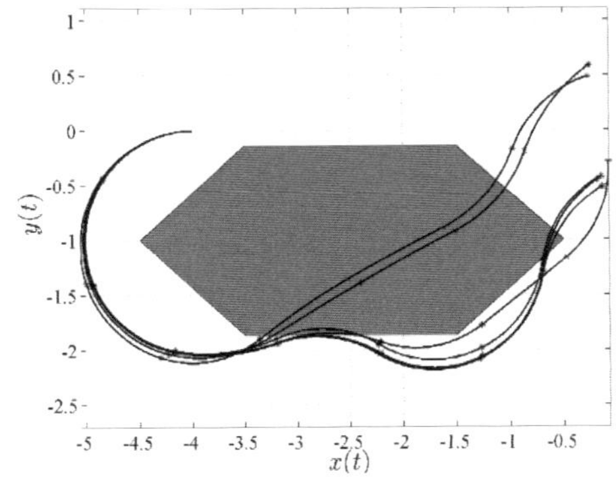

Fig. 6. Dubins car trajectories in a heterogeneous environment (online variant, full time 9 sec)

The main disadvantage of evolutionary computing, which is the excessive computation time necessary for the analysis of a large number of alternative variants, can be overcome in this way. In the absence of obstruction, one can recommend the online calculation variant combined with the control process. This variant allows significantly reducing the computation time and improving the quality of the solutions found. In a heterogeneous environment, it is advisable to use the offline variant of pre-computation the complete solution.

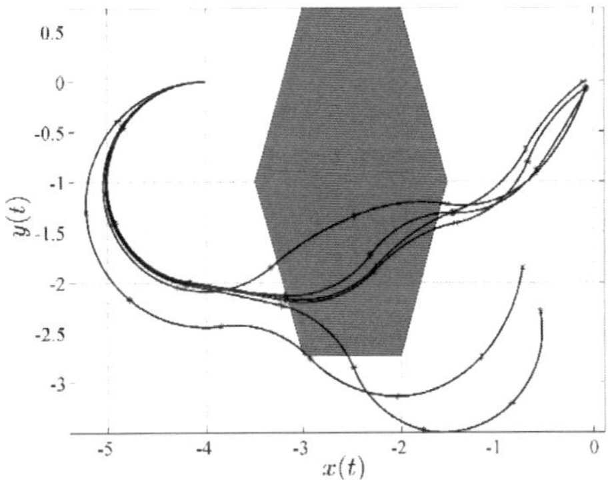

Fig. 7. Dubins car trajectories in a heterogeneous environment (online variant, full time 9 sec)

This work was financially supported by Ministry of Education and Science of Russian Federation (basic part of government contract).

References

1. *Cyber-Phisical System. Driving force for innovation in mobility, healthy, energy and production.* (Springer, 2011)
2. *Living in networked world. Integrate research agenda Cyber-Physical Systems (agenda CPS)* (ACATECH (2015)
3. R. van. Kranenburg, *The Internet of Things. A critique of ambient technology and the all-seeing network of RFID* (Amsterdam, 2008)
4. G.N. Rogachev, Automatic control and computer sciences, **48**, 5 (2014)
5. G.N. Rogachev, Vest. SSTU. Ser: Tech. sci., **41** (2006)
6. L.E. Dubins, American Journal of Mathematics, **79**, 3 (1957)

ITM Web of Conferences **10**, 02007 (2017) DOI: 10.1051/itmconf/20171002007
2017 Seminar on Systems Analysis

A Cross-lag Analysis of Longitudinal Associations between Non-verbal Intelligence and Math Achievement

Tatiana Tikhomirova[1, *], *Ekaterina* Misozhnikova[1], *Yulia* Kuzmina[2] and *Sergey* Malykh[1]

[1]Psychological Institute of Russian Academy of Education, 125009 Moscow, Russia
[2]Natinal Research University Higher School of Economics, 2101000 Moscow, Russia

Abstract. The article presents the results of a longitudinal study of the relationship of nonverbal intelligence with success in teaching mathematics. A cross-lag analysis showed that at primary school age the empirical data is best described with the theoretical model of indirect influence of non-verbal intelligence. According to this model, non-verbal intelligence measured at Grade 3 of schooling affects the success in mathematics by the end of Grade 3, which, in turn, influences the success in mathematics by the end of primary school.

1 Introduction

Relationship between intelligence and academic success is observed in a number of cross-sectional studies carried out in different socio-economic contexts, educational conditions and ages [1–7]. These studies, including meta-analyses, reported high correlations of intelligence and academic success in various school subjects - from 0.37 to 0.63 [7, 8].

At the same time, the question of the causal relationship of intelligence and academic success requires further longitudinal studies, in which both analyzed constructs are measured in the same respondents over a certain time period [9]. For example, in a five-year longitudinal study of 70,000 British schoolchildren it was shown that intelligence measured at the age of 11, explains almost 60% of the variability in standardized test scores in mathematics at the age of 16 [5].

At the same time, the results of other longitudinal studies indicate that the most important factor affecting the increase in the mean intelligence score with age is schooling [10, 11]. Thus, in natural experiments involving children who are unable to study at school, it was found that these children show intellectual deficit of two standard deviations [11].

Thus, schooling might affect the mean values of non-verbal intelligence. It is possible that the differences in educational systems (both formal and conceptual) might mediate the relationship of intelligence and academic success in the course of development [1, 4, 11, 12]. The purpose of this longitudinal study is to investigate the causal relationship between non-verbal intelligence and success in mathematics at primary school age in the Russian sample.

2 Methods

2.1 Participants

The sample included students of the municipal educational institution participating in a longitudinal study of academic success. The present study analyzed the data of 133 students of Grades 3 and 4.

The average age of participants at the time of the first testing was 9.82 years (SD = 0.30), with 45.1% being boys, and 54.9% – girls.

The average age of the participants during the second testing was 10.82 years (SD = 0.30), the number of boys was 45.1%, the number of girls – 54.9%.

Each participant took part in the study twice – at the end of Grades 3 and 4.

2.2 Measures

2.2.1 Intelligence

Non-verbal intelligence was measured with the 'Raven Progressive Matrices' test (RPM, [13]). It consists of 60 tasks grouped in 5 series. In series A, participants have to complement the missing part of an image. In series B they are asked to find correspondence between pairs. In series C the tasks are related to geometrical principles in figure changes. In series D participants have to find the structure in shuffling of figures. Series E requires the ability to analyze figures and add it to the missing parts. Each correct answer was counted as 1 score. Total scores were calculated.

* Corresponding author: tikho@mail.ru

2.2.2 Mathematical achievement

Academic success was indicated by term grades for mathematics as marked by a primary school teacher. In the statistical analysis the mean of four term grades was used.

2.2.3 Statistical Analyses

At the first stage the descriptive statistics were calculated for each of the analyzed variables recorded at the end of Grades 3 and 4.

At the second stage a correlation analysis of nonverbal intelligence and success in learning mathematics, as measured at the end of Grades 3 and 4, was carried out. Spearman correlation coefficients were calculated (SPSS 20.0 package).

At the third stage, a confirmatory factor analysis was conducted to develop a measurement model of nonverbal intelligence as a latent variable. This is due to the fact that one of the main conditions of latent growth modeling is factorial invariance [9]. The total scores for five series of Raven Standard Progressive Matrices were used as indicators of the latent variable, nonverbal intelligence. To compare the models of nonverbal intelligence as a latent variable obtained on the data in Grades 3 and 4, chi-square values and degrees of freedom were used (MPlus package).

At the fourth stage, cross-lagged structural equation modeling was used for the analysis of the developmental structure of causal relationships between nonverbal intelligence and success in mathematics, measured twice at primary school age. Cross-lag analysis allowed to assess: 1) autoregressive correlations reflecting the stability of each trait over time, 2) contemporaneous correlations, estimating the total variation of the variables within each of the two measurements, and 3) cross-lag correlations showing how the variation of one trait at one time point explains the variation of another trait measured in the next time point.

To compare the models, the following criteria were used: chi-square test ($p > 0,05$); root mean square error of approximation (RMSEA $\leq$ 0.06, 90% confidence intervals – RMSEA low = 0.00 and RMSEA high < 0.08); comparative fit index (CFI > 0,95); Tucker-Lewis index (TLI> 0,90); Akaike Information Criterion (AIC), Bayesian information criterion (BIC) and sample-size adjusted BIC.

Five competing models of the relationship of non-verbal intelligence and success in mathematics measured at two points in time during the early school age were sequentially compared. In all structural models non-verbal intelligence was analyzed as a latent construct based on test scores for the series of Raven Progressive Matrices, and success in mathematics – as the mean of four term grades.

Model 1, autoregressive: non-verbal intelligence and success in mathematics only correlate within each measurement, none of the indicators affects the other one measured in the next time point.

Model 2, with a direct effect: non-verbal intelligence, measured in Grade 3, predicts the success in learning mathematics in Grade 4.

Model 3, with a direct effect: success in learning mathematics in third grade predicts nonverbal intelligence at Grade 4.

Model 4, reciprocal: non-verbal intelligence measured in Grade 3, predicts success in mathematics in Grade 4, and success in mathematics in Grade 3 test predicts non-verbal intelligence measured in Grade 4.

Model 5, with indirect effects: includes two indirect effects, where non-verbal intelligence measured in Grade 3 serves as a predictor, and success in learning mathematics in third grade as a mediator. The first effect involves the influence of non-verbal intelligence measured in Grade 3 on the success in learning mathematics in Grade 4 through success in mathematics in Grade 3. The second effect suggests that non-verbal intelligence in Grade 3 predicts non-verbal intelligence in Grade 4 through the success in learning mathematics in Grade 3.

3 Results

Table 1 presents the descriptive statistics for all indicators of non-verbal intelligence (scores for series A – E and the total score for the test) and success in learning mathematics (mean of four term grades) in Grades 3 and 4.

Table 1. Descriptive statistics of non-verbal intelligence and success in learning mathematics in Grades 3 and 4.

Measure	Mean (SD)	
	3rd grade	4th grade
Non-verbal intelligence, series A	10,64 (1,50)	11,07 (1,07)
Non-verbal intelligence, series B	10,22 (2,16)	10,62 (1,64)
Non-verbal intelligence, series C	8,02 (2,33)	8,47 (2,29)
Non-verbal intelligence, series D	8,03 (2,60)	8,20 (2,31)
Non-verbal intelligence, series E	3,43 (2,52)	3,60 (2,46)
Non-verbal intelligence, total score	40,63 (7,86)	42,02 (7,13)
Success in learning mathematics	4,17 (0,61)	4,15 (0,63)

Table 1 shows the mean values and standard deviations for the analyzed indicators. The maximum score for each series in the Standard Progressive Matrices is 12, for the total score – 60. The minimum and maximum values for success in mathematics are 2 and 5, respectively.

According to Table 1, means of non-verbal intelligence (on the series and the entire test) increase from the third to Grade 4 with narrowing of variability of individual differences (standard deviation slightly decreases). Indicators of success in learning mathematics, on the other hand, demonstrate the stability of the means and variation range. Similar data on the age-specific ratios of cognitive development and success in learning were obtained in cross-sectional studies on the samples of Russian schoolchildren [7]. A decrease in the means from series A to E in the Raven Progressive Matrices, as well as an increase in the standard deviation, confirms the principle of progressive complexity of tasks underlying the test of nonverbal intelligence.

3.1 Correlation between intelligence and Math achievement at Grade 3 and Grade 4

In the correlation analysis we studied the structure of the relationship of nonverbal intelligence and success in learning mathematics in the third and fourth grades.

Overall, statistically significant correlations – from low to high – were observed between nonverbal intelligence and success in mathematics in Grades 3 and 4. To the greatest extent success in mathematics was associated with nonverbal intelligence as indicated by the total score and the scores for D series. Thus, in Grade 3 the correlations reach 0.45 and 0.44, respectively, and in Grade 4 – 0.42 and 0.41 at $p < 0.01$. Success in mathematics is weakly associated with nonverbal intelligence as indicated by the C series of tasks in Grade 3 (r = 0.29, $p < 0.05$) and series E and C in Grade 4 ($r = 0.23$ and 0.24, respectively, $p < 0.05$). This wide range of the correlation coefficients for success in learning mathematics with different test parameters of intelligence necessitates the analysis of non-verbal intelligence as a latent construct based on the scores on the five series of the 'Raven Progressive Matrices' test. The studies have shown that for a more adequate assessment of the relationship intelligence should be considered not as a test score, but as a latent construct, allocated on the basis of performance on a number of tests [14, 15].

The correlation between non-verbal intelligence scores measured twice at an interval of one academic year is 0.53, $p < 0.01$, and between indicators of success in mathematics reaches 0.90 at $p < 0.01$, confirming the available literature on the stability of high success rates based on teachers' assessments [14, 16].

There is a tendency to a certain weakening of the relationship between measures of nonverbal intelligence and success in mathematics from Grade 3 to Grade 4. However, generally, the structure of the relationships remains stable.

3.2 Cross-lag analyses of causal associations between intelligence and Math achievement

Within the cross-lag analysis five competing models of the relationship of non-verbal intelligence and success in mathematics at primary school age were considered, first four models with direct effects, then one model with two indirect effects. Table 2 shows the fit indices for the models of the relationship between non-verbal intelligence and success in learning mathematics.

According to Table 2, among the models with direct effects a reciprocal model described the empirical data best, suggesting that intelligence in Grade 3 predicts the success in learning mathematics in Grade 4, and on the contrary, success in learning mathematics in Grade 3 predicts intelligence in Grade 4.

All autoregressive and contemporaneous relationships were statistically significant. An exception is the connection between non-verbal intelligence in Grade 3 and success in mathematics in Grade 4. Estimation of the model parameters shows that non-verbal intelligence in Grade 3 does not make a statistically significant contribution to the variation in success in learning mathematics by the end of primary school (β = 0.07, $p > 0.05$).

Table 2. Fit indices for the models of the relationship between non-verbal intelligence and success in learning mathematics.

Indices		M 1	M 2	M 3	M 4	M 5
AIC / BIC	AIC	4925,6	4925,9	4921,4	4922,5	4922,5
	BIC	5019,2	5022,3	5017,8	5021,6	5021,6
	adj. BIC	4911,8	4911,7	4907,2	4907,9	4907,9
χ2	value	71,5	69,86	65,31	64,42	64,42
	df	56	55	55	54	54
	p	0,07	0,08	0,16	0,16	0,16
RMSEA (CIs)	Estim.	0,05	0,05	0,04	0,04	0,04
	90% CI	0,00–0,08	0,00–0,08	0,00–0,07	0,00–0,07	0,00–0,06
CFI / TLI	CFI	0,97	0,97	0,97	0,98	0,99
	TLI	0,97	0,97	0,97	0,98	0,98

Note: AIC – Akaike Information Criterion; BIC – Bayesian information criterion; adj. BIC – sample-size adjusted BIC; χ2 (value, df, p) – chi-square test (value, degrees of freedom, p-value); RMSEA (Estim., CIs) – root mean square error of approximation (value, 90% confidence intervals); CFI – comparative fit index; TLI – Tucker-Lewis index

However, in the vast majority of research intelligence is seen as cognitive predictor of success in learning, including studies on the Russian sample [5 – 7]. Therefore, in the further analysis a model with indirect effects was tested where non-verbal intelligence in Grade 3 acts as a predictor, and success in learning mathematics in Grade 3 is considered as a mediator.

Estimation of the model with indirect effects indicates that autoregressive coefficients are statistically significant ($p < 0.01$) and reach values: 0.46 for non-verbal intelligence and 0.79 for the success in learning in Grades 3 and 4.

The regression coefficients of contemporaneous associations of intelligence and success in mathematics measured at each of the two time points are significantly different. Thus, in Grade 3 the relationship of non-verbal intelligence and success in mathematics is well pronounced (β = 0.53 with $p < 0.001$). In Grade 4, however, the strength of the association between these indicators significantly reduced (β = 0.11 at $p < 0.05$). One of the reasons for the observed differences might be a high autoregressive factor between success in mathematics in Grades 3 and 4. According to the literature, the high temporal stability of one construct might weaken the contemporaneous association [9].

The Model 5 analyzed indirect cross-lag relationships between non-verbal intelligence and success in learning mathematics in a two-year period of primary school. According to the analysis, non-verbal intelligence in Grade 3 affects the success in learning mathematics in Grade 4 through success in mathematics in Grade 3.

Statistically significant standardized weight of this indirect path is 0.42 ($p < 0.001$), after controlling for the variations related to autoregressive and contemporaneous associations.

The regression weight of the second indirect association – non-verbal intelligence in Grade 3 predicts intelligence in Grade 4 through the success in learning mathematics in Grade 3 – is significantly lower ($\beta = 0.11$, $p < 0.05$).

Thus, the cross-lag analysis showed that non-verbal intelligence in Grade 3 predicts 49% of variance of success in mathematics in Grade 4 through success in mathematics in Grade 3.

4 Discussion

The study investigated the causal relationship between non-verbal intelligence and success in learning mathematics by means of cross-lagged structural equation modeling.

The analyzed indicators were measured twice – in Grades 3 and 4. The cross-lag analysis allowed to assess: a) the temporal stability of nonverbal intelligence and success in mathematics in the early school years, b) the total variation of the variables within each of the two measurements in Grades 3 and 4, and c) the causal relationship between non-verbal intelligence and success in mathematics in primary school.

The statistical analysis showed that among the analyzed indicators the success in learning mathematics as measured by teachers' assessments was most stable at primary school age. It is reported that teachers' marks as indicators of success in schooling are highly stable [16], which makes it difficult to analyze longitudinal relationships with other variables at each subsequent measurement. However, teacher's assessment is the only measure of success of Russian students in learning, which can be used in longitudinal studies throughout the school years – from second to eleventh grades.

For non-verbal intelligence lower autoregressive correlations were obtained in comparison with the success in mathematics, but in general they suggest the temporal stability of this psychological construct, after controlling for variation related to contemporaneous and cross-lag associations. The results correspond to the results of studies of age dynamics of intelligence (e.g., [17]). In particular, these studies reported that intelligence indicators are more stable from early adolescence to late adulthood, whereas before adolescence intelligence develops unevenly [17, 18].

The analysis of contemporaneous correlations showed that the relationship of nonverbal intelligence and success in learning mathematics differ in Grades 3 and 4. In Grade 3 strong relationships are observed between these variables, which are fully consistent with the results of cross-sectional studies involving school-age children. A strong relationship was reported between intelligence and academic success – from 0.37 to 0.63 [5, 7, 8]. In Grade 4 a much weaker correlation was obtained, which, as was indicated above, is due to the high autoregressive coefficients obtained for the success in learning mathematics in Grades 3 and 4.

Among the models including direct paths between non-verbal intelligence and success in mathematics, the reciprocal model assuming a bidirectional relationship of constructs over time best describes the empirical data. However, in this model the influence of non-verbal intelligence measured at an earlier time point on success in learning mathematics recorded at a later time point was not statistically significant. On the contrary, the success in learning mathematics in Grade 3 explained 21% of the variance of nonverbal intelligence in Grade 4 ($p < 0.05$). This result is consistent with the available literature on the significant influence of learning on the 'Raven Progressive Matrices' test performance [10, 11, 19]. However, in a longitudinal study conducted on a sample of American students [20], influence the success in learning on intelligence was not confirmed, which may be due to differences in the measurement of academic success.

The theoretical model, suggesting an indirect effect of non-verbal intelligence in Grade 3 on the success in mathematics in Grade 4 best describes the empirical data. The success in learning mathematics in Grade 3 acts as a mediator. Consequently, non-verbal intelligence in Grade 3 and success in mathematics a year after are associated through an indirect causal relationship: 'early' intelligence acts as a predictor of 'later' academic achievement in mathematics.

These results might reflect the specifics of the relationship of cognitive functioning and academic success in terms of the Russian system of education.

This study was supported by the grant from the Russian Science Foundation [grant RSF № 15-18-30055].

References

1. T.N. Tikhomirova, S.B. Malykh, M.G. Tosto, Y.V. Kovas, Psychological journal, **35**, 41 (2014)
2. T.N. Tikhomirova, A.D. Modyaev, N.M. Leonova, S.B. Malykh, Psychological journal, **36**, 43 (2015)
3. T. Tikhomirova, I. Voronina, J. Marakshina, E. Nikulchev, I. Ayrapetyan, T. Malykh, SHS Web of Conferences, **29**, 02039 (2016)
4. S.B. Malykh, T.N. Tikhomirova, C. Zhou, W. Wei, M. Rodic, E.B. Misozhnikova, Y.A. Davydova, Y. Kovas, Voprosy psihologii, **5**, 133 (2012)
5. I.J. Deary, S. Strand, P. Smith, C. Fernandez, Intelligence, **35**, 13 (2007)
6. L.A. Verbitskaya, S.B. Malykh, Y.P. Zinchenko & T.N. Tikhomirova, Psychology in Russia. State of the Art, **8**, 91 (2015)
7. T.N. Tikhomirova, I.V. Voronin, E.B. Misozhnikova, S.B. Malykh, Theoretical and experimental psychology, **8**, 55 (2015)
8. D. Luo, L.A. Thompson, D.K. Detterman, Intelligence, **34**, 79 (2006)

9. T.D. Little, K.J. Preacher, J.P. Selig and N.A. Card, International Journal of Behavioral Development, **31**, 357 (2007)
10. C.N. Brinch, T.A. Galloway, Proceedings of the National Academy of Sciences, **109**, 425 (2012)
11. R. Nisbett, J. Aronson, C. Blair, W. Dickens, J. Flynn, D. Halpern, E. Turkheimer, American Psychologist, **67**, 130 (2012)
12. M. Rodic, X. Zhou, T. Tikhomirova, W. Wei, S. Malykh, V. Ismatulina, E. Sabirova, Y. Davidova, M. Tosto, J-P. Lemelin and Y. Kovas, Developmental Science, **18**, 165 (2015)
13. J. Raven, Cognitive Psychology, **41**, 1 (2000)
14. Y.V. Kovas, T.N. Tikhomirova, S.B. Malykh, Voprosy psihologii, **6**, 67 (2011)
15. R. Colom, F.J. Abad, L.F. Garcı´a, M. Juan-Espinosa, Intelligence, **30**, 449 (2002)
16. B. Oliver, N. Harlaar, M. Hayiou-Thomans, Y. Kovas, S. Walker, F. Spinath, S. Petrill, P. Dale and R. Plomin, Journal of Educational Psychology, **96**, 504 (2004)
17. S. von Stumm and R. Plomin, Intelligence, **48**, 30 (2015)
18. E.M. Tucker-Drob and D.A. Briley, Psychological Bulletin, 140, 949 (2014)
19. S.A. Brouwers, F.J.R. van de Vijver, D.A. van Hemert, Learning and Individual Differences, **19**, 330 (2009)
20. M.W. Watkins, P.W. Lei and G.L. Canivez, Intelligence, **35**, 59 (2007).

DOI: 10.1051/itmconf/20171002008

Development of the Automated Information System for Monitoring of Results of Accounting Object Activities Using Semantic Networks

Valeriya V. Tishkina[1,*], *Alexander N.* Pylkin[1], *Alexander V.* Kroshilin[1], and *Svetlana V.* Kroshilina[1]

[1]Ryazan State Radio Engineering University, 390005 Ryazan, Russia

Abstract. Currently, any management object is characterized by a large amount of information. This information is contained in various documents: in the financial statements, regulations, laws, etc. For information on management object must be converted to a certain type, since the information in the future will need to be analyzed. Knowledge about management object allows making effective and informed decisions. So now the task of not only the collection and storage of information, but also to the transformation of information suitable for the analysis of the user view. Thus, the article focuses on the process of developing a system that allows you to analyze the data about management object and based on the analysis to conclude about the state of the object.

1 Introduction

At the present time, factors such as the globalization of trade, market uncertainty and fierce competition involve a decrease in profit in the enterprise. There is a need to reduce the probability of erroneous decisions in enterprise management. Two key aspects to achieving this goal are the vitality and competitiveness of enterprises, which is largely dependent upon the effectiveness of decision-making related to the activities of the enterprise. For this reason, the companies took on the task of developing more effective management information systems in order to help decision-makers exploit the data and models that enrich and improve the decision-making process.

The developed system should be improved in order to deal with the large number of available data and heterogeneity of the existing approaches to modeling.

Most of the data arising from the activities of the enterprise, it is in the form of electronic and paper documents. All aspects of economic activity are either document, or can be formally reduced to the document. Today is dominated by relational database management systems that provide a convenient way to store information in the form of tables.

The relational model is sufficient for modeling the subject areas, but the very design of database in terms of the relationship is often very difficult. The need for designers in more convenient and powerful means of presenting the subject area has caused the emergence of semantic modeling.

2 Intelligent methods in automated analysis of activity of objects of management

The advantage of automated systems for analysis is the ability to discover hidden knowledge in large volumes of data. Need exists for the use of artificial intelligence methods in systems for analysis of the activity of management objects.

Computational intelligence methods in recent decades have received the development and implementation of activities in the analysis of management objects. These methods include artificial neural networks, genetic algorithms and fuzzy systems [1]. The use of fuzzy sets is popular with enterprise management. Financial indicators characterize certain aspects of the current financial situation of the company. These indicators are business activity, the turnover, profitability, solvency, financial stability, etc. For some indicators are known standard values.

One of the areas of research in the field of artificial intelligence is the problem of knowledge representation. This line solves the problem of knowledge representation in expert systems. Knowledge should have the following features: internal interpretability, structured, connectivity.

The basic models of knowledge representation in expert systems are: production model, frame model, a neural network, the logical model, a semantic network.

After analyzing the advantages and disadvantages of existing models of knowledge representation, we can conclude that the most appropriate model for the

* Corresponding author: LeraTishkina@mail.ru

DOI: 10.1051/itmconf/20171002008

monitoring of the results of activities of the management object is a model based on semantic networks. Semantic network is a model of knowledge representation, which is based on graph-oriented network structure. Any subject area can be represented by objects and links between them. Semantic network provides domain objects (nodes) and relations between them (the arcs). Models of knowledge based on semantic networks have a number of advantages: the ability to transform into other knowledge representation models; a visual representation of the causal relationships between objects; presentation of data about real objects and relations between them [2].

Figure 1 shows a model of a semantic network for represent of object of management. G1, G2, G3 – different types of analysis (marketable assets, current liquidity, absolute liquidity). Relationship (U13, U14 and U15) between objects made using different degrees of dependency. Status of control object is evaluated based on the degree of relatedness of objects. You can make individual conclusions for each management object.

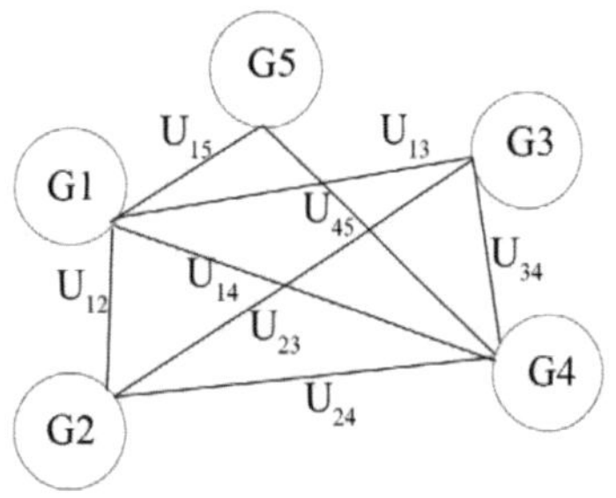

Fig. 1. Model of a semantic network

3 Development of a system for monitoring the results of activity of accounting objects

Develop software and information system allows you to analyze the state of the control object on the basis of information about it. An object of management can be analyzed with the help of different types of analysis: financial stability, business activity, profitability, liquidity, management efficiency.

The basis of the developed system is fuzzy logic methods. These financial ratios are analyzed using fuzzy sets theory. A number of parameters of the enterprise is not available to accurately measure.

The developed software system has the following features:

- The possibility of adding new data;
- Entering accounting data;
- Downloading data from the financial statements Excel;
- Monitoring of various parameters of the management object: assessment of business activity, financial stability, management efficiency, liquidity and solvency;
- Reporting on the data of different types of analysis of object of management;
- Analysis of the financial ratios using the theory of fuzzy sets.

In the future we plan to develop for software:

- Choice of the kind and branch of object of management;
- The addition of new analysis methods;
- The addition of new metrics analysis;
- The conclusion and recommendations of the analysis of the situation, depending on the type of industry and enterprise.

The fundamental difference from the existing systems of this type is integration. The intuitive interface of the system makes it easy to train staff to operate the system. The developed system saves staff time. Financial analysis system allows drawing conclusions about the real situation on the management object.

References

1. M. Moharrampour, M. Moharrami, A. Akson, Journal of current research in science, **2** (2014)
2. Hilovska K., Koncz P, Acta VSFS, **6** (2012)

 DOI: 10.1051/itmconf/20171002009

Model of Forecasting the Social News Events on the Basis of Stochastic Dynamics Methods

D.O. Zhukov [1]*, *A.M.* Zamyshlyaev[2], and *O.A.* Novikova[1]

[1] Moscow Technological University, Moscow, Russia
[2] Researches and Design Institute of Information Technology, Automation and Telecommunications on Railway Transport (JSC "NIIAS"), Moscow, Russia

Abstract. For a description of the information space it is introduced a vector representation of the constituent text documents that are bound by the events described in the timeline. The predicted event is also represented by a vector obtained on the base of its text description. The mean value of projections of the information space in the direction of the vector of predicted events at different time points is considered as a set of information system states. It is also entered the change values of states. To describe transitions between states is used a probabilistic approach and the difference transition scheme. This makes it possible to get the dependence of the time for the value of the probability density for the event "detection information system in a state" in the form of a second order differential equation. On the basis of this equation is formulated and solved the boundary problem. Carried out by the authors the analysis of the stochastic dynamics of achievement a threshold of realization of news events has allowed the establishing of the ability to increase the probability of transition almost simultaneously with the beginning of the process of the news cluster structure changing. This is due to the presence of the memory of previous states in the information system and the possibility of self-description, as a result of accounting in the differential model information processes on the basis of the second derivative over time. In addition, the proposed model demonstrates the possibility of sudden changes in the probability of crossing the threshold of events and takes into account the presence of oscillations in her behavior. Based on the model developed it is proposed the algorithm for analysis of news clusters relationship in the information field with the possibility of occurrence of the predicted event, and determined the possible time of its implementation.

1 Introduction

There is currently the theory put forward by Nassim Nicholas Taleb, which deals with the nature of the emergence and implementation the information of unexpected events. According to his theory, these phenomena must meet the following criteria [1] :

1. The event is unexpected (for experts);
2. The event has significant consequences;
3. Upon the occurrence, in a retrospective, the event can be given a rational explanation, as if it was expected.

In his theory Nassim Taleb suggests that humanity is not able to successfully predict their future and the confidence in their knowledge advances ourselves and knowledge produces the phenomenon of "over-reliance" [1].

Since in the real world, there are cause-and-effect relationships, then we think we can not say that this problem has no solution, and in our present work, we denote some possible ways to solve it [2]. When creating a news event forecasting model it requires a mathematical tool that would allow formalization the nature of the data and bringing them to a common measurement scale [3]. Obviously, it is impossible to carry out calculation operations in one model, for example, estimates the linguistic and metric scale values without displaying procedures on the formal dimensionless set [4].

The essence of the proposed approach for the prediction of news events is as follows:

1. On the basis of existing methods of mathematical linguistics the description of information space can be formalized in the form of vectors, presenting a set of texts on natural languages. Thus, it is supposed to solve the problem of the heterogeneity of the data and units of various processes settings (measurement scales deliberately roughened and become linguistic, but all the data are formalized in a unified manner).

2. On the natural language it is possible to describe and provided a vector representation of interest (intended) news event for which it will be held forecasting of its implementation.

3. Taking into account that information space is a reflection of the real world in which there is a cause - effect relationships between events, it is possible to assume the implementation of the law of conservation of the information space. And as a hypothesis to test it is

* Corresponding author: zhukovdm@yandex.ru

possible put forward the idea that existing in the information space formalized textual knowledge can shape the image of the projected events of interest.

2 A model the stochastic dynamics of transitions between states in the information space

2.1. Contact meaningful clusters of information space with a predicted event

Take a collection of text documents. Using the methods of mathematical linguistics, they will create a vector representation of the information space. Carry out the clustering of semantic groups at a time t. We define the vectors (z_1, z_2, ...,z_k, z_j,...), defining the position of the centers of the clusters in a given time. Then spend a textual description of the forecast news events and set its vector X_{hs}.

As a hypothesis, we assume that the information space already has some data on projected event, and we can assume that there should be and the evolution of existing semantic groups of news events in the event that we predict. In the description of evolution in our opinion the most acceptable is the use of the parameters used in informational search whilst determining the relevancy of search requests: finding the distance between the vectors and determination of cosine of the angle between them.
We choose as the evolutionary parameter the finding the projection of x_j vectors defining the position of the centers of the information clusters at any given time $z_1, z_2, ..., z_k, z_j$, in the direction of the vector X_{hs}, which determines the appearance of the predicted events. Each of the projections x_k is defined as the product of the corresponding vector z_k and cosine of the angle between the directions of the vectors z_k and X_{hs} ($x_k = z_k \cdot \cos(\alpha_k)$), that is, in fact, we use the cosine measure, adopted in informational search.

After a certain period of time (called an interval measurement T) values of the vectors defining the position of the information centers of clusters vary to some values Δ_j (j — represents the considered vector). To illustrate, for example, vector z_{01} and z_{02} determine the position of the centers of clusters of news in the information space at a time t, and the vector z_1 and z_2 z2 – after a time interval T (at time $t + \tau$). In these cases, $\Delta_1 = z_1 - z_{01}$ and $\Delta_2 = z_2 - z_{02}$. Similarly, they determined the changes for positions of the centers of all clusters in the information space at a time τ.

The values x_{01}, x_{02}, x_1 and x_2 are to assign values corresponding to the projections of the vectors defining the position of the news centers of the clusters 1 and 2, in the direction of the vector of predicted events, at times t and $t + \tau$. Note that some values of x_k projections may be larger than the preceding x0k values (for the same group of news data), and some smaller; in the information space of two trends of behavior coexist. One of the projections is to increase the values, the other is to reduce that must be considered in the framework of the developed model. We introduce for any time the concept of the average value $< x_t >$ of all values of the projection vectors that define the position of the centers of clusters of news in the information space on the direction of the axis of the predicted events. For a group of K news cluster at a time t the average value $< x_t >$ is defined as: $< x_t >= (\Sigma x_{t,j}) / K$ (the summation is from $j = 1$ to K) where $x_{t,j}$ denote the corresponding values of the vectors of the projections, defining the position of the news centers of clusters, on the direction of the axis of the predicted events in the time t. After a period of time τ: $< x_{t+\tau} >= (\Sigma x_{t+\tau,j}) / K$ (the summation is from $j = 1$ to K). To take account of trends to increase and decrease the values of the projection of the vectors defining the position of the news centers of clusters, on the direction of the axis of the predicted events it can proceed as follows. Based on the analysis x_t the values, j and $x_{t+\tau,j}$ we divide the set of x_t, j into two subgroups, one $(x_{t,j})_{\text{I}}$ will have all the news clusters for which over the time interval τ there was a decrease the quantities of values of the projections $x_{t+\tau,j}$ (denote the number of such clusters as an R), and the second $(x_{t,j})_{\text{II}}$ – increase (denote the number of such clusters as the K–R), and find for each of these the average values $(< (x_{t,j})_{\text{I}} >= (\Sigma(x_{t,j})_{\text{I}} / R$ (the summation is from j =1 to R) and $< (x_{t,j})_{\text{II}} >= (\Sigma\, (x_{t,j})_{\text{II}} / (K - R))$ projections of vectors defining the position of the centers of these news clusters. Further, we offer the following approach to accounting trends to increase and decrease the values of the projection of the vectors defining the position of the news centers of clusters, on the direction of the axis of the predicted events. Since taking into account the trend it makes sense to talk about the average values, then we will consider the transition to the time interval τ to the point $< x_{t+\tau} >$ of point $< (x_{t,j})_{\text{I}} >$, which is on the axis of events forecasting to the right of $< x_{t+\tau} >$ and the point $< (x_{t,j})_{\text{II}} >$ which is located to the left of $< x_{t+\tau} >$. In themselves the transitions are random events, and their size can be determined as follows: $\xi_t =< (x_{t,j})_{\text{I}} > - < x_{t+\tau} >$ and $\varepsilon_t =< x_{t+\tau} > - < (x_{t,j})_{\text{II}} >$. After the next step, we determine the new values of τ $\xi_{t+\tau}$ and $\varepsilon_{t+\tau}$: $\xi_{t+\tau} =< (x_{t+\tau,j})_I > - < x_{t+2\tau} >$ and $\varepsilon_{t+\tau} =< x_{t+2\tau} > - < (x_{t+\tau,j})_{\text{II}} >$, etc. At any stage n values $\xi_{t+n\tau}$ and $\varepsilon_{t+n\tau}$ may have different random (or almost random) values. Therefore, it is necessary to detect any in their behavior characteristic features (for example, the dependences $\xi_{t+k\tau}$ and $\varepsilon_{t+k\tau}$ from time to time may have self-similarity at not random behavior) or, if they have the characteristics of a uniform distribution, it is possible their averaging over a sufficiently long time period of observation and usage in the model of the average of random values

$\xi = \Sigma\xi_{t+k\tau} / N$ and $\varepsilon = \Sigma\varepsilon_{t+k\tau} / N$ (the summation is from k = 1 to N), where N – number of steps (time intervals τ) monitoring). Note that depending on the values $\xi_{t+k\tau}$ and $\varepsilon_{t+k\tau}$ from time to time can obey a certain distribution law and then its parameters can be set according to obtained data.

2.2. The Construction of difference schemes of transition probabilities between states

In the developed model of processes taking place in the information space, the value of the average value of the current state of vectors projections xi, characterizing the position of the news centers of clusters in the information area on axis of projecting event can randomly increase due to the fact that the value of ε greater than the value ξ at each step (or several successive steps) or randomly decrease if the value is less than the value of ε £. Eventually, state xi would be near the threshold of projected event that equal to vector value X_{bs}.

All set of states will be denoted by X. The state observed at time t can be denoted as $x_i(x_i \in X)$. The observed state is determined by economic and political processes taking place in society. In addition, we introduce a time interval τ, for which is possible to change the state x_i. In this case, any of the current value of time $t = h\,\tau$, where h — the transition step number between states (the transition between states is becoming a quasi-continuous infinitesimal time interval τ), h = 0, 1, ..., N. The current state x_i at step h, after the transition to step $h+1$ can occur due to accidental factors increase by a certain amount ε, or decrease by an amount ξ, and respectively be equal to $x_i + \varepsilon$, or $x_i - \xi$. We introduce the concept of probability of the system stated in a particular condition. Suppose that after a certain number of steps h about the described system it can be said that:

- $P(x-\varepsilon,\ h)$ – the probability that it is in a state $(x - \varepsilon)$;
- $P(x,\ h)$ – the probability that it is in a state x;
- $P(x + \xi,\ h)$ – the probability that it is in a state $(x + \xi)$.

After each step, the state x_i (hereinafter index i can be omitted for brevity) may vary by an amount ε or ξ.The probability P $(x,\ h + 1)$ – that at the next $(h + 1)$ step, the system (or process) in a state x will be equal as follows (see Fig. 1.):

$$P(x,h+1) = P(x-\varepsilon,\ h) + P(x+\xi,\ h) - P(x,\ h). \quad (1)$$

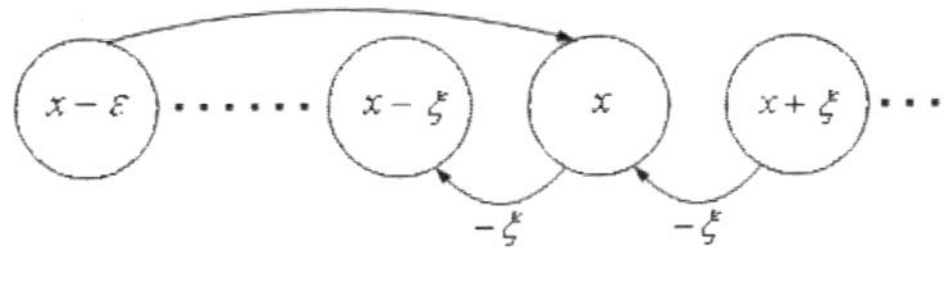

Fig.1. Diagram of the possible transitions between states of the system (or process) to h + 1 step.

Let us explain the expression (1) and shown in Figure 1 the scheme. The probability of a transition in the state x in step h $P(x,\ h+1)$ is the sum of the probabilities of the transitions in this state of the states $(x - \varepsilon)$ – $P(x - \varepsilon,\ h)$, and $(x + \xi)$ – $P(x + \xi,\ h)$ in which the system is located on the step h, net of the transition probability $(P\ (x,\ h))$ system from the state x (where she was on the step h) to any other state in the h + 1 step. In this case, we will assume that the transitions themselves are carried out with probability equal to 1.In an actual situation it may remain the memory of the previous state. Therefore, the proposed model must take it into account. We define the probability $P(x-\varepsilon,\ h)$, $P(x + \xi,\ h)$ and $P(x,\ h)$ through the states at the h–1 step. Similarly, the scheme shown in Figure 1is possible to compose schema of the corresponding transitions and write as follows:

$$P(x-\varepsilon,h) = P(x-2\varepsilon,h-1) + P(x-\varepsilon+\xi,h-1) - P(x-\varepsilon,h-1) \quad (2)$$

$$P(x+\xi,h) = P(x+\xi-\varepsilon,h-1) + P(x+2\xi,h-1) - P(x+\xi,h-1) \quad (3)$$

$$P(x,h) = P(x-\varepsilon,h-1) + P(x+\xi,h-1) - P(x,h-1) \quad (4)$$

Having substituted (2), (3) and (4) into the equation (1) and taking into account that $t = h\tau$, where t – time of the process, h – step number, τ – duration of a single step, we move of h to t, and will hold corresponding Taylor series expansion and having limited only by second derivatives, we write:

$$\partial P(x,t)/\partial t = a \cdot \frac{\partial^2 P(x,t)}{\partial x^2} - b \cdot \frac{\partial P(x,t)}{\partial x} - \tau \cdot \frac{\partial^2 P(x,t)}{\partial t^2} \quad (5)$$

where $a = (\varepsilon^2 - \varepsilon\xi + \xi^2)/\tau$; $b = (\varepsilon - \xi)/\tau$.

A member of equations of the type $\partial P(x,t)/\partial x$ – describes an orderly transition to a state when it increases $(\varepsilon > \xi)$, or when it decreases $(\varepsilon < \xi)$; a member of equations of the type $\partial^2 P(x,t)/\partial x^2$ – describes random change of state (uncertainty). A member of equations of the type $\partial P(x,t)/\partial t$ – can be defined as the rate of overall change in condition of the system over time; a member of equations of the type $\partial^2 P(x,t)/\partial t^2$ – describes the process by which the states themselves become sources of occurrence of other conditions (self-organization and acceleration as the ordered $(\partial P(x,t)/\partial x)$ and random $(\partial^2 P(x,t)/\partial x^2)$ transitions). From the point of view of the applicability of the model area it should be considered a limitation on the coefficient $a = (\varepsilon^2 - \varepsilon\xi + \xi^2)/\tau$ of the second derivative in x, which takes into account the possibility of accidental changes in the state. It should satisfy the condition $(\varepsilon^2 - \varepsilon\xi + \xi^2) \geq (l - x_0)^2$, the meaning of which is that the transition from the initial state x_0 to achieve the threshold events l may not occur in less than one time step τ. If $(\varepsilon^2 - \varepsilon\xi + \xi^2) < (l - x_0)^2$, the system moves through the door events to achieve in one step.

2.3 The formulation and solution of the problem

Assuming that the function $P(x, t)$ continuous, is possible to go on the probability $P(x, t)$ (equation (5)) to the probability density $\rho(x, t) = dP(x,t)/dx$ and formulate the boundary value problem, the solution of which will describe the process of transition between the states.

$$\frac{\partial \rho(x,t)}{\partial t} = a \cdot \frac{\partial^2 \rho(x,t)}{\partial x^2} - b \cdot \frac{\partial \rho(x,t)}{\partial x} - \tau \cdot \frac{\partial^2 \rho(x,t)}{\partial t^2} \quad (6)$$

The first boundary condition. The first boundary condition will choose for the following reasons: the state $x = 0$ defines a complete lack of any kind of the processes, which occur in the information space, with their corresponding measured parameters. The actual probability of detection such a condition can be different from zero (though it should be close to zero), but the probability density, which determines the flow in a state $x = 0$, must be set equal to 0 (state of the system cannot go to negative values (it is realized reflection condition), i.e.:

$$\rho(x,t)\big|_{x=0} = 0$$

The second boundary condition. Let us consider the state of the information space with a value of the vector located near the boundary of possible values of its states, denote this limit value as a possible states L. The actual probability of detection such a state will be different from 0.

However, the probability density, which determines the state of flow in the $x = L$, must be set equal to 0 (state of the system cannot go to the range of values greater than the maximum possible value (it is realized the condition of reflection from the boundary)), i.e.:

$$\rho(x,t)\big|_{x=L} = 0$$

Since at time $t = 0$, the state of the system may already be set to a certain value x_0, the initial condition is given in the form:

$$\rho(x,t)\big|_{t=0} = \delta(x - x_0)$$

Since the initial condition contains a delta function, the solution $\rho(x,t)$ is split into two regions at $x > x_0$ and $x \le x_0$. Using the methods of operational calculus for the probability density $\rho_1(x,t)$ and $\rho_2(x, t)$ detection condition in one of the values in the interval from 0 to L, you can get the following system of equations.

When $x > x_0$

$$\rho_1(x,t) = A(x,t) \cdot \Sigma(-1)^n \cdot B(x,t) \cdot \sin\left(\tfrac{\pi n x_0}{L}\right) \cdot \sin\left(\tfrac{\pi n(L-x)}{L}\right);$$

When $x \le x_0$

$$\rho_2(x,t) = A(x,t) \cdot \Sigma(-1)^n \cdot B(x,t) \cdot \sin\left(\tfrac{\pi n(L-x_0)}{L}\right) \cdot \sin\left(\tfrac{\pi n x}{L}\right),$$

where

$$A(x,t) = -(2\exp(-t \cdot k \cdot (x - x_0)/2\tau))/L,$$

$$k = (\varepsilon - \xi)/(2(\varepsilon^2 - \varepsilon \cdot \xi + \xi^2)),$$

$$B(n,t) = ch(t \cdot (k\varepsilon\xi/(2(\varepsilon - \xi)) - \pi^2 n^2 (\varepsilon - \xi)/(2kL^2))^{1/2}/\tau)$$

Amounts are calculated by n = 1 to ∞. If we calculate the integral $P(l, t)$:

$$P(l,t) = \int \rho_2(x,t)dx + \int \rho_1(x,t)dx \quad (7)$$

where the first integral is calculated between 0 and x_0, and the second from x0 to l, then the function $P(l, t)$ will set the probability that the system state at time t time is in the interval from 0 to l ($l = X_{bs}$), i.e., the I threshold event will not be achieved.

Accordingly, the probability $Q(t)$ that the limit event l at time t reached or surpassed can be determined as follows:

$$Q(l,t) = 1 - P(l,t) \quad (8)$$

The analysis shows that $\rho_1(x,t)$ and $p_2(x,t)$ for all values of t and x are non-negative, for the function $Q(l, t)$ as t→∞ following condition is satisfied $Q(l, t) \to 1$ ($P(l, t) \to 0$).

2.4 Analysis of the solution of the boundary problem for the dynamics of self-organization of the social conditions in the community

Let us analyze the results. To simulate the process we will assume that the initial (at the start of follow-up) value of condition vector of the system (information space) is x_0 ($x_0 = 0.05$ conditionally accepted the value), the value t_0 assumed to be 1 standard unit of time, ε =0.02 and $\xi = 0.01$, $l = 2$ – conditionally accepted quantity.

The results of the solution of equation (8) using (7), function $\rho_1(x,t)$, $\rho_2(x,t)$ and a predetermined above mentioned set of parameters and different event thresholds (note that in this case the predicted event is observed during the growth of the value of the vector of system state), selected in the simulation are presented in graphical form in Fig. 2.

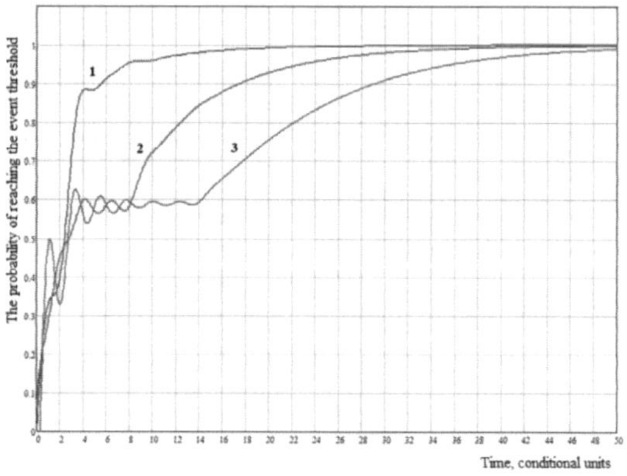

Fig. 2. Graphical representation of the results of modeling to overcome the percolation threshold of negative attitudes in society.

Curve 1 in Figure 1 is constructed for the event threshold equal to 0.1; curve 2 for the magnitude of event threshold equal to 0.2, and curve 3 for the event threshold value of 0.3.

The course of the curves in Figure 1 shows the possibility of the growth of the transition probability threshold of event almost immediately after the start of the process, which is associated with the presence of the memory about the previous state of the system in a model developed by us, and the possibility of significant self-description of the system due to differential equation of the model member which has the type – $\partial^2\rho(x,t)/\partial t^2$.

Curves 2 and 3 in Fig. 2 show that the nearer value of x_0 of the system state at the start of observation to the threshold event, the faster the transition probability increases (curve 1 is built for event threshold of 0.1, and curve 2 for 0.2, with the same initial value of the system state vector – 0.05). The course of the curves in Fig. 2, shows the possibility of the growth of the transition probability of percolation threshold, almost immediately after the start of the process, this is due to the presence of the memory of the previous state of the system in our model developed, and the possibility of self-description of the system as a result of the account in the differential equation model of the member which has the form $\partial^2\rho(x,t)/\partial t^2$.

The second feature of our proposed model is the possibility of several abrupt changes across the threshold the transition probability event.

The third feature of our proposed model is the existence of phenomena in the wave-like behavior for the value of achieving the threshold event.

The developed model takes into account many of the basic properties of rare events: a time uncertainty of their existence, stochastics with unknown characteristics, and the presence of memory in a system the event occurs, the self-organization of information.

Our model allows us to analyze the possibility of predicting the rare news event in conjunction with the various clusters in the information space. An analysis of the values of times achieving the rare events may allow them to make a fairly accurate prediction for a given level of probability to realize (for example 0.90 or 0.95).

It should be noted that every rare news event has the poorly structured and poorly defined precursor, the appearance of which was not revealed, but they are meaningful indicators in a retrospective to give the usual rationalized definition the phenomenon occurring. The study of self-similarity of information processes may allow us to determine the period or interval of self-similarity, which is important from the prognostic point of view.

3 Conclusions

The proposed model considers the uncertainties in the occurrence of events in the information space, and is not based on the statistical characteristics of a pre-supposed law distribution.

The proposed model shows the possibility of the growth of the transition probability threshold to achieve news event in the information space almost immediately after the start of its process of developing, due to the taking into account the memory of previous states of the system and the possibility of significant self-description due to differential model of the second derivative by time.

The proposed model shows the possibility of abrupt changes for the transition probability through the event threshold and takes into account the presence in her behavior wavelike phenomena.

The developed model allows creating algorithm of analyzing the relationship of information clusters in information space with the possibility of realization of any event, as well as to determine the predicted time of its occurrence.

The work is executed due to financing by the Ministry of Education and Science of the Russian Federation as the competitive part of government tasks of higher education and scientific organizations for the implementation the initiative scientific projects; the number of the project 28.2635.2017 / IF named "Development of models of stochastic self-semistructured information and implementation of memory in predicting the news events array-based natural language texts.

References

1. N.T. Nassim, *The Black Swan: The Impact of the Highly Improbable* (Random House, 2007).
2. J. M. Hofman, A. Sharma, D. J. Watts, Science, **355**. 486 (2017)
3. D. Roy, D. Ganguly, M. Mitra, G. J. Jones, Neu-IR'16 SIGIR Workshop on Neural Information Retrieval, Pisa, Italy (2016)
4. J.R. Bellegarda, C. Monz, Computer Speech & Language, **35**, 163 (2016)

ITM Web of Conferences **10**, 03001 (2017) DOI: 10.1051/itmconf/20171003001
2017 Seminar on Systems Analysis

On Suboptimal Solution of Antagonistic Matrix Games

Alexander Goryashko [1], *

[1] Moscow Technological Institute, 119334 Moscow, Russia

Abstract. The paper examines resource allocation games such as Colonel Blotto and Colonel Lotto games with the goal to develop tractable method for building suboptimal solution in mixed strategies of these games without solving the relevant optimization problem. The foundation of proposed method lies in the specific combinatorial properties of the partition games. It turned out that as far as distribution of resource along battlefield is concerned that pure strategies participating in ε-optimal solution possessed specific structure. Numerical experiments showed that these specific structural peculiarities can be easily reproduced utilizing previously found combinatorial properties of partition. As a result, we get ε-optimal solution of partition games and support set mixed strategies can be computed in polynomial time.

1 Introduction

In 1921 Borel published the seminal work [1] in which he studied a two-player constant-sum game, where the players strategically distribute a fixed amount of resources n over a finite number of m contests (called as "battlefield"). The player who assigns a battlefield a higher amount of resources wins this one. The objective of the players is to maximize the number of battlefields won. (This work – as some researches reasoned – became the cornerstone of the game theory). After Second World War Borel's model takes the name "Colonel Blotto game" brought into the scope of game theory the field of allocation games or a 'winner-takes-all' conflicts with applications in the areas such as R&D races, presidential elections, auctions, tournaments (for an overview of research works on allocation games, see [2]). Hart [3] considered a discrete version of the Blotto game, called Colonel Lotto game where the battlefields are assumed indistinguishable. More exactly the difference between Colonel Blotto and Colonel Lotto games can be explained as follows.

Let $\boldsymbol{\alpha} = (\alpha_1, \ldots, \alpha_m)$ and $\boldsymbol{\beta} = (\beta_1, \ldots, \beta_m)$ be pure strategies of players A and B in these games. Then for Blotto game payoff function H_B is defined as

$$H_B(\boldsymbol{\alpha},\boldsymbol{\beta}) = (1/m) \sum_i \mathrm{sign}(\alpha_i - \beta_i).$$

For Colonel Lotto game, in accordance with Hart [6], payoff function H_L is defined as

$$H_L(\boldsymbol{\alpha},\boldsymbol{\beta}) = (1/m^2) \sum_i \sum_j \mathrm{sign}(\alpha_i - \beta_j).$$

In [3] it was shown that Colonel Blotto game (n, m) and the Colonel Lotto game (n, m) have the same value.

The Colonel Blotto or Colonel Lotto games are the games, which are easy to formulate, yet analytically quite challenging. In general, these games have multiple mixed strategy equilibria only.

In [4, 5] model of partition games was introduced to describe the classes of Colonel Blotto and Colonel Lotto games. Recall that an (n, m)-partition of n into m parts is a sequence of non-negative integers $a_1 \geq a_2 \geq \cdots \geq a_m \geq 0$, such that $n = a_1 + a_2 + \cdots + a_m$. See [6] for details on partition theory.

The antagonistic partition game [4] is a two-player constant-sum game. The playoff function H_P is defined as

$$H_P(\boldsymbol{\alpha}, \boldsymbol{\beta}) = (1/|\Theta(\boldsymbol{\alpha})|) \sum_{\Theta(\alpha)} \sum_i \mathrm{sign}(\alpha_i - \beta_j),$$

where $\Theta(\boldsymbol{\alpha})$ is permutation set for $\boldsymbol{\alpha}$.

In spite of great interest in optimal solution of Colonel Blotto and Colonel Lotto games to the best of our knowledge are not works where numerical minimax solutions were was produced and analyzed. In [3] was shown that Colonel Blotto game has a mixed strategy equilibrium in which the marginal distributions are uniform on $[0.2n/m]$ along all battlefields. In this way for Colonel Blotto game (120,6) for example the support set should contain more than 10^8 strategies taken with equal probabilities each.

On the other hand by seminal theorem of Carathéodory [7] the games like Colonel Blotto admit equilibrium mixed strategies involving at most more than $(n+1)\cdot m+1$ the pure strategies. Nevertheless, theorem of Carathéodory was existence theorem only for a long time.

The payoff matrix of Colonel Blotto and Colonel Lotto games has a huge size even for small values n and m. For example, for Colonel Blotto game (120, 6) the size of payoff matrix is about $10^{10} \times 10^{10}$. Therefore, it is not surprising that traditional optimization techniques fail to find optimal solutions Colonel Blotto and Colonel Lotto games. Up to now it was common believe that solving minimax problem for antagonistic matrix games with constant sum like colonel Blotto or colonel Lotto games are intractable because the number of pure strategies grows exponentially with games' parameters (for partition games it is total resource n

* Corresponding author: petrovich4you@gmail.com

DOI: 10.1051/itmconf/20171003001

and number of part m). So all previous investigation efforts was concentrated on finding marginal distributions of the available resources that are the best for equilibrium [2, 3].

Recently in [8] so called LMO-based decomposition techniques were proposed. In particular, there was investigated the case where these techniques allow to reduce a huge, but *well organized matrix game*[a] to a small saddle point optimization problem.

Fortunately, Colonel Blotto game (and partition game, accordingly) is the case when the matrices for each player are well organized. Specifically, in [8] the game "attacker vs defender" was considered. This game is more general version of Colonel Blotto game – the different battlefields are allowed to have different weights. The method from [8] as applied to Colonel Blotto games (more exactly "attacker vs defender" game) allows to solve the game in polynomial time. In reality, the method is capable to find in reasonable time *near-optimal* solutions to rather large (with m, n about 100) games within accuracy, in terms of the payoffs of the players, like 0.02.

Besides this method provides support set with few pure strategies (in our experiments it is significantly below Carathéodory bound). However, this method – as any other computational method – does not allow to understand *a priori* what kind of pure strategies will enter to the supports of ε-optimal mixed strategies. At the same time, previous results [4] allow to find a set of "appropriate" pure strategies (for ε-optimal support set) without solving optimization problem [8].

In this paper, we present the first, to our knowledge, method to approximate the ε-optimal solutions of partition games. Essentially our method is as follows: we employ the knowledge about given partition's parameters (peculiar resource and permutation balance [4]) to design the set of pure strategies "similar" to those participating in ε-optimal solution [8]. ("Similarity" here means the ability to find of a game value within accuracy, in terms of the payoffs of the players, like 0.02–0.04). To check the quality of our solutions and to get the support set (the set of pure strategies with probability values) we have to solve a small matrix minmax problem by well-known method [9]. Results of the numerical simulation yield strong reasons to believe that in the case of colonel Blotto-like antagonistic games our approach is quite competitive with the techniques from [8].

The rest of the paper is organized as follows. In section 2 "Analysis of the ε-optimal support set" we analyzed the support sets of ε-optimal solutions obtained by methods from [8] as applied to Colonel Blotto games (120, 6), (36, 6) and (100, 10) with symmetrical resources and demonstrate some combinatorial peculiarities of pure strategies participating in these solutions. In section 3 "Experimental Design: synthesis suboptimal solution for symmetric partition games" the basic stages of experimental procedure to compute equilibrium solutions are presented. The accuracy of obtained suboptimal solutions is compared with ε-optimal solutions was estimated by numerical simulations. Section 4 contains our concluding remarks.

[a] matrix B(KxL) is well organized if, given $x \in R^K$, it is easy to identify the columns _B[x], B¯[x] of B making the maximal, resp. the minimal, inner product with x [3].

2. Analysis of the ε-optimal support set

First of all we checked ε-optimal support sets for colonel Blotto games (36,6), (120,6) and (100,10). These solutions in mixed strategies contain about two hundreds strategies. As example, fig.1 demonstrates first ten strategies of Colonel Blotto game (120, 6) for two players A vs B. Here first value is probability p(**α**) for associated strategy **α** = [a_1, $a_{2,\dots,}$ a_6] and $a_1+a_2+\dots+a_6$ =120, i.e. in support set player must use strategy **α** with probability p(**α**).

Altogether support set contains 227 pure strategies for player A and 229 pure strategies for player B This support set allows to get ε-optimal game value with guarantee accuracy $-2.587182 \cdot 10^{-002}$ for player A and $2.040023 \cdot 10^{-002}$ for player B.

Such accuracy is sufficient for most practical application

A	B
0.0181590, [22, 0, 39, 21, 29, 9]	0.01668, [2, 27, 20, 3, 39, 29]
0.0170577, [9, 37, 20, 34, 7, 13]	0.01645, [30, 28, 34, 7, 11, 10]
0.0169868, [5, 40, 25, 40, 5, 5]	0.01652, [13, 8, 23, 28, 15, 33]
0.0148952, [36, 30, 7, 4, 18, 25]	0.0153, [23, 15, 17, 15, 24, 26]
0.0134729, [37, 17, 32, 28, 3, 3]	0.01375, [14, 10, 39, 39, 13, 5]
0.013079, [14, 16, 6, 16, 37, 31]	0.013087, [5, 3, 24, 35, 21, 32]
0.012941, [25, 29, 5, 20, 19, 22]	0.012786, [6, 21, 40, 37, 3, 13]
0.012619, [13, 19, 39, 14, 15, 20]	0.012661, [8, 5, 14, 40, 34, 19]
0.0125790, [40, 10, 8, 5, 39, 18]	0.012351, [34, 32, 5, 6, 40, 3]
0.01171438, [17, 5, 16, 36, 40, 6]	0.0119, [35, 10, 25, 17, 12,21]
…	…

Fig. 1. First ten strategies and their probability from support set of Blotto game (120, 6) A vs B

We emphasize that there is essentially discrepancy between well-known condition on resource allocation for optimal support set [5] and resource allocation in ε-optimal support set. For example, for colonel Blotto game (120,6) value of maximal resource in each battlefield for player A is (59, 62, 53, 40, 53, 64), and for player B – (53, 46, 51, 51, 50, 48). It is common knowledge that the value of maximal resource for any battlefield in accordance [5] must be less than $(2n/m)+1$, i.e. for colonel Blotto game (120,6) less than 41. What more, resources in each battlefield based on the univariate distribution function $(mx/2n)$ where $x \in [0, 2n/m]$. But if all *pure strategies in* ε-optimal support set will be represented as partitions $\alpha = \alpha_1, \dots, \alpha_m$, where $\alpha_i \geq \alpha_{i-1}$, $i = 1,\dots, m$ and m is even, resource allocation in these partitions are far from requirement of uniformity imposed on model in [2]. So it is desirable examine how with point of resource allocation all partition support sets constructed.

Let $\Theta_{n,m}$ is set of all (n, m)-partitions and subset $\Im \subseteq \Theta_{n,m}$. For any $\boldsymbol{\alpha} \in \Im$ define function $Q(\boldsymbol{\alpha})$ as

$$Q(\alpha) = \{S^1(\alpha) - S^2(\alpha)\}/n = \; 2S^1(\alpha)/n - 1, \; (1)$$

where $S^1(\alpha) = \sum_{j=1}^{m/2} \alpha_j$, $S^2(\alpha) = \sum_{j=m/2+1}^{m} \alpha_j, \tilde{a}^{m}_{j=m/2+1} a_j$.

For set $\Theta_{n,m}$ next boundary estimates holds

$$0 \le Q(\Theta_{n,m}) \le 1. \quad (2)$$

Here $Q(\boldsymbol{\alpha} = n/m, n/m, \ldots, n/m) = 0$ and $Q(\boldsymbol{\alpha} = (n, 0, \ldots, 0) = 1$. The shape of distribution $Q(\Theta_{n,m})$ depends on the relation between n and m.

For example, Fig.2. demonstrated the distribution of $Q(\Theta_{100,10})$. Analysis of the moments of frequency distribution $Q(\Theta_{n,m})$ as a function of parameters n and m shows that value of first moment essentially depends on these parameters (see Fig.3)

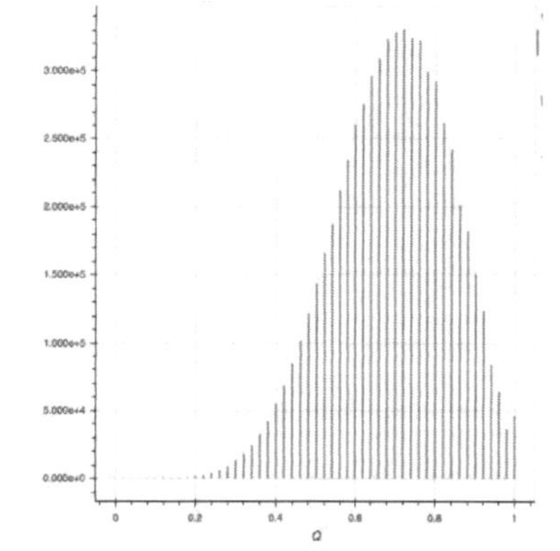

Fig. 2. Number of function from set $\Theta_{100,10}$ as a function of $Q(\Theta_{100,10})$

n	m	m^2/n	$M(Q_{n,m})$	$\lvert M-\ln 2\rvert$
90	16	2.8	0.764	0.071
100	10	1	0.691	0.002
120	6	0.3	0.632	0.061
120	20	3.3	0.780	0.087
144	12	1	0.698	0.005

Fig. 3. Average value of $Q(\Theta_{n,m}) \equiv M(Q_{n,m})$ *as a function of n, m.*

Last column of Fig.3 shows deviation of the first moment $M(Q_{n,m})$ from ln 2. This value is asymptotical approximation of $M(Q_{n,m})$ if n,m are sufficiently large (this statement is readily apparent from [10]). From Fig.3 we see that when $n = m^2$ a deviation of the first moment $Q(\Im_{n,m}')$ from ln 2 is very small (about 0.003) but for all other cases this deviation significantly more.

There is important characteristics of partitions what is known as peculiar resource [4]. The value of peculiar resource is maximal when the partition $\boldsymbol{\alpha} = \alpha_1, \ldots, \alpha_m$ is well-ordered, i.e. $\alpha_1 > \alpha_2 > \ldots > \alpha_{m-1} > \alpha_m$. In this case the partition has all different parts.

Let $PR_{n,m} \supset \Theta_{n,m}$ is partition set where each partition has a maximal peculiar resource.

Proposition. For $PR_{n,m}$ are true:

For any $\boldsymbol{\alpha} \in PR_{n,m}$, $\boldsymbol{\alpha} = \alpha_1, \ldots, \alpha_m$

1) $\min \sum_{i=1}^{m/2} \alpha_i = \dfrac{n+2m}{2}$; $\max \sum_{i=1}^{m/2} \alpha_i = n - \left(\frac{m}{2}+1\right)\frac{m}{4}$.

2) $\min \sum_{i=m/2+1}^{m} \alpha_i = \left(\frac{m}{2}+1\right)\frac{m}{4}$; $\max \sum_{i=m/2+1}^{m} \alpha_i = (n-2m)/2$.

3) $2m/n \le Q(PR_{n,m}) \le 1 - (m^2/4n) - m/2n$.

This is evident from proposition above that if $n = m^2$

$$1/3 \le Q(PR_{n,\sqrt{n}}) \le 2/3. \quad (3)$$

Let $\Omega^*_{n,m}$ is set of the pure strategies of ε-optimal support set. Numerical simulations show that as a rule

$$0.5 \le M(Q(\Omega^*_{n,m})) \le 0.7, \quad (4)$$

Hence, the bigger diversity of the pure strategy the greater the chance to see this strategy in the optimal support set.

3. Experimental Design: synthesis suboptimal solution for symmetric partition games

The main body of numerical experiments was focused on finding of suboptimal solution by simulation of the antagonistic symmetric partition game between two players AC and AS.

The player AC is set of pure strategies $\Omega^*_{n,m}$ (ε-optimal solution) which get by approach [4].

The player AS is a synthetic (artificial) set of the partitions $\Xi_{n,m}(PR_{n,m}, \boldsymbol{pb})$ where $PR_{n,m}$ is some set partitions with maximal value of peculiar resource each and some value of permutation balance $\boldsymbol{pb} \in [pb_o, 0]$ (the value of left border pb_o is set by experiments). The convex optimization program developed to calculate the game value between AC and AS. It is reasonably safe to suggest that the small difference of game values between AS and AC mean that these players could be used interchangeably.

Stages of the numerical simulation partition game between AC and AS.

1. Set the values n,m (resource and number battlefields) for n,m-partition game
2. Get ε-optimal support set $\Omega^*_{n,m}$ for "attacker vs defender" game with fixed parameters n and m by program based on method [4].
3. From $\Omega^*_{n,m}$ pick first N pure strategies (the strategies in $\Omega_{n,m}$ are ordered by probabilities).
4. To build up synthetic set partition $\Xi_{n,m}(PR_{n,m}, \boldsymbol{pb})$ it is sufficient to choose by chance some number M partitions from $\Xi_{n,m}(PR_{n,m}, \boldsymbol{pb})$.
5. Get game value for antagonistic symmetric game between $\Xi_{n,m}(PR_{n,m}, \boldsymbol{pb})$ and $\Omega_{n,m}$ by special program based on CVXPY library [9].
6. The previous steps are repeated $\boldsymbol{I}$ times to calculate the average game value.

Evidently that in our experiments there are three free parameters only: N, M and $\boldsymbol{pb}_o$. Therefore, basic part of experimental works was centered on finding most appropriate parameters of the partition set, i.e. such values of free parameters which permit to build "almost ε-optimal" support sets. By way of example, Fig.4 shows the difference game value of the (100,10)-partition game between set out of 100 and 200 strategies for ε-optimal

 DOI: 10.1051/itmconf/20171003001

solution and set which contains M of synthetic strategies (M = 100, 200, …, 600).

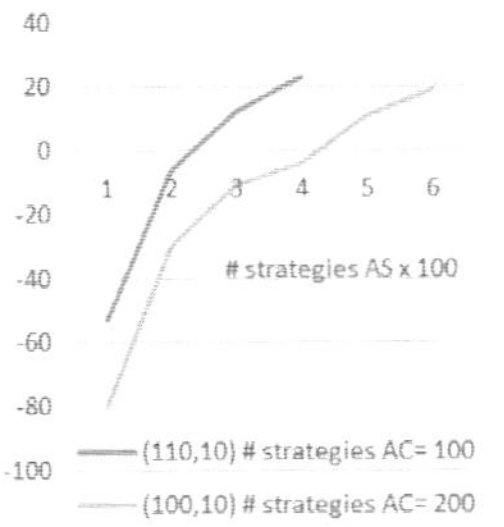

Fig. 4. Difference game values AC vs AS for (100,10)-partition game

From this figure, we notice that if numbers of synthetic strategies (player AC) twice as many strategies of ε-optimal solution (player AS) the difference between games value is practically negligible (no more 0,02)

However, on the base of experiments described above, it is impossible to make final conclusion about behavioral identity AS and AC. Actually, players AC and AS could be showing different results when meeting with other players. Therefore, to investigate these cases was created the test set strategies $\Im$. The player T_M is defined as set of strategies $M_\Im$ ($M_\Im \in \Im$). These $M_\Im$ strategies is chosen out of $\Im$ by chance.

By way of example, Fig.5 shows the experimental results of game value (case 120,6-partition) if AC and AS playing with T_{200} ([0, –0,85], $PR_{n,m}$) and T_{400}([0, –0,85], no more 0.5 $PR_{n,m}$). Here the first argument is interval of partition balance value and second – a value of peculiar resource).

In Table (Fig.5) AC and AS game values are average values of twenty experiments. During each experiment, a partition balance and peculiar resource of player T_M is selected randomly from preset range (see above).

# test Strat.	#AC Strat.	#AS Strat.	AC game value	AS game value	Diff. game value
200	100	100	0,02	0,052	0,03
		200	0,059	0,054	0,005
		400	0,084	0,047	0,027
	200	100	0,015	0,07	-0,058
		200	0,059	0,054	0,005
		400	0,057	0,076	-0,018
400	100	100	-0,034	0,009	-0,04
		200	0,009	0,003	0,006
		400	0,033	0,002	0,03
	200	100	-0,028	0,026	-0,055
		200	0,0088;	0,0288	-0,02
		400	0,034	0,031	0,0027

Fig. 5. Experimental results for games AC and AS with test players T_{200} and T_{400}

4 Conclusions

Results of the numerical simulation provides reason enough to suppose that outlined approach offered serious competition to ε-optimal solution [4], at least, in case of antagonistic matrix games such as Colonel Blotto game. This method with accuracy and computing complexity comparable to [4] allows to get of approximation of ε-optimal solution without decision of relevant optimization problem.The models of strategic multidimensional resource allocation (and in particularly partition games model), has been utilized in many real life applications, such as military conflicts, advertising resource allocation, political campaigns, and development portfolio selection. Nevertheless, using of these models is impossible without design of tractable decision methods. The results [4] was of crucial importance to attain these ends. In our turn we tried to make next step along this line and have discovered that complexity of the problem in question may be strongly diminished at the expense of accuracy. Certainly, validating the experimental results with help of some analytical methods seems imperative and it is our nearest goal. The simplicity of our suboptimal solution method is main advantage for the fields of behavioral game theory [10]. This method can be used to develop of new experimental approaches. For example, in the laboratory experiments [11] where a version of the classic Colonel Blotto game to understand when human decision consistent with equilibrium predictions were investigated. What is more, the special features of our method offer a clearer view of why human being could be smarter than supposed in iterative reasoning model [12].

Author is much grateful to A.C. Nemirovski for his instructive explanations, and P.S. Bocharov who aids in computing experimental work.

References

1. E. Borel, Comptes Rendus de l'Academie, 173, 1304 (1921) [Eng. Transl.: Econometr. **21** (1953)]
2. B. Roberson, Econ. Theory. **29**, 1–24 (2006)
3. D. Kovenock, B. Roberson, *Conflicts with multiple battlefields* (CESifo working paper no. 3165, 2010)
4. B. Cox, A. Juditsky, A. Nemirovski, J. Opt. Theory and Applications, **172**, 402 (2016)
5. P. Bocharov, A. Goryashko, E.V. Nikulchev, Applied Mathematical Sciences, **9**, 5149 (2015)
6. S. Hart, Int. J. of Game Theory, **36**, 441 (2008)
7. J. Eckhoff, *Helly, Radon, and Carathéodory type theorems. Handbook of Convex Geometry*, pp. 389–443 (Amsterdam, North-Holland, 1993)
8. P. Bocharov, A. Goryashko, E. Nikulchev, Int. Review on Modelling and Simulations, **9**, 11 (2016)
9. S. Boyd, L. Vandenberghe, *Convex Optimization* (Cambridge University Press, 2004)
10. A.M. Vershik, Yu.V. Yakubovich, Mosc. Math. J., **1**, 457 (2001)
11. C.F. Camerer, *Behavioral Game Theory* (Princeton University Press, 2003)
12. A. Arad, A. Rubinstein, J. of Economic Behavior & Organization, **84**, 571 (2012)

DOI: 10.1051/itmconf/20171003002

Non-Verbal Intelligence in Primary School Students: A Cross-Cultural Study

Yulia Davydova[1], *Ilia* Zakharov[2], *Irina* Lysenkova[1], *Tamara* Malykh[2] and *Victoria* Ismatullina[2,*]

[1]Kyrgyz-Russian Slavic University, 720000 Bishkek, Kyrgyzstan
[2]Psychological Institute of Russian Academy of Education, 125009 Moscow, Russia

Abstract. In this article we present the results of a cross-cultural study of non-verbal intelligence in primary school students. Significant differences with the effect size of 9% were found in non-verbal intelligence scores of 1057 students from Russia and Kyrgyzstan. The differences were also found for city and countryside residents (effect size of 10%). These results might be explained both by the features of educational systems and socio-economic development level in Russia and Kyrgyzstan.

1 Introduction

Cognitive abilities play an important role both in the life of an individual and the whole society [1 – 4]. Therefore, individual differences in intelligence may be the basis for the academic as well as professional success. Naturally, cognitive abilities studies has been drawing researchers' attention for many years [5, 6].

One of the methods for studying the formation of individual differences in psychological traits is the cross-cultural analysis. Cross-cultural studies consider the cultural context as a source of individual differences and seek to reveal universal and culture-specific patterns of individual differences [7].

Studying these abilities in different cultures, thus conducting a large-scale natural experiment, is a way to assess the influence of culture, spoken and written language, nurturing and educational system on their development (for example, [8]). Several papers showed that these factors contribute significantly to the individual differences in non-verbal intelligence [3, 9]. Cross-cultural differences are explained often by differences in features like thinking, for example, in East Asian (holistic thinking) and western (analytical thinking) cultures [9], differences in the structure of the language, such as Chinese characters and the Russian alphabet (e.g., [10]), and the type of cultural communities (ratio of the scales 'collectivism – individualism' and 'independence – interdependence'). In particular, a significant positive effect of education on individual differences in intelligence was found in the Norwegian natural experiment, when as a result of the reform of public education two additional years of study after the seventh grade were introduced [11]. According to this study, the effect of prolonged educational process in adolescence on intelligence is significant at the age of 19 years [11]. It was also found that students who miss one year of schooling in the future show slightly lower results on intelligence tests [9]. Poor performance on intelligence tests in a number of studies was also associated with long summer holidays, when there is no systematic educational impact [9].

The present study is aimed at studying cross-cultural differences in non-verbal intelligence in Russian and Kyrgyz primary schoolchildren. Inclusion of students from these countries is of particular importance.

Firstly, these states have different human development index. According to the United Nations Development Programme, Russia occupies 55th place in the ranking of countries by the human development index and is included in the group of countries with high human development rate, whereas Kyrgyzstan occupies 125th place, which corresponds to the average level of human development. Secondly, the education systems in Russia and Kyrgyzstan are similar. Third, the quality of teaching high school students differs in the two countries. It was shown that in the Programme for International Student Assessment 15-year-old Russian schoolchildren were slightly below average (38–43) and the results of Kyrgyz students were at the last 65th position.

These macro-environmental similarities and differences allow specifying universalism and cultural specificity in non-verbal intelligence at primary school age.

2 Methods

In total, the sample included 1057 primary school students aged from 7 to 9: 629 Russian (53.9% boys) and 428 Kyrgyz (45.3% boys).

* Corresponding author: victoria2686@gmail.com

We used Raven's Progressive Matrices (SPM) to assess their non-verbal intelligence [12]. It should be noted that, on the one hand, the test 'Raven Progressive Matrices' is positioned as independent of cultural context among intelligence tests. The literature emphasizes the central position of this test: it is assumed that the test 'Raven Progressive Matrices' is the most 'pure' of the existing measures of intelligence as a latent characteristic [13]. These characteristics are achieved through the use of abstract stimuli that are able to neutralize the influence of the cultural context in the strict compliance with the test instructions and differential item functioning analysis (DIF-analysis).

3 Results and discussion

First, we analyzed sex and age differences in non-verbal intelligence. Table 1 presents the descriptive statistics for non-verbal intelligence in Russian and Kyrgyz boys and girls. One-way ANOVA did not show any significant sex differences neither for the Russian ($p = 0.908$) nor for the Kyrgyz sample ($p = 0.076$).

Table 1. Means and standard deviations for non-verbal intelligence in primary school students in Russia and Kyrgyzstan (boys and girls).

	Boys	Girls
Russia	38.72 (9.4)	38.63 (8.5)
Kyrgyzstan	30.77 (9.67)	32.38 (9.01)

In order to assess the age differences in both samples, three groups were compared in the analysis: 7-, 8- and 9-year-old Russian and Kyrgyz students (table 2).

Table 2. Means and standard deviations for non-verbal intelligence in 7-, 8- and 9-year-old primary school students in Russia and Kyrgyzstan.

	7 years	8 years	9 years
Russia	23.67 (3.2)	35.8 (9.46)	40.2 (8.34)
Kyrgyzstan	29 (11.5)	29.87 (9.19)	32.71 (9.28)

The results suggest that there is a tendency for non-verbal intelligence to increase with age. The extent of this growth was different for each country: from 23.67 to 40.2 in Russia and from 29 to 32.71 in Kyrgyzstan. After the Bonferroni correction, the statistically significant differences were shown for all age groups in the Russian sample ($p = 0.001$) and for the 8- and 9-year-olds in the Kyrgyz sample ($p = 0.01$). The age factor explains about 6.6% and 2.4% dispersion of the non-verbal intelligence in Russian and Kyrgyz samples, respectively.

These results may be related to the quality and effectiveness of the educational system in these countries. The pre-school and primary school systems are similar in Russia and Kyrgyzstan as both of them have roots in the USSR practice: children start attending kindergarden at the age of 3, followed by pre-school classes at 6 to 7 years old, then entering primary school at about 7 years of age. During the Grades 1-4, that constitute primary education in both countries, the general disciplines, such as mathematics, Russian, reading and natural sciences are all taught by one teacher.

Despite the observed similarity, the Kyrgyz educational system is less centralized and less effective. For example, even though there are general requirements for the primary program in all Kyrgyz schools, they may differ a lot due to the choice of specific textbooks. Moreover, the educational standards vary across regions, as well as the age of school entrance ranges from 6 to 8 years. Due to the Federal state educational standards in Russia, this particular system is much more centralized. As for the pre-school education quality, it is shown that more than 90% of the children in Russia have access to the kindergarden – whereas the rate is only 10 to 16% in Kyrgyzstan. The quality of school education itself is also a subject for differences: the Programme for International Student Assessment (PISA) places Russian students at the 38 to 41 place in the world rankings, whereas Kyrgyz students take the last (65th) place. The other meaningful indicator is the teachers' education level: 68.4% of all the primary school teachers pass the required pedagogical training. In Russia it is only after you have the professional training or the specialized high education in pedagogy that you are allowed to teach at any level.

We suppose that the differences in the effectiveness and quality of primary education in Russia and Kyrgyzstan mentioned above may account for the differences in non-verbal intelligence in these two samples.

The analysis of the role of social and cultural characteristics (such as the type of the living area or country) in the individual differences in non-verbal intelligence of primary school children showed that on average the Russian students scored higher than the Kyrgyz. Russian children living in the city showed the highest mean score, while the Kyrgyzstan schoolchildren from the rural area showed the lowest mean score.

Two-way ANOVA (table 3) with the factors of country and living area showed significant effect on non-verbal intelligence. The interaction of factors was also significant.

Table 3. Results of 2-way ANOVA.

Factor	Sum of squares (SS)	F	p-value	η^2
«Country»	7658,42	107,13	0,000	0,09
«Living area»	8672,24	121,31	0,000	0,10
Interaction	1089,83	15,24	0,000	0,01

According to table 3, the effect size of the country factor was 9%. The best score was showed by Russian schoolchildren (mean = 36.81), with the difference = 0.40. The living area factor accounted for 10% of the variance. The city schoolchildren's mean was 37.01, the difference with the rural schoolchildren was 0.19. The interaction effect was significant though the effect size was small (1%). Non-verbal intelligence was higher in

DOI: 10.1051/itmconf/20171003002

Russian children living in the city than for those in Kyrgyzstan and both Russian and Kyrgyz children living in rural areas. There were no significant diffrences between Russian and Kyrgyz children living in rural areas.

4 Conclusions

Overall, the results of our study show that social-cultural characteristics such as country or living area type affects individual differences in non-verbal intelligence of primary school children. The differences we found may be related to the educational system features as well as the socio-economic status of the countries. According to the UN Human Development Report, Russia and Kyrgyzstan have different Human Development Index. Russia is in the high index group (50th rank), while Kyrgyzstan is in the medium group (120th rank). Future research may address the informative analysis of the educational factors that lead to the cross-cultural differences in cognitive functioning.

The fact of the extent of cross-cultural differences increasing with the complexity of the test tasks is an additional argument about the educational effects on intellectual performance. As for the mechanisms of the relationship 'education – intelligence', it should be noted that the effect of education 'applies' not only to the increase in knowledge, but it also stimulates development of mental operations. Thus, a number of studies have documented the effect of education on both crystallized and fluid intelligence [14]. Possibilities of enhancing non-verbal intelligence with a variety of educational activities are described in a number of formative experiments (e.g., [15]). For example, in one of these studies it was shown that working memory training using verbal and visual-spatial stimuli improves the scores for 'Raven Progressive Matrices' [15]. It is assumed that the relationship of macro-environmental conditions and nonverbal intelligence might be mediated by training sessions aimed at cognitive processes that underlie successful performance on intelligence tests (e.g., speed of information processing, spatial memory).

References

1. K.V. Petrides, T. Chamorro-Premuzic, N. Frederickson, A. Furnham, British Journal of Educational Psychology, **75**, 2 (2005)
2. W. Johnson, M. McGue, W.G. Iacono, Developmental Psychology, **42**, 3 (2006)
3. R.J. Sternberg, *Wisdom, intelligence and creativity synthesized* (Cambridge, 2006)
4. P. Hagmann-von Arx, J.T. Gygi, R. Weidmann, A. Grob, Frontiers in Psychology, 7 (2016)
5. U. Neisser, G. Boodoo, T.J.J. Bouchard, A.W. Boykin, N. Brody, S.J. Ceci, D.F. Halpern, J.C. Loehlin, R. Perloff, R.J. Sternberg, S. Urbina, American Psychology, **51**, 2 (1996)
6. R.B. Cattell, *Abilities: their structure, growth, and action* (Houghton Mifflin, 1979)
7. D. Matsumoto, F.J.R. van de Vijver. *Cross-cultural research methods in psychology* (Cambridge University Press, 2011)
8. A. Demetriou, Z.X. Kui, G. Spanoudis, C. Christou, L. Kyriakedes, M. Platsidou, Intelligence, **33**, 2, (2005)
9. R. Nisbett, J. Aronson, C. Blair, W. Dickens, J. Flynn, D. Halpern and E. Turkheimer . Intelligence: New findings and theoretical developments, American Psychologist, **67**, 130–159 (2012)
10. M. Rodic, X. Zhou, T. Tikhomirova, W. Wei, Malykh S., Ismatulina V., Sabirova E., Davidova Y., M. Tosto, J-P. Lemelin and Y. Kovas, Developmental Science, **18**, 165–174 (2015)
11. C.N. Brinch and T.A. Galloway (2011). *Schooling in adolescence raises IQ.* Oslo, Norway: Research Department of Statistics Norway.
12. J. Raven, *Occupational user's guide: Raven's advanced progressive matrices & mill hill vocabulary scale* (Oxford Psychologists Press Ltd., 1994)
13. P.A. Carpenter, M.A. Just, P. Shell, Psychological review, **97**, 404–431 (1990)
14. H. Rindermann, C. Flores-Mendoza and M. Mansur-Alves, Learning and Individual Differences, **20**, 544–548 (2010)
15. S.M. Jaeggi, B. Studer-Luethi, M. Buschkuehl, Y.-F. Su, J. Jonides and W.J. Perrig, Intelligence, **38**, 625–635 (2010)

Evolutionary-Simulative Methodology in the Management of Social and Economic Systems

V.A. Konyavskiy[1], *V.E.* Liechtenstein[2] and *V.P.* Los[2,*]

[1]Research and Design Institute of Information Technology, Automation and Telecommunications on Railway Transport (JSC "NIIAS"), 109029 Moscow, Russia
[2]Moscow Technological University, 119454 Moscow, Russia

Abstract. The article outlines the main provisions of the evolutionary-simulative methodology (ESM) which is a methodology of mathematical modeling of equilibrium random processes (CPR), widely used in the economy. It discusses the basic directions of use of ESM solutions for social problems and economic management systems.

1 Introduction

Evolutionary-simulative methodology (ESM) is a methodology of mathematical modeling of equilibrium random processes (CPR). The discovery of CPR, the development of ESM, the creation Decision, the system providing instrumental optimal decision making in risk conditions and uncertainties, enable to implement programmatically the mathematical models CPR, designed by V.E. Liechtenstein and G.V. Ross [1, 2], the authors.

Based on ESM they have been developed the models of various objects and processes in economics, physics, biology and robotics [2–5]. It has been created CPR, the theory [1, 2], which managed to build on the axiomatic principle. The main scientific results are protected by the following patents: "A method for optimizing the characteristics of equilibrium stochastic process" [6]; "Method of optimal control equilibrium stochastic process" [7]; "The method for selecting the external environment parameters agreed with the optimal management of equilibrium stochastic process" [8].

Reporting about Decision computer system is placed on the site of high technologies in Russia [9]. To date, as part of this research area they were defended more than 30 doctoral and master's theses.

2 Evolutionarily – simulative methodology

ESM includes generalized (structural) formulation of evolutionary-simulative model represented by correlations presented below in (1) - (9) and universal search optimization algorithms realized in Decision. Let us consider the evolutionary-simulation models, following 1.3 in [3].

$$Fa_1 = \rho_1(f_1, \ldots, f_n) \quad (1)$$

$$Fa_2 = \rho_2(f_1, \ldots, f_n) \quad (2)$$

$$F_1 = \rho_3(PL, Fa_1, f_1, \ldots, f_n), \ if \ PL > Fa_1 \quad (3)$$

$$F_2 = \rho_4(PL, Fa_2, f_1, \ldots, f_n), \ if \ PL < Fa_2 \quad (4)$$

$$\Phi(PL, Fa_1, Fa_2) = \{F_1, \ if \ PL > Fa_1 and \ F_2, \ if \ PL < Fa_2\} \quad (5)$$

$$\min_{PL}\{max\{M\{F_j\}\}\}, \ j \in \{1; 2\} \quad (6)$$

$$\min_{PL}\{M\{\Phi(PL, Fa_1, Fa_2)\}\} \quad (7)$$

$$P(PL > Fa_1) = P^0 \ or \ P(PL > Fa_2) = P^0 \quad (8)$$

$$r = \rho_5(PL) \quad (9)$$

Symbols and meaningful sense of correlations (ratio - ?) is convenient to consider as an example marketing planning tasks. A block diagram of planning is shown in Fig. 1.

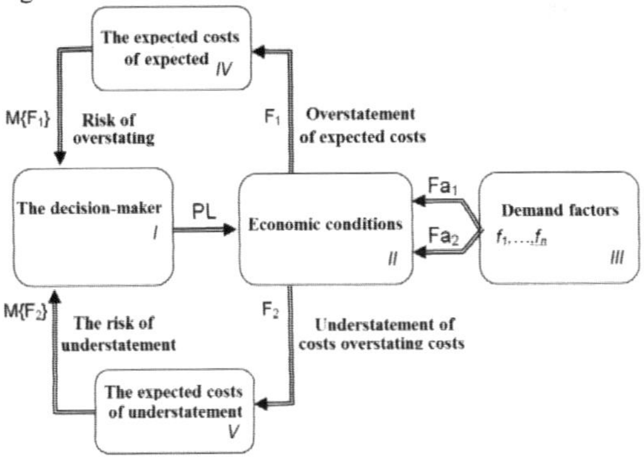

Fig. 1. Block diagram of the control based on the planning.

The decision-maker (DM) (block I), at the beginning of the plan period sets the sales plan (marked as *PL*), and by the end of the planning period it appears the actual volume of sales (Fa_1 – excluding sales outside the market, such as pre-signed contracts; Fa_2 - with their account). Fa_1 and Fa_2 depend on random factors (Block III), such as for example: the number of buyers (f_1),

* Corresponding author: los-vladimir@yandex.ru

income buyers (f_2), customer preferences (f_3), rivalry (f_4), the comparative quality of goods (f_5), and others.

Sales Plan *PL* deterministic, and the actual volume of sales and Fa_1, Fa_2 — random variables. It is possible one of two situations: $PL > Fa_1$, or $PL < Fa_2$. If the plan proved to be more than demand, i.e., if $PL > Fa_1$, the economic environment (Block II) determine the costs of overvaluation (marked as F_1) and the risk of overstatement (marked as $M\{F_1\}$, where M — a sign of the expectation). Costs of overstatement — it is the costs of queue time or waiting time and loss of quality of the goods in the amount of $PL - Fa_1$, as well as the freezing of funds invested in its production. If the plan was less demand ($PL < Fa_2$), then there are the costs of understating (marked as F_2) in the form of lost profits from the pent-up demand in volume $Fa_2 - PL$ and the loss of market share. In developing the plan a decision maker is trying to anticipate the expected costs of overstatement (unit IV) and understating costs (block V), and to compare risks.

Psychologically, the risk of overstatement $M\{F_1\}$ – this irrational fear of a decision maker to spend funds ("cowardice"), and the risk of understating $M\{F_2\}$ – fear of missed profit ("greed"). Moderate presence of these sensations is necessary for proper intuitive orientation in the environment. Charts of risk depending on the plan are shown on Fig. 2.

The risk of overstatement is presented by nondecreasing dotted line, and understating risk – not increasing dotted line with a dot. The solid line represents a risk difference module of overstatement and understatement. PL Plan, in which the difference between the risk of overstatement and understatement turns to zero, is the optimum by the criterion (6). It is proved (see chap. 3 in [2] or [16]) that the risk of balance concept of overstatement and understatement is a generalization of the concept of balance of demand and offers, that is, that the PL plan which is optimum by the criterion (6), is the optimal by correlation on demand and offers. The fine dashed line is a graph of the amount of risk lines. PL plan of the minimal amount of the risk, is optimal by the criterion (7).

The meaning of the model correlations (1)–(9) is that:

– ratio (1) and (2), they indicate that the dependence of demand of Fa_1 and Fa_2 and factors $f_1, ..., f_n$ is represented in the form of simulation models ρ_1 and ρ_2;

– ratio (3) and (4), they indicate that the dependence of overstatement costs of F_1 and understating costs F_2 respectively the *PL*, the fact Fa_1 (or Fa_2) and factors $f_1, ..., f_n$ are represented in the form of simulation models and ρ_3 ρ_4;

– ratio (5), it introduces a penalty function *F*;

– ratio (6), it expresses the minimax principle of optimality, which is used in the planning of (at least the solid line in Fig. 2);

– ratio (8) shows the probability P^0 of meeting or even exceeding (reliability) of PL plan;

– ratio (9) indicates the existence of a vector calculation indices *r*, dependent on the optimum sales plan *PL*.

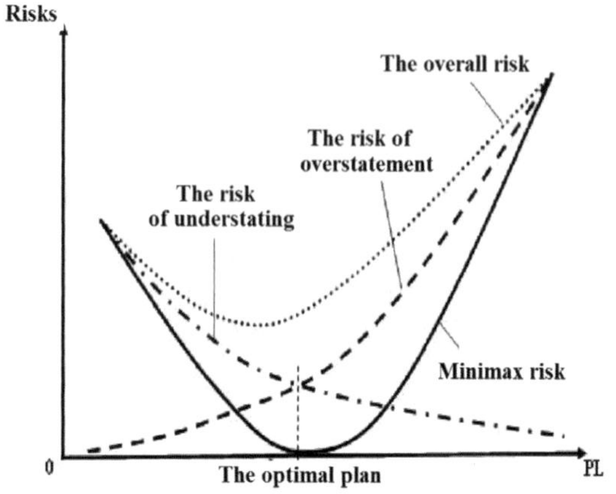

Fig. 2. Market risks and minimax strategy of the company in the market.

Evolutionary-simulative model has three modifications, each of which provides a mathematically correct definition of the PL optimal plan:

1) comprises of (1)–(6) and (9);

2) comprises of (1)–(4), (7), (9);

3) relation comprises of (1), (8), (9) or (2), (8), (9) (it is applicable if known beforehand reliability P^0).

3 Conclusion

There are several areas of application of ESM in the management of social and economic systems. Some of these areas can be called traditional in the sense that the ESM opens the possibility of developing new, more effective and versatile tool to solve traditional business tasks, such as marketing planning (ch. 3 [3]), forecasting and planning of various processes and trends in microeconomics (inflation, taxation, etc., 4.2 in [3]) and macroeconomics (the budget, employment and others., 5.2 in [3]), the valuation of stocks (ch. 1 in [3]) and al.

In addition, ESM provides new direction for the economy. Based on the ESM was able to formulate and prove a number of theorems (see chap. 3 in [2] or [16]), which reveal the mechanisms of negative tendencies and processes, such as randomization (Chapter 4 in [5]), economic measurement distortion (Chapter 3 [5]), lack of control of financial flows (chapter 3 in [2]).

It follows from the theory that the primary source of all problems is the formation of total and global criterion of maximizing the average unit profitability with taking into account the risks (denote the *D*) (see. [17]). Every economic agent is increasingly forced to rely on the criterion $D \rightarrow \max$. The state, not in opposition to the market, is intended to rid the economy of the criterion $D \rightarrow \max$.

This criterion should be replaced by a requirement of economic justice, for which it is necessary to maintain approximate equality *D* for the economic agents and activities. And we are not talking about how to withstand this equation perfectly. In this case, they will stop all movement of capital and lost the incentive to rivalry and economic competition. ESM allows the creation of tools for management of these processes.

References

1. V.E. Liechtenstein, G.V. Ross, *New approaches in the economy* (Finance and Statistics, 2013)
2. V.E. Liechtenstein, G.V. Ross, *The equilibrium stochastic processes: Theory, Practice, Infobusiness* (Finance and Statistics, 2015)
3. V.E. Liechtenstein, G.V. Ross, *Information technology in the business. Application Decision System tool in micro- and macroeconomics* (Finance and Statistics, 2008).
4. V.E. Liechtenstein, G.V. Ross, *Information technology in business. Application Decision System tool for solving practical business tasks* (Finance and Statistics, 2009)
5. V.I. Avdiysky, V.M. Bezdenezhnykh, V.E. Liechtenstein, G.V. Ross *Economic justice and security of economic agents* (Finance and Statistics, 2016)
6. Patent for invention number 2229741 (2002)
7. Patent for invention number 2557483 (2014)
8. Patent for invention number 2558251 (2014)
9. http://www.rushightech.com

DOI: 10.1051/itmconf/20171003004

Psychometric Properties of the Big Five - Children Questionnaire, Russian Version

Sergey Malykh[1], *Georgy* Vasin[1], *Ivan* Voronin[1], and *Tatiana* Tikhomirova[1,*]

[1]Psychological Institute of Russian Academy of Education, 125009 Moscow, Russia

Abstract. Studying personality traits in children and adolescents is valuable, because they can predict a number of important outcomes. The Big Five Questionnaire – Children (BFQ-C) is a questionnaire for 9-14 year-olds used to measure the Big Five personality traits. No analogous psychometric instruments exist or Russian-speaking children of this age group, so our goal was to adapt it into Russian and assess the psychometric properties of the adapted version of the questionnaire. We show evidence of adequate factorial validity and internal consistency of the adapted version in two groups of school-age Russian students.

1 Introduction

Use A4 paper size (210 x 297 mm) and adjust the margins to those shown in Table 1. The final printed area will be 172 x 252 mm.

The 5-factor structure of personality, or Big Five, is one of the few well-replicated constructs in psychology today. This structure has been observed in child and adult samples from many different cultural backgrounds [1-6]. Even though the names of some of the factors may differ between studies [7], the 5 factors are generally referred to as Neuroticism, Extraversion, Openness, Agreeableness, and Conscientiousness [8].

The Big Five factors are broad and their exact composition is still up for debate, however a set of lower order factors, or facets, can be identified. For Neuroticism they are anxiety, impulsivity, reflectiveness and fragility. Extraversion includes sociability, activity level and positive emotionality. Openness is comprised of imagination, creativity and open-mindedness. Agreeableness includes trust, altruism, straightforwardness and humility. Finally, the facets of Conscientiousness are competency, orderliness, self-discipline and a drive towards accomplishment.

The Big Five has been very popular with researchers and a number of questionnaires have been developed to measure it. In Russian-speaking populations the most popular questionnaire is the NEO-PI-R [8], adapted into Russian by V.E. Orel and I.G. Senin [9]. This questionnaire was designed to measure personality traits in adults and adolescents, but is unsuitable for younger adolescents and children [9].

This leaves researchers without a measurement instrument to study the Big Five personality traits in Russian-speaking children. At the same time studies show that personality traits can predict several important outcomes in school-age children – from academic achievement to behavioral problems [10-12].

The Big Five Questionnaire – Children (BFQ-C) is a self-reported phrase-based questionnaire used to measure personality traits in children from 9 to 14 years old [13]. It was developed by Barbaranelli and colleagues in 2003, the original version was in Italian, and an English version was later created by the same authors. The aim of our study is to adapt the English version of BFQ-C for Russian-speaking populations. In order to study the psychometric properties of the translated Russian version of the questionnaire, we assessed the factor structure of the questionnaire and the internal consistency of its scales in a sample of school-age children.

2 Methods

2.1 Participants

The sample included 250 students from Primary school (Grades II-IV, mean age 9.47 years, SD=0.64 years, 51% were female) and 280 students from Secondary school (Grades VI-VIII, mean age 13.21 years, SD=1.31 years, 53% were female). For all participants the informed consent of a parent was provided. The data were collected anonymously; each participant was assigned with a unique ID.

2.2 Measures

The original version of the "Big Five Questionnaire – Children Version" (BFQ-C) comprises 65 sentences apprehensible for children [13]. The authors report satisfactory psychometric properties of BFQ-C. Factor analysis exposed five factor structure–corresponding to the "Big Five" personality traits–in both Primary school

* Corresponding author: tikho@mail.ru

and Secondary school students. All scales also showed moderate consistency across the report types (child report, mother report, teacher report).

In the original BFQ-C the scales quantify the Big Five personality traits: Extraversion, Neuroticism, Openness, Agreeableness, and Conscientiousness. Each scale is measured with 13 items. Each item is a sentence which expresses behavior. The participants have to rate to what extent the sentence describes their behavior using either 3-point or 5-point Likert scale, depending on age. The sentences were translated by the members of the Laboratory of the Developmental Behaviour Genetics, Psychological Institute of Russian Academy of Education, Moscow. The Russian translation of the sentences was then checked by reverse translation.

The Extraversion scale assesses the level of activity and self-assurance ("I like to joke"). The Neuroticism scale measures emotional instability, anxiety, discontent, and anger ("I easily get angry"). The Openness scale reflects the breadth of interests, the ability to search and adopt new knowledge, the creativity ("I easily learn what I study at school"). The Agreeableness scale indices empathy, helpfulness and care ("I trust in others"). The Conscientiousness evaluates self-discipline, punctuality and responsibility ("I play only after I have finished my homework").

A confirmatory factor analysis was used to study the factor structure of BFQ-C. We fit the model with five latent factors (corresponding to the Big Five traits) and 65 observed variables (the items). Each factor was associated with 13 items according to the original factor structure of BFQ-C. The model included 335 free parameters in total.

The model parameters were computed by means of WLSMV estimator which shows best performance on the ordinal data [14]. We used the following criteria of model fit: Comparative Fit Index (CFI), Tucker-Lewis Index (TLI), Root Mean Square Error of Approximation (RMSEA), and Weighted Root Mean Square Residual (WRMR). CFI and TLI > 0.9, RMSEA < 0.05, and WRMR close to 1 index the good model fit [15].

We computed Cronbach alpha and split-half reliability with Spearman-Brown correction as the indices of scale reliability. The values over 0.6 were considered sufficient and over 0.7 – satisfactory. The computations were performed using Mplus.

3 Results

3.1 Factor structure of questionnaire

After fitting the five factor model three items were removed: items 39 and 56 showed reverse factor loadings, and the factor loading of item 9 was statistically non-significant. The result was replicated in both age groups. These 3 items were removed from further analysis. The final model included 5 latent factors, 62 observed variables (items), 320 free parameters in total.

The fit indices of the model are reported in the Table 1. The fit indices obtained in two age groups are highly similar. The model shows tolerable fit according to RMSEA (0.031 and 0.045). CFI and TLI do not reach the critical level, however similar values were reported in the study of original BFQ-C (0.87 and 0.90, for details see [13]).

Table 1. The fit indices of the BFQ-C five factor model

	CFI	TLI	RMSEA	WRMR
Primary school	0.86	0.86	0.031	1.1
Secondary school	0.86	0.86	0.045	1.4

CFI = Comparative Fit Index, TLI = Tucker-Lewis Index, RMSEA = Root Mean Square Error of Approximation, WRMR = Weighted Root Mean Square Residual

3.2 Analysis of reliability

The reliability indices are reported in Table 2,3. On the sample of the Secondary school students all scales showed high reliability (0.7-0.8). In Primary school all scales showed high reliability (up to 0.84) except Extraversion (Cronbach α = 0.60 and split-half reliability = 0.64).

Table 2. The reliability indices of the BFQ-C scales

Scale	**Primary school**	
	Cronbach α	Split-half
Extraversion	0.60	0. 64
Agreeableness	0.75	0.72
Conscientiousness	0.77	0.75
Neuroticism	0.84	0.84
Openness	0.70	0.72

Table 3. The reliability indices of the BFQ-C scales

Scale	**Secondary school**	
	Cronbach α	Split-half
Extraversion	0.76	0.72
Agreeableness	0.72	0.78
Conscientiousness	0.80	0.76
Neuroticism	0.80	0.79
Openness	0.74	0.73

4 Discussion

In this study we aimed to adapt the BFQ-C for Russian-speaking children. We translated the items, tested them on a sample of Russian-speaking children and assessed the psychometric properties of the Russian version of the questionnaire. Based on our results, the Russian version of the BFQ-C is adequate for measuring the Big Five personality traits in Russian-speaking children between 9 and 14 years old. We have observed the intended 5-factor structure of the original in the adapted version. The scales are sufficiently internally consistent. Unfortunately we could not study the convergent validity of the adapted version's results, because no analogous questionnaires are currently available in Russian.

In summation, the BFQ-C Russian version is reliable instrument with adequate factorial validity, when used to

DOI: 10.1051/itmconf/20171003004

study the Big Five personality traits in 9-14 year old children.

This study was supported by the grant from the Russian Science Foundation [grant RSF № 14-18-03764].

References

1. D.W. Fiske, Journal of Abnormal and Social Psychology, **44**, 3 (1949)
2. W.T. Norman Journal of Abnormal and Social Psychology, **66**, 6 (1963)
3. R.R. McCrae, P. Costa., T.A. Martin et al., Journal of Research in Personality, **38**, 2 (2004)
4. M.J. McLarnon, J.J.Carswell, Personality and Individual Differences, **54**, 5(2013)
5. E.S. Nizamova, M.V. Ptukha, M.M. Lobaskova, Teoreticheskaya i eksperimentalnaya psikhologiya, [Theoretical and experimental psychology], **6**,4, (2013)
6. S.B. Malykh, I.A. Voronin, V.I. Ismatullina, I.M. Zakharov, T.N. Tikhomirova, Teoreticheskaya i eksperimentalnaya psikhologiya, [Theoretical and experimental psychology],**7**,4, (2014)
7. S.B. Malykh, T.N. Tikhomirova,Voprosy Psychologii [Question of Psychology], **2**, (2015)
8. P.T. Costa, R.R.McCrae. Professional manual. – Odessa, FL: Psychological Assessment Resources, (1992)
9. V.Orel,I.Senin, Manual, Yaroslavl, (2008)
10. P.Leeson, J.Ciarrochi, P.Heaven, Personality and Individual Differences. **45**, (2008)
11. N.Kuncel, S. Hezlett, D.Ones, Journal of personality and social psychology, **86**,1, (2004)
12. *T.Chamorro-Premuzic, A.Furnham,* Journal of Research in Personality, **37**, 4, (2003)
13. *C.Barbaranelli, G.Caprara, A.Rabasca, C.Pastorelli,* Personality and Individual Differences, **34**, (2003)
14. *C.-Y.Yu & B.Muthén,* Paper presented at the annual meeting of the American Educational Research Association, New Orleans, LA. (2002)
15. *C.Geiser,* Data Analysis with Mplus, New York: Guilford, (2012).

ITM Web of Conferences **10**, 03005 (2017) DOI: 10.1051/itmconf/20171003005
2017 Seminar on Systems Analysis

Methodical Errors of the SWOT-Analysis in Applied Research

Aleksey Murzinov[1], and *Tatiana* Zhubreva[1,*]

[1]Moscow Technological Institute, 199334, Moscow, Russia

Abstract. The article discusses the methodology is widely known the SWOT-analysis and suggests approaches to increase confidence in the results of the analysis. Some typical methodological errors are Illustrated by examples and discussed. Recommendations that increase the value of the method in strategic analysis and increase its effectiveness are given. The recommendations could be useful for companies' managers of different levels in the strategy development and advancement of strategic alternatives, Diploma Thesis supervisors as well as for students and graduates of MBA programs.

1 Introduction

One of the most widely known methods of strategic analysis – SWOT analysis – has found wide application in practice of development planning of enterprises into various fields of business. However, not everyone who uses this method, familiar with the intricacies of filling in the 'magic squares', designed to ensure business prosperity of a company or an enterprise.

Methodically incorrect application of the method at best generates distrust to the analysis and its results, and at worst leads to incorrect conclusions.

Considerable experience of the authors in the application of the SWOT analysis and generalization of the other researchers' experience allows identifying the main methodological errors, which occur in the analysis process, including when it is done as a part of business research in the frame of Diploma Thesis preparation in the MBA programs.

2 Literature Review

2.1 The basic principles of SWOT analysis

The methodology of the SWOT-analysis is seemingly simple to use. The essence of the analysis is to perform sequential steps: identification of favorable and unfavorable factors of the external and internal environment, formulation of the list of main opportunities and threats offered by the external environment, strengths and weaknesses that characterize the company. The mapping of internal and external factors follows this [1, 2].

However, the implementation of this methodology in practice leads to the fact that "the output is a mess of randomly-chosen insights and factors that is why proposals based on them become unreliable and light weighted" [3]. The main reason usually is the incorrect interpretation of external and internal factors, methodically incorrect 'binding' of various factors to a particular company. In sufficiently detailed manner the methodological characteristics identifying essential factors in the external environment when developing strategy according to the methodology of SWOT analysis are described in the articles [4, 5].

2.2 The main causes of methodological mistakes in SWOT analysis

One of the main reasons of methodological errors is *the subjectivity of the analysis*, the prevalence of the intuitive approach to the extension of favorable and unfavorable factors on the analytical methods for their detection. A widespread approach that involves the identification of favorable or unfavorable factors in the external environment and the identification of opinions about the strength and weaknesses of the company with the help of managers (working with the analyzed company) through individual surveys or discussion groups is not tenable. Manager's judgment about the company and its environment could be important, but employees do not always comprehend the real, based on facts, situation. Mostly often, their judgments are rather subjective. In addition, practice shows that employees of the company, even if they know the ins and outs of the business, are not always willing publicly disclose it.

As a result staff opinions may contain "nuggets of gold, but mixed with a fair amount of gangue and inclusions, just looking like gold, which often leads away from the solution of the task facing him. Naturally, such an outcome is not inevitable, but it's a strong possibility" [3].

* Corresponding author: tjoubreva@mti.edu.ru

 DOI: 10.1051/itmconf/20171003005

To reduce the influence of subjective judgment, both external and internal factors should be identified on a rational basis. With this purpose, one should use a few key ways to determine the true external and internal factors influencing the company's operations, its success in the short and long term.

These include:

• Secondary data review;
• Expert survey;
• Investigations and experiments.

3 Research Methods

To identify the causes of systematic errors when conducting a SWOT analysis the research was conducted within the phenomenological paradigm related to the understanding of human behavior within this paradigm "...social reality depends on the mind" [6, p. 53] of the participants; the studied phenomenon and the researcher cannot be separated from each other.

To find the ways for increasing the level of the SWOT analysis validity analytical qualitative approach to the research was used, as according to this methodology, "the researcher goes beyond describing the characteristics of analyzing and explaining why and how it occurs" [6, p. 11].

General population includes the SWOT analyses prepared in the process of the consulting activities of the authors, and also those that had been presented in Diploma Thesis of MBSH students ("distance education with a tutor taking an active role" [7]) for the past 3 years. The final papers were those where MBSH tutors performed the role of academic supervisors. In a random sample, there were students and graduates, who applied for advice and assistance when conducting a SWOT analysis in the framework of their professional activities. Bough are classified as primary data [6, 8].

4 Findings

4.1 Generalization of secondary data when conducting a SWOT analysis

Information and analytical data published in the media and Internet, as well as data from the analyzed companies are a good source of necessary information. The information gleaned from publications, can be very useful. Especially if these data or overviews presented by well-known political scientists, economists, analytical agencies. However, this information suffers from redundancy; opinions are often inconsistent, and sometimes biased. There is another difficulty when working with secondary information: all information from secondary sources, including statistical materials, is created for specific purposes, and for the purposes of the second researcher could be useful only in part. For this reason, the study of secondary information is obligatory, but not sufficient method to obtain objective data. The best results could be obtained only after consideration of the information gathered from the experts.

In other words, to reduce the subjectivity in identifying the factors it is advisable to pre-assemble factual material on the analysis of the external and internal environment, not limited to the fixation of certain opinions of the company employees.

4.2 Identification and synthesis of expert opinions

The method provides the most objectivity in the identification and estimation, since the experts are the most knowledgeable people. The main difficulty lies in the selection of people, whom we could rightly call experts. Given that companies for a number of reasons are the most often orientated on their own employees, people with expert knowledge on all aspects of analysis are difficult to find. Therefore, before conducting, the expert survey should prepare the relevant data and to allow the persons involved in the evaluation, to be acquainted with the available secondary information. Furthermore, expert evaluations are usually unequal; in any case, you should pay attention to the consistency of expert opinions (defined by the coefficient of concordance of Kendall). These features require us to conduct expert interviews on procedure, contributing to increase the objectivity of the results [9].

4.3 Investigations and experiments

In many cases, for identifying environmental factors it is necessary to carry out primary investigation among customers and competitors. In this case, people use such methods as focus groups, surveys, and benchmarking. In the case of the internal environment analysis researchers use applied methods of analysis of financial and economic activities, methods of personnel analysis, including, where appropriate, and questionnaires.

Each of these ways has advantages and disadvantages, so they are used in combination. In other words, the detection (identification) of external and internal factors and their assessment should be based on facts. Judgments and personal assessments of facts could still take some place, but only on the stage of a comparison of the facts.

Factors are relative, relative to vision and goals. Favorable and unfavorable factors of the external environment, as well as the strengths and weaknesses of the company do not have absolute values. The event, phenomenon in the external environment can carry the threat for one company, and create a rare opportunity for others. Similarly, strengths and weaknesses are relative. Depending on the purposes of different companies, even operating in the same market, these companies can consider the same factors as strong for one and weak for other ones.

This means that there is no absolute strong and weak points, they are relative in relation to the objectives of the company and to the context in which the entity operates. For example, strengths and weaknesses will help or hinder the achievement of specific vision and strategy. Upon changing the strategy, strengths might lose their importance, and the weaknesses gain strength. Similarly, external opportunities and threats are important in the certain situation. It is considered that the external factors act on the company throughout the industry. Do so, however, the influence for each specific company is very concrete since the possible consequences are different.

In this regard, the detection and evaluation of both external and internal factors for SWOT analysis should focus on the vision and goals of the company and the context in which the company exists, especially to competitors. You should to compare the performance of the company with the efficiency of other companies in the same industry or to the average efficiency in the industry.

4.4 Identify the factors in a systematic manner

The widely used algorithm of SWOT analysis is based on identifying external and internal factors based on the experience and knowledge of the employees. As a rule, this leads to unsystematic, random appearance factors. Very often, important for company characteristics of external environment or a substantial parts of the company remain without attention. The company even related to small businesses, are economic system, the elements of which are closely linked, moreover, they are part of a more general economic system. Therefore, the company should be considered systematically and identification of the factors should be conducted on a systematic basis. Moreover, the identification of factors must be undertaken using a methodological approach that would allow identifying the maximum number of factors that affect the company in all spheres of activities. I.e. systematically and consistently, considering the company and its environment from all the sides.

Among the most common methods for systematic search of the external environment factors researchers use PESTEL analysis and 5FP (analysis five forces of Porter). When searching for the internal factors the most popular approaches are such as Porter's value chain and managerial examinations, which consider all aspects of the company activities.

External factors are *events*. As external factors (opportunities and threats) there should be used events, phenomena, and trends that characterize the external environment and are for the company either favorable (comfortable) or unfavorable factor. Opportunities and threats exist in the external environment regardless of the object of study. As a rule, in practice, external factors that characterizes the 'threats' are formulated correctly. Threats always come from outside. Errors occur in the formulation of 'opportunities'.

This is due to the perception of the word 'opportunity', which is mentally formulated as "I, we, can do this or that, we have the opportunity". At the same time, 'opportunities' in SWOT analysis are factors that operated in the external environment, and regardless of the object of consideration that can contribute (create) opportunities. To avoid that conflict we recommend in Russian language using the definition 'favorable external factors' instead of 'opportunities' that will reduce the number of errors.

When identifying the environmental factors it should be noted another circumstance. Quite often an external factor, the researchers use the qualitative characteristics of the environment or the description of the situation. For example, 'bad (good) economic situation in the country' or 'favorable / unfavorable investment climate'. To characterize the situation in such a way is just enough to watch a news program on TV. However, the situation is a product of a plurality of events, so it is a blurred concept. The impact of the situation on the company includes a significant touch of uncertainty. It is rather difficult to identify clear causal relationships. At the same time, the situation is the sum of events and generates event [10]. These particular events have more or less clear cause and affect companies.

For example, another analogy, based on natural events. "The clouds had gathered over the city, the air smells of a storm" (the words from Mark Bernes song) – *this is a situation*. However, this means that soon it will rain and storm (*expected event*). That is precisely an approaching storm, which will bring heavy rainfall and may cause damage to both population and the city itself. Similarly, when fulfilling the analysis of the external environment, one should take as external factors not the situation but the event. The event occurs with a certain probability and leads to certain consequences. The situation has a general impact, it is some background, and the specific event caused by this situation has a direct impact. To quantify the situation is extremely difficult, and not necessary, but events can bring direct measurable damage or create a specific (concrete) opportunity. By the way, in risk management exactly the event is concerned as a risk.

Another circumstance worthy of consideration. Without exception, all the researchers use the data characterizing the state of a particular segment of the external environment. For example, evaluating the degree of importance of external environment factors on the enterprise for the production of feminine hygiene, the researchers used such 'factors' as the level of inflation, fall in GDP, decreasing of oil prices, devaluation of the local currency, and the credit rating of the country.

All the listed above parameters, undoubtedly, characterize the economy of the country. At the same time, the economy affects the enterprise manufacturing personal products of feminine hygiene, nevertheless, as other companies in other industries. However, these parameters characterize the situation in the economy and are very important for macroeconomic planning, but none could assess this impact to a specific company. If to omit the chain of causality, the poor state of the economy leads eventually to a drop in living standards and a drop in demand or a shift in demand to cheaper products. Decline in demand, as an external factor affecting the particular company, is much easier to assess than the impact of the macroeconomic indicators.

The situation is *an uncertainty*, in the sense that the description of the situation contains no information about probable future events, that is, the situation is not amenable to evaluation. With the exception of the dynamic situations. If the situation changes for better or worse, this is trend (a sequence of unidirectional events). If we have identified a trend, we can expect the next event matching this trend. The impact of this event could be easily traced. Therefore, *the situation leads to events; events exactly affect a company. They have to find events and use them as external factors.*

Internal factors are resources and capabilities. Internal strengths and weaknesses of the company one should search among the resources and abilities that it has. Resources could be material, nonmaterial, and human resources.

However, a variety of resources owned by the company can be considered as its strong point, which may lead to competitive advantage only if the company has the organizational abilities (core competencies) in the usage of these resources. The mere existence of resources does not guarantee victory in the competition. Companies have to dispose these resources adequately [11]. Capabilities hierarchy. In business, processes of companies have the form of nested dolls. The high-level processes consist of a series of processes on a lower level, you can draw them as 'a tree model of business processes' or as business processes network. Similarly, the capabilities of the company can be divided into general and functional, and specialized skills and abilities of a lower level. In other words, the general capabilities of the company, which are determined for the whole company, are the result of the integration of functional and specialized abilities of the lower level.

As an example, consider the key ability of "Scientific center of cardiovascular surgery named after A. N. Bakulev": the ability of the Centre to treat cardiovascular disease. This ability is determined by the integration capacities of the center in the delivery of patient diagnosis, surgery, preparation of patient for surgery and providing him/her post-operative care, and many other abilities. In the formation of this ability, the effectiveness of support services and administration play role.

Functional capabilities include a number of specialized abilities, providing separate tasks accomplishing. The top-level capabilities require the implementation of cross-functional integration. For example, the ability to develop new products requires the integration of R&D, marketing, strategic planning, operations and finance. A key capacity for innovative development of new products, which is common for many companies, is the abilities integration to analyze the market situation, the organization of research and experimental activities, identifying the best forms of commercialization, etc. Unique in this sense, is the 3M Company. For 3M, this key ability (the ability to develop new products and related functions) and 3M's capability in new product introduction have been maintained over several generations of employees [12].

It must be emphasized that very often in the literature, especially in the Internet publications; they suggest using the estimated company's activities in particular functional areas as the strengths and weaknesses of that company. For example, the strategy is strong or weak, finances are strong or weak, the staff is qualified or not qualified, etc. Such a generalized notion of strong and weak sides of the company for the purpose of strategic analysis is not valid. Strong (Strengths) and weak (Weaknesses) this is not a general assessment of the company, but its specific characteristics (resources and abilities).

If the company made a clear, definite, understandable, effective, feasible, and shared by all stakeholders' strategy, it is indisputable plus of the company. However, a strong side in this case is the ability (in this case ability as a resource) for strategic analysis and choosing of the appropriate strategy. Moreover, this ability requires evidence. It is unlikely that after one developed strategy the company manages can brag about their potential for strategic planning.

There is no reason to consider the fact of the strategy existence as an important resource. The story is that strategy manages adopt at present time; the results of its execution will be visible only in the future, so in this future someone can boast that in the past the right strategy has been developed. At the same time, the absence of any strategy undoubtedly is the weak side of the company.

In general, the assessment of the overall financial condition of the company for the purpose of strategic analysis is also not suitable. It is important for the analysis the existence of the source for innovations and development activities financing. Therefore, strong sides for the purpose of strategic analysis include the availability of retained earnings, access to cheaper resources, or the ability of the company financiers to find common language with creditors.

Personnel assessment cannot be one-sided. On one hand, it is the skills possessed by the staff, and on the other is the adaptability of the employees and their social skills (ability to work in a group). In addition, it is the responsibility and loyalty of employees. If the researchers for the purposes of strategic analysis declare that the company has qualified personnel, it means that their knowledge of staff is extremely low. Not the overall rating is important, for example, of personnel, but the identifying specific competence that could be put in the basis of strategy development.

Difficulties in understanding factors do not stop there. Very often, they argue that internal factors can present opportunities and threats for the company, so, they say analysts need to use not only the external opportunities and threats but internal opportunities and threats also. From the point of view of the Russian language is acceptable. For example, our company can expand markets or increase market share. There is such a possibility. Acceptable from the point of view of linguistic practice, but not acceptable from the point of view of logic laid down in the SWOT analysis. The company's ability to expand markets or increase market share, is not our strength, it is our desire, intention, goal in the end, based on available resources, experience and market needs.

DOI: 10.1051/itmconf/20171003005

5 Conclusions

The synthesis of described in the literature experience of the SWOT analysis and discussed in this paper the results of conducting SWOT analysis in the process of counselling and tutoring activities of the authors, their supervising the Diploma Thesis of MDSH students allows to draw the following conclusions.

To eliminate the subjectivity of the analysis and the uncertainty of the results of the SWOT analysis everyone should identify external and internal factors systematically using the full procedure of the expert survey.

As external factors (opportunities and threats), is wise to use events, phenomena, and trends that characterize the external environment and represent favorable (comfortable) or unfavorable factors or the company. When determining the internal strengths and weakness of the company parties, it is important to understand that this is not a general assessment of the company, but characteristic of its specific features (resources and abilities).

References

1. K. Fleischer, B., Bensussan. *Strategic and competitive analysis. Methods and tools for competitive analysis in the business* (Moscow, BINOM, 2017)
2. 2. N. S. Otvarukhina, V. R. Vesnin. *Contemporary strategic analysis* (Moscow, Urait, 2016)
3. P. Jenster, D. Hussey. *Analysis of the strengths and weaknesses of the company. Identification of strategic opportunity* (Moscow, Williams, 2003)
4. A.V. Murzinov. Proc. 11 conf. Educational environment today and tomorrow, 302 (2016)
5. A.V. Murzinov. Proc. 11 conf. Educational environment today and tomorrow, 304 (2016)
6. J. Hussey, R. Hussey, *Business Research. A practical Guide for Undergraduate and Postgrad. Students* (Macmillan Press LTD, 1997)
7. T. Zhubreva, SHS Web of Conferences, **29**, 02047 (2016)
8. D.R. Cooper, P.S. Schindler. *Business Research Methods* (Irwin/McGraw-Hill, 2001)
9. A.I. Orlov. *Expert assessments* (Moscow, 2002)
10. R.R. Popova, Bulletin of TGGPU. Series 1. Psychological and pedagogical Sciences, **25**, 2011
11. R. Grant, M. Robert. *Contemporary strategy analysis* (*John Wiley Sons Ltd*, 2010)
12. M.H. Zack (Ed), *Knowledge and Strategy* (Butterworth-Heinemann, 2008)
13. O. Chapelle, V. Vapnik, O. Bousquet, S. Mukherjee, Machine Learning, **46**, 131 (2002)
14. L. Yu, S. Wang, K. K. Lai, L. Zhou, *Bio-Inspired Credit Risk Analysis. Computational Intelligence with Support Vector Machines* (Springer, 2008)

ITM Web of Conferences **10**, 03006 (2017) DOI: 10.1051/itmconf/20171003006
2017 Seminar on Systems Analysis

Non-Stationary Single-Channel Queuing System Features Research in Context of Number of Served Queries

Sergey Porshnev[1] and *Ivan* Korelin[1,*]

[1] Ural Federal University, Institute of Radioelectronics and Information Technologies, 620002, 32 Mira street, Yekaterinburg, Russia

Abstract. This work devoted to researching of mathematical model of non-stationary queuing system (NQS). Arrival rate in studied NQS $\lambda(t)$ is similar to rate which observed in practice in a real access control system of objects of mass events. Dependence of number of serviced requests from time was calculated. It is proven that the ratio value of served requests at the beginning of event to all served requests described by a deterministic function, depending on the average service rate $\bar{\mu}$ and the maximum value of the arrival rate function $\lambda(t)$.

1 Introduction

The most of the known analytical solutions considered in the theory of queuing systems (QS) are obtained with assumption that QS is stationary and the input of requests is Poisson flow[1]. In addition, there are analytic solutions for:

1. QS with Erlang flow of requests (QS with limited aftereffect [5]).
2. QS with the flow of requests, representing a Markov process with a finite or countable state space [6].
3. QS with the flow of requests, rate of which is a semi-Markov process with discrete state space, (MC-flows or imbedded Markov chains) [2].

There is substantially less analytical solutions for the QS receiving random input flow of requests with rate λ, depending from the time of $\lambda = \lambda(t)$. Moreover, this class includes a large number of really existing QS, such as turnstiles, providing passages to the objects of mass events [4], passenger monitoring device in airports and train stations, etc.

The results of research of this class of QS can be used as a scientific basis for the making decision at the design stage for design and modernization of this type QS. In this regard, the study of this class of QS it is an urgent task for today from both scientific and practical points of view.

However, for instance, the issue about possibility of describing NQS characteristics, which were chosen as the research object, using deterministic functions which link the measured practical characteristics flow of requests (visitors) and the average serving rate of the operational device is opened.

In this paper are presented the results of a research of the NQS using the statistical modeling. The analysis of this results allowed us to offer analytical formulas describing the dependence of the NQS characteristics from maximum input flow rate $\lambda = \lambda(t)$ and the average service rate of the operational devise $\bar{\mu}$.

2 Mathematical model of non-stationary queuing system

Block diagram of a non-stationary model of single-channel QS with unlimited queue is shown in Figure 1. Queue-discipline is first in first out (FIFO).

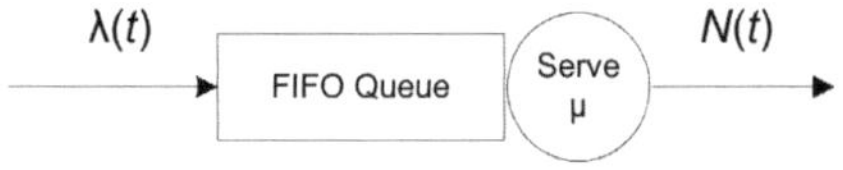

Fig. 1. The scheme of non-stationary QS model

This scheme shows that in this model QS input request flow with rate $\lambda = \lambda(t)$ is changing in time. Speed of service of incoming requests is determined by service rate, which is a random variable with probability density:

$$p\{\xi\} = \begin{cases} 0, \text{ then } \xi < 1, \\ \dfrac{2}{9(M[\xi]-1)}(\xi - 1), \text{ then } 1 \le \xi < M[\xi], \\ \dfrac{2}{9(M[\xi]-10)}(\xi - 10), \text{ then } M[\xi] < \xi \le 10, \\ 0, \text{ then } \xi > 10, \end{cases} \quad (1)$$

where $\xi \in [1,10]$. The used probability density (1) provides, that $\bar{\mu} \in (6,60)$.

Selection of arrival rate dependence from time type based on statistical analysis of real data, carried out in

---
[*] Corresponding author: korelin.ivan@gmail.com

[4]. Typical dependence $\lambda_{exp}(t)$ which was obtained in the football match between football clubs "Ural" and "Anji" at the Central Stadium (CS) of Ekaterinburg 27.09.2012 shown in Figure 2.

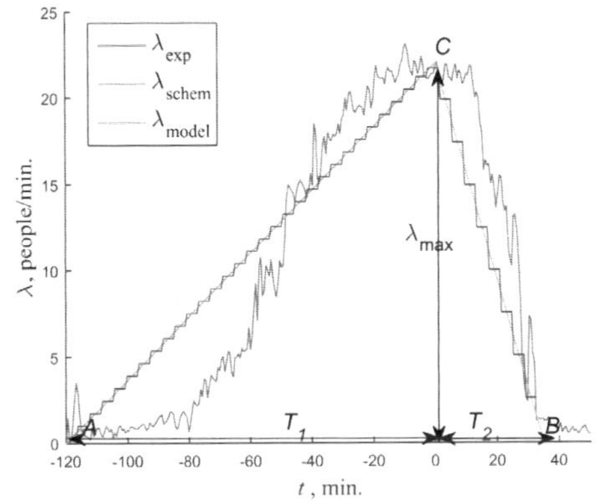

Fig. 2. Dependencies λ (*t*) non-stationary queuing system (the beginning of the match, *t* = 0)

Figure 2 shows that access to CS was opened for 2 hours prior to the football game. In the considered NQS after the opening of the turnstiles during time $T_1 = 120$ minutes the arrival rate of requests (visitors) was growing from 0 people/min to $\lambda_{max} = 22$ people/min. After the beginning of match during the time interval $T_2 = 30$ minutes arrival rate or requests (visitors) has decreased from $\lambda_{max} = 22$ people/min to 0 people/min. Thus, mean number of persons passed in the CS through a single turnstile amounted to 1700 people.

$$N = \int_{-120}^{30} \lambda(t)\,dt \tag{2}$$

Piecewise-linear law depending on $\lambda(t)$ was used in the simulation because the main objective of the research was to study opportunity of describing of non-stationary queuing systems using deterministic functions. On the time interval T_1 [-120; 0] min $\lambda(t)$ increases linearly from 0 to λ_{max}, further time interval T_2 [0, 30] min decreased linearly from 0 to λ_{max}. At the same time, λ_{max} is chosen so that the total number of people served in NQS is 1700. Piecewise constant approximation was used in carrying out statistical tests for the chosen law $\lambda_{schem}(t)$

Following [3], chosen approximation interval duration is equal to 30 seconds and the rate value for the corresponding interval was as average rate for this range.

3 The methodology of the computational experiments

The diagram of algorithm used for statistical modelling is described in detail in [3]. During statistical tests, parameter $T_2 = 30$ min was fixed and parameters T_1, λ_{max} varied so that the total number of requests (visitors) N was equal to 1700 (Fig. 3). It is enough to change one of the parameters, for example T_1, because for fixed N and T_2 parameters T_1, λ_{max} are linearly independent from each other:

$$\lambda_{max} = 2 \cdot N/(T_1 + T_2), \tag{3}$$

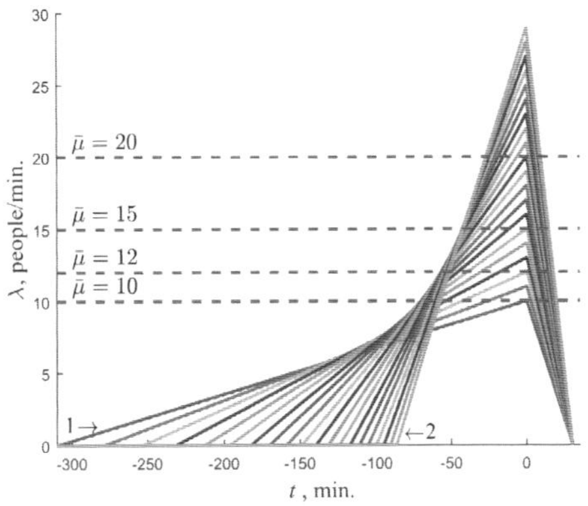

Fig. 3. Dependencies arrival requests rate from time with different values λ_{max} and T_1

In conducted studies parameter T_1 was varied in the range $[-310;-87]$ minutes and the value λ_{max} varied in the range of $[10,29]$ people/min. (Plots 1 and 2 in Figure 3, respectively). Analysis of the characteristics used for describing the features of the operation of studied NQS [3] showed that for their quantitative description can be used, for example, the dependence of the number of visitors entered to the stadium (in terms of QS - number of serviced requests) from time:

$$N = N(\lambda_{max}, \bar{\mu}, t_k),$$

where $t_k = T_1 + \frac{T_2 - T_1}{K}(k-1)$, $k = \overline{1,K}$, K – the number of intervals of the piecewise linear approximation $\lambda(t)$. In the simulation, Monte Carlo method was used. It had average values of function $N = N(\lambda_{max}, \bar{\mu}, t_k)$ with over the ensemble of realizations of independent values:

$$\bar{N}(\lambda_{max}, \bar{\mu}, t_k) = \frac{1}{m}\sum_{j=1}^{m} N_j(\lambda_{max}, \bar{\mu}, t_k), \tag{4}$$

where m – the number of independent trials in the Monte-Carlo method.

4 Analysis of the experimental results

The results of calculations of the functions $\bar{N}(T_1, T_2, \lambda_{max}, \bar{\mu}, t_k)$ are showed below. During simulation the number of intervals of the piecewise linear approximation of the dependence $\lambda(t)$ K was equal to 680. The number m of independent statistical tests was 1000. Dependencies $\bar{N} = \bar{N}(T_1, T_2, \lambda_{max}, \bar{\mu}, t_k)$ for $\lambda_{max} \in [10,29]$ people/min, $T_1 \in [-310;-87]$ min, $T_2 = 30$ min., $\bar{\mu} \in \{10;12;15;20\}$ people/min shown in Fig. 4.

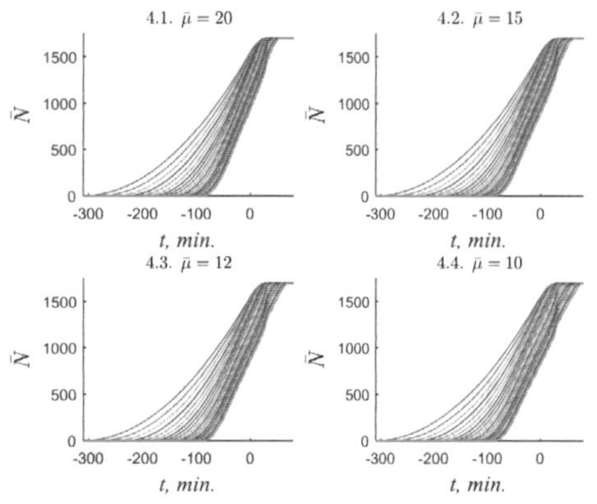

Fig. 4. Dependencies $\bar{N}(\lambda_{max}, \bar{\mu}, t)$ (the beginning of the match, $t = 0$) for different values of parameters $\lambda_{max}, \bar{\mu}$

Considering to figure 4:

1. Dependence $\bar{N}(T_1, T_2, \lambda_{max}, \bar{\mu}, t_k)$ monotonically increases from zero up to 1700 people in selected range of parameters in any combination. Service of all requests (visitors) ends before time $T_2 = 30$ min for parameters in range given in the Table. 1. For ranges of values of the parameters listed in Table. 2, maintenance of visitors continues after finishing of coming requests in the system.

2. The average number of applications served by the moment $t = 0$ is a function:

$$\bar{N}_0 = \bar{N}(\lambda_{max}, \bar{\mu}),$$

To calculate the coefficient characterizing the ratio of serviced requests at the moment $t = 0$ minutes to the total number of requests serviced (1700) using this function:

$$P_0 = \bar{N}_0 / 1700, \quad (5)$$

The physical sense of this characteristic for football stadium is fullness of visitors at the beginning of a football match.

Table 1. Parameter values for which service of requests ends before $T_2 = 30$ min.

$\bar{\mu}$, people/min	20	15	12	10
λ_{max}, people/min	$[10,20]$	$[10,19]$	$[10,17]$	$[10,16]$

Table 2. Parameter values for which service of requests continues after $T_2 = 30$ min.

$\bar{\mu}$, people/min	20	15	12	10
λ_{max}, people/min	$[21,29]$	$[20,29]$	$[18,29]$	$[17,29]$

The surface defined by the function $\bar{N}_0(\lambda_{max}, \bar{\mu})$ shown in Fig. 5.

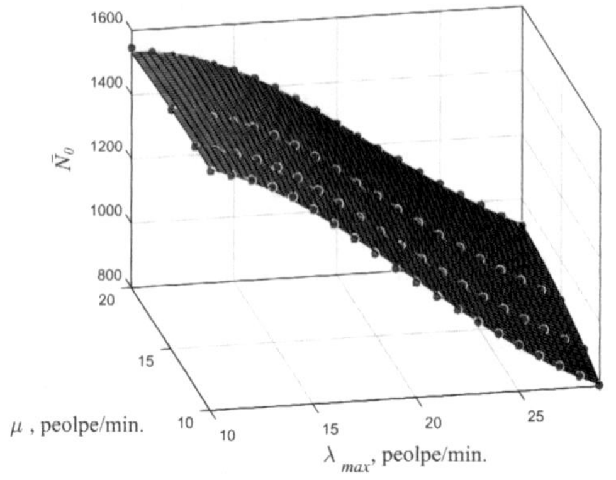

Fig. 5. Function $\bar{N}_0(\lambda_{max}, \bar{\mu})$ graph

Figure 5 shows that dependencies $\bar{N}_0(\lambda_{\max}, \bar{\mu})$, $P_0(\lambda_{\max}, \bar{\mu})$ can be approximated by functions of the form:

$$\bar{F}_0(\lambda_{\max}, \bar{\mu}) = a_0 + a_1\lambda_{max} + a_2\bar{\mu} + a_5\bar{\mu}^2 + a_4\lambda_{max}\bar{\mu} + a_3\lambda_{max}^2 + a_6\lambda_{max}^3 + a_7\lambda_{max}^2\bar{\mu} + a_8\lambda_{max}\bar{\mu}^2, \quad (6)$$

Respective coefficient values a_i, $i = \overline{0,8}$, are calculated using the method of least squares. Coefficient values are presented in Table 3.

Table 3. The values of the coefficients of functional dependencies $\bar{N}_0(\lambda_{\max}, \bar{\mu})$ and $P_0(\lambda_{\max}, \bar{\mu})$

	$\bar{N}_0(\lambda_{\max}, \bar{\mu})$	$P_0(\lambda_{\max}, \bar{\mu})$
a_0	1570±110	93±6
a_1	41±11	2,4±0,6
a_2	−28±12	−1,7±0,7
a_3	−5,8±0,5	−0,34±0,03
a_4	4,1±0,7	0,24±0,04
a_5	0,1±0,4	0,003±0,023
a_6	0,106±0,008	0,0062±0,0004
a_7	−0,061±0,011	−0,0036±0,0006
a_8	−0,033±0,020	−0,0020±0,0011

The sections of the functions $\bar{N}_0(\lambda_{max}, \bar{\mu})$ are dependencies $\bar{N}_0(\lambda_{max}, \bar{\mu}_k = \text{const})$, there $k = \overline{1,4}$, $\bar{\mu}_1 = 20$, $\bar{\mu}_2 = 15$, $\bar{\mu}_3 = 12$, $\bar{\mu}_4 = 10$, shown in Figure 6.

Fig. 6 shows:

1. When $\lambda_{max} = 10$ people/min values of the function $\bar{N}_0(\lambda_{max}, \bar{\mu})$ are the same for each of the used values of $\bar{\mu}$

2. When $\lambda_{max} = 15$ people/min values of the functions $\bar{N}_0(\lambda_{max}, 10)$, $\bar{N}_0(\lambda_{max}, 20)$ differ from each other by 3.67%.

3. When $\lambda_{max} = 20$ people/min values of the functions $\bar{N}_0(\lambda_{max}, 10)$, $\bar{N}_0(\lambda_{max}, 20)$ differ from each other by 9.79%.
4. When $\lambda_{max} = 25$ people/min values of the functions $\bar{N}_0(\lambda_{max}, 10)$, $\bar{N}_0(\lambda_{max}, 20)$ differ from each other by 12.86%.

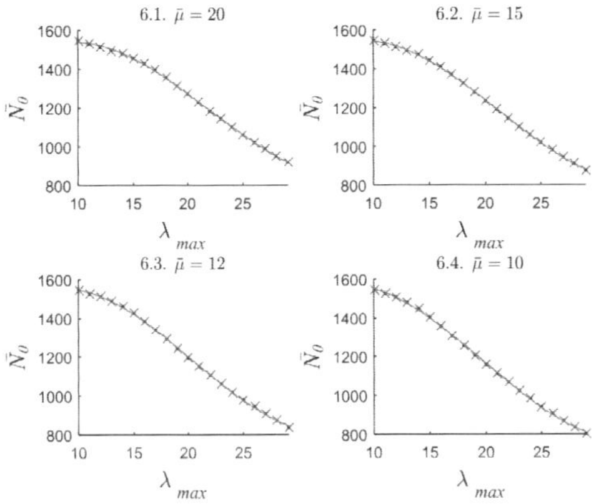

Fig. 6. Dependencies $\bar{N}_0(\lambda_{max}, \bar{\mu} = \text{const})$

Thus, in the considered range of values filling of stadium at the beginning of the match will be increase by no more than 12.86% after doubling the average service rate of a server and respectively a proportional increase of its cost.

5 Conclusion

Results of the study suggest the possibility of describing the characteristics of the selected studied type of NQS (ratio of the number of serviced requests for the selected point in time to the total number of serviced requests) using a polynomial that depends on two variables: the maximum arrival rate and the average service rate. The obtained dependence can be used in the design phase of information systems checkpoints (ISCP) objects of mass events, in choosing specifications ISCP turnstiles. The designer is free from the need for simulation modeling NQS. Analysis of other quantitative characteristics studied NQS is the subject of subsequent publications.

References

1. B.V. Gnedenko, I.N. Kovalenko, *Introduction to queuing theory* (Moscow, Nauka, 1966)
2. D.G. Kendall, The Annals of Mathematical Statistics, 24, 338. (1953)
3. S.V. Porshnev, I.A. Korelin, D.A. Jakob, 26th International Crimean Conference "Microwave and Telecommunication Technology" (CriMiCo), Moscow, Minsk, 4 (2016)
4. S.V. Porshnev, D.A. Jakob, *The study of the functioning of information systems checkpoints objects of mass events* (Ekaterinburg, Institut jekonomiki UrO RAN Publ., 2014)
5. S.V. Porshnev, *Mathematical models of information flows in the backbone high-speed Internet channels* (Moscow, Gorjachaja linija–Telekom Publ., 2015)
6. N.U. Prabhu, Yixin Zhu, Queueing systems, 5, 215–246 (1989)

Serial and Parallel Implementations of Hybrid Fluid Model of Information Flows in Networks with Complex Topology

Dmitry Basavin[1*], and *Sergey* Porshnev[1]

[1]Ural Federal University named after first President of Russia B.N. Yeltsin, 620002 Yekaterinburg, Russia

Abstract. This paper is dedicated to the issue of modeling information flows in networks with complex topologies and it describes a comparison of the sequential (written in the MATLAB language) and parallel (based on GPGPU technology) software implementations of the hybrid fluid model (HFM) of Internet traffic. Obtained performance estimates of both software implementations indicate a higher performance of parallel software implementation HFM. The directions of further research, the results of which will be the basis for the later development of parallel software implementation HFM are proposed.

1 Introduction

In order to research features of the information flows, generated in modern computer networks with large number of different devices and applications, fluid model (FM) of network traffic [1] and its further modification – hybrid fluid model (HFM), which was proposed in [2], are used. FM and HFM represent the following coupled sets of nonlinear differential equations:

$$\frac{dW_i(t)}{dt} = \frac{\boldsymbol{l}_{(W_i(t)-M_i)}}{R_i(t)} - \frac{W_i(t)}{2} \cdot \lambda_i(t), \tag{1}$$

$$\frac{dq_l(t)}{dt} = -\boldsymbol{l}_{q(t)} \cdot C_l + \sum_{i \in N_l} A_i^l(t), \tag{2}$$

where $W_i(t)$ is TCP window size of a class i flow at time t, $\boldsymbol{l}_{f(t)}$ – Heaviside step function, $R_i(t)$ – round trip time of a class i flow at time t, $\lambda_i(t)$ – the loss indication rate experienced by a class i flow, $q_l(t)$ – queue length of a l link at time t, C_l – bandwidth of a link l, $A_i^l(t) = W_i^l(t) / R_i^l(t)$ – arrival rate of class i flow at link l at time t.

FM and HFM take into account the finiteness of data transmission time from one link to another (the delay), as well as feedback provided by *TCP* protocol, transmission rate control policies, active queue management algorithms as well as the interference of modeling flows.

Type of function $\lambda_i(t)$ is determined by links characteristics and traffic shaping algorithms, i.e. Rate limiting and AQM. From a physical point of view, these models are Bernoulli's fluid balance equations for corresponding links.

Due to lacking analytical solutions of ODEs, used in HFM, there is a need in finding their numerical solutions and consequentially developing appropriate software implementations. A version of HFM software implementation with sequentially executable code has been introduced in [3]. However, experience of its practical usage showed that the speed of data flows characteristics calculations is very slow even for relatively simple network configurations. In this regard, it was conjectured in [4] about the possibility of significantly increasing computational speed through the use of *GPGPU* technology. Authors have developed the parallel software implementation of *HFM* using *GPGPU* for networks with a single router in order to confirm it, and analysis of it was presented in [5].

The article touches upon the results of computational speed comparison of sequential and parallel software implementations of HFM for networks with multiple routers. Sequential implementation written with script programming language MATLAB [2] and parallel implementation written with C programming language and OpenCL framework were used in the experiments. Due to the fact of correspondence of computed numerical results obtained with sequential implementation of HFM and real network traffic was earlier proved in [2], we take convergence of sequential and parallel implementation as testifying criterion for correctness of parallel implementation.

2 The experiments methodology

As a part of experiments, it is suggested to carry out modeling of data flows in networks, which conceptual topology diagram is shown in Fig. 1.

Fig. 1 shows that network topology diagram of the described experiments, — is a collection of smaller networks, each of which is a subnet, consisting of two TCP-senders, one router, one receiver and three links. The total number of subnets for k-th experiment is $m = 2^{k-1}$, $k = 1, ..., 9$.

Each TCP class starts data transmission throughout the simulation time to maximize the algorithmic and computational hardware resources loading for performance evaluation and analysis of HFM software implementations. Variable HFM characteristics within a single experiment are as follows: the number of modeled TCP-senders, routers and receivers. Other HFM characteristics remain unchanged. This approach allows

*Corresponding author: basavind@gmail.com

us to conduct identical experiments on sequential and parallel implementations of HFM.

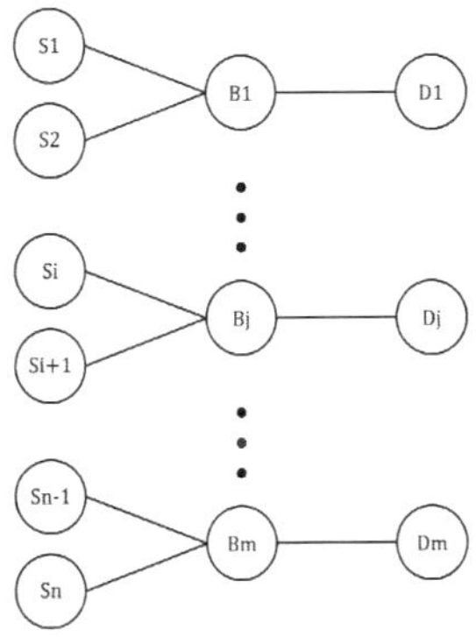

Fig. 1. Conceptual network topology diagram for experiment k, where S is TCP-sender, B – router and D – receiver

We are using next HFM characteristics in k-th experiment:

• Simulation time – 5 s,
• Number of TCP-classes – $n = 2^k$,
• Number of routers – $m = 2^{k-1}$,
• Average link propagation delay – 4 ms,
• Links bandwidth – 1 Mbps,
• Committed information rate (Rate Limiting algorithm) – 1 Mbps,
• Committed burst (Rate limiting algorithm) – 100 Kb,
• Excess burst (Rate limiting algorithm) – 1000 Kb.

Time measurements will be conducted before and after simulation, excluding initialization operations. We will compute 20 independent HFM solutions for experiment plan with obtained average computational time measurements over this ensemble of solutions. For each experiment all HFM solutions will be checked for consistency between sequential and parallel implementations.

The same hardware and operational system will be used for eliminating influence of external factors during the performance of each of the implementations during the experiments.

3 Analysis of experimental results

Comparison of the averaged over the ensemble of the independent solutions system of ODE (1)–(2), obtained using the sequential and parallel implementations HFM, showed that their differences from each other remained within the error due to the finite precision of the computer calculations.

Averaged over the ensemble of implementations of time simulation measurements for the 8 experiments plans, are described below in Fig. 2. As we can see from Fig. 2, computational time of sequential HFM implementation with any number of TCP-classes exceeds the same amount, and is measured in experiments with a parallel HFM implementation, indicating a higher performance of the latter. For a quantitative confirmation of this conclusion, Table 1 shows quantitative values of the computation time.

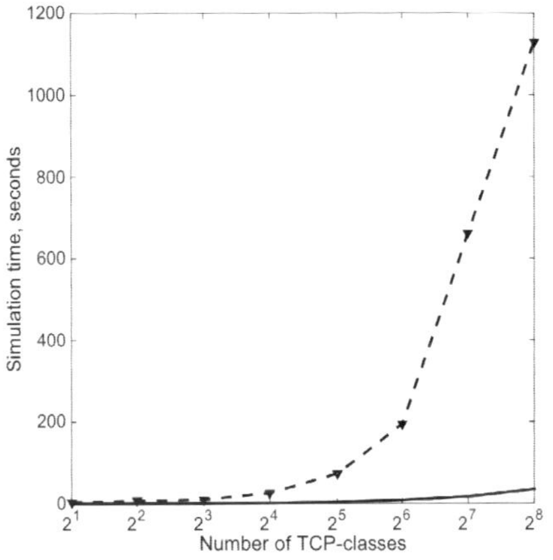

Fig. 2. The dependence of simulation time for the number of TCP classes: dotted line – sequential HFM implementation, solid line – parallel HFM implementation

Table 1. Comparative analysis of software implementations

Count of TCP-classes	Time of modeling in GPU, seconds	Time of modeling in MATLAB, seconds	Acceleration, time
2^1	0.684	3.760	5.494
2^2	0.818	6.823	8.338
2^3	1.186	10.245	8.635
2^4	2.084	26.224	12.583
2^5	4.083	73.505	18.005
2^6	8.329	194.542	23.357
2^7	16.960	661.531	39.005
2^8	34.699	1128.521	32.524

We should note, that, when using parallel processing algorithms on the central processor (CPU) (for example, embedded in the language MATLAB), the computational speed will decrease inversely proportional to the number of processor cores. However, even when using CPU with 8 cores computational time, it will obviously be more than when it is obtained with using a parallel implementation HFM. Analysis of the experience of using the sequential software HFM implementation, written with C language [5], shows that it provides higher speed of calculations in comparison with a software implementation, written with MATLAB script language, however, it will still be inferior to the parallel HFM implementation. But one of the main pros for using CPU implementations is the opportunity to use large amounts of RAM memory for storing parameters and calculation results, therefore, modeling a larger number of TCP classes of Internet traffic (according to our estimates, their number may reach 2^{17}) and networks with difficult topology.

As a part of a further improvement of the parallel software implementation, it is planned to develop a system architecture, which allows using dynamic-link modules in order to implement new algorithms AQM, TCP etc.

4 Conclusion

The efficiency of parallel HFM implementation, developed with usage of *GPGPU* technology, is confirmed. It is shown that its usage provides a significant increase in computation speed compared to the sequential HFM implementation, written in MATLAB language. Parallel HFM implementation, Created by the authors, in contrast to the packet simulators, i.e. NS-2, provides the possibility of modeling high speed Network with difficult topology.

References

1. V. Misra, W. Gong, and D. Towsley, Proceedings of ACM Sigcomm, 151 (2000).
2. M.K. Grebenkin, S.V. Porshnev, *Gibridnaia zhidkostnaia model magistralnogo Internet-kanala* (LAP LAMBERT Academic Publish., 2012) [In Rus]
3. M.K. Grebenkin, S.V. Porshnev, *Programmnaia realizatciia gibridnoi zhidkostnoi modeli informatcionnykh potokov v vysokoskorostnykh magistralnykh internet-kanalakh* (2012). [In Rus]
4. D.A. Basavin, S.V. Porshnev, *Proceedings of Aktualnye voprosy v nauchnoi rabote i obrazovatelnoi deiatelnosti*, 12 (2013) [In Rus]
5. D.A. Basavin, S.V. Porshnev, Proceedings of CriMiCo 2013 – 2013 23rd International Crimean Conference Microwave and Telecommunication Technology, 424 (2013).

Algorithms of the UML Class Diagram Analysis and Their Effectiveness: Strategy and Interface Insertion Transformations

Olga Deryugina[1,*] and *Evgeny* Nikulchev[1,2]

[1]Moscow Technological University (MIREA), 119454 Moscow, Russia
[2]Moscow Technological Institute, 119334 Moscow, Russia

Abstract. A number of studies have investigated different means of the software refactoring. The question is whether there are any effective methods that could provide automated refactoring of the architecture on the design stage with no source code available yet. With the aim of evaluating this possibility, the algorithms of the UML class diagrams analysis were proposed. In addition, the computational experiment was conducted to evaluate the algorithms' performance depending on the initial diagram size.

1 Introduction

Model-Driven Architecture (MDA) approach [1], which was developed by the Object-Management Group (OMG), introduces a new software development paradigm. This paradigm proposes a design process, which starts with the creation of the PIM (Platform Independent Model). Then the PIM is automatically transformed into the PSM (Platform Specific Model).

MDA approach sets out a new research agenda of creating mathematical methods and software tools of model creation, transformation, storage and interchange.

Standards, developed to support the MDA conception, include MOF (Meta-Object Facilities) [2], UML (Unified Modelling Language) [3], XMI (XML Metadata Interchange) [4], etc.

One of the possible research challenges for MDA is the problem of model refactoring. The question is whether there are any effective methods that could provide automated refactoring of the architecture on the design stage with no source code available yet.

A number of studies have investigated different means of the model refactoring. There are two main approaches introduced by researchers.

The first one is based on the SBSE methods, which include GA, Simulated annealing, Swarm intelligence algorithms, etc. An algorithm receives a UML diagram and a fitness function as an input and gives a result diagram as an output [5-10].

The problem is that the result, maximizing the fitness function, can be unsatisfactory for the software designer. This can be solved by the interaction with the user on each step of the algorithm [11].

Software tools based on the SBSE approach include Dearthóir [12], Darwin [11], CODe-Imp [13], Bunch tool [14], etc.

That is why the second approach is connected with the developing frameworks of automated model refactoring, where the main role is given to the software designer. Framework analyses the model and gives recommendations for the refactoring aimed at the maximizing the fitness function, for example.

Software tools based on the second approach include AchE [15], UML Refactoring tool [16], etc.

In addition, various methods of UML class diagram transformation has been developed. The first one is a deterministic algorithm of transformation. However, the disadvantage of this approach is the lack of modifiability: the user cannot add new transformations to the database.

The second approach is usage of XML transformation facilities: XQuery [17] and XLST [18], for example. UML model should be exported to the XMI format, transformed and then imported from the XMI. The disadvantage is connected with the difficultness of understanding the transformations.

Nowadays the QVT (Query/View/Transformation) standard [19] has been developed by OMG. It defines a set of languages for model transformation. It gives the possibility of developing tools, which could allow users to add new transformation rules to the database.

The aim of this paper is to propose algorithms of UML class diagram analysis, which suggest Strategy and Interface transformations in order to minimize/maximize fitness function value.

The rest of this paper is organized as follows: First, the problem of the automated UML class diagram refactoring is formulated in Section 2. Then the UML Map abstract data structure, which stores elements of a UML class diagram in hash maps, is introduced in Section 3. In Section 4, the Strategy transformation analysis algorithm is proposed. In addition, the

* Corresponding author: o.a.derugina@yandex.ru

DOI: 10.1051/itmconf/20171004002

experimental results of applying this algorithm to class diagrams of different size are presented. After that, in Section 5 the Interface transformation analysis algorithm is proposed including the experimental results of applying it to class diagrams. In Section 6, the role of the proposed algorithms in the UML Refactoring Tool is introduced before concluding in Section 7.

2 The problem of the automated UML class diagram refactoring

UML class diagram transformation t can be described as the following mapping function:

$$t(d,E): d \to d', \quad (1)$$

where d is a UML class diagram, E is a set of diagram elements $e_i \in d, e_i \in \{C,R,I\}$, d' is a UML class diagram attained as a result of applying the transformation t to the diagram d.

Then the problem of the diagram refactoring can be formulated as searching such a set of pairs $\{t,E\}$, that:

$$d' = t(d,E), \Delta f(d') < 0 \quad (2)$$

To be able to conduct the automated UML class diagram refactoring it is important to do the following:

1) formalize the semantics of UML class diagrams, which give an opportunity to check whether transformations keep the invariance of the semantic value;

2) formulate a refactoring criteria – fitness function $f(\cdot)$;

3) define a list of semantically equivalent transformations, which can be automatically performed by the refactoring algorithm.

The problem of the automated UML class diagram refactoring is connected with several difficulties.

First, it is hard to formulate a fitness function. Recent advances in UML class diagram quality evaluation provide a wide range of metrics [20–24]. However, it is hard to interpret most of these metrics. Scientists have conducted experiments aimed at evaluating the influence of different metrics (CBO, DIT or NOC [20], for example) on the level of the quality criteria [25–27]. So far, the results of these investigations sometimes are contradictory. In addition, the ways of measuring such quality criteria as the maintainability and understandability stay subjective.

Secondly, the way of searching parts of the diagram to be transformed depends on the transformation type: there is no general-purpose algorithm.

3 UML Map abstract data structure

To allow analysis and transformation of UML class diagrams the UML Map abstract data structure has been developed. It stores hash maps of the diagram's classes, interfaces and relations (see Fig. 1) to make diagram processing faster.

For example, the complexity of searching a class with the xmi:id = "X" in an XMI text document is evaluated as $O(n)$, while the complexity of searching in a hash map storing pairs of keys and values {xmi:id, Class} is evaluated as $O(1)$.

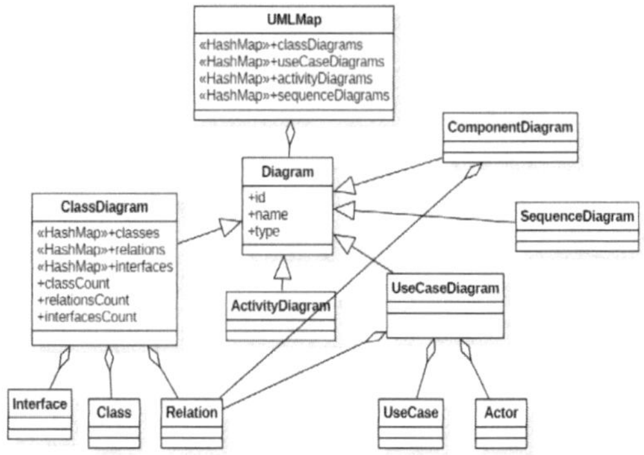

Fig. 1. Reduced class diagram of the UML Map abstract data structure

Special Translator has been developed to translate an XMI file to the UML Map and from the UML Map to an XMI file.

With the UML Map, it is possible to calculate metrics, search elements where transformation application is convenient, automatically transform diagrams, etc.

4 Strategy transformation analysis algorithm

The Strategy transformation means the encapsulation of several algorithms to provide their interchangeability (see Fig. 2 and Fig. 3).

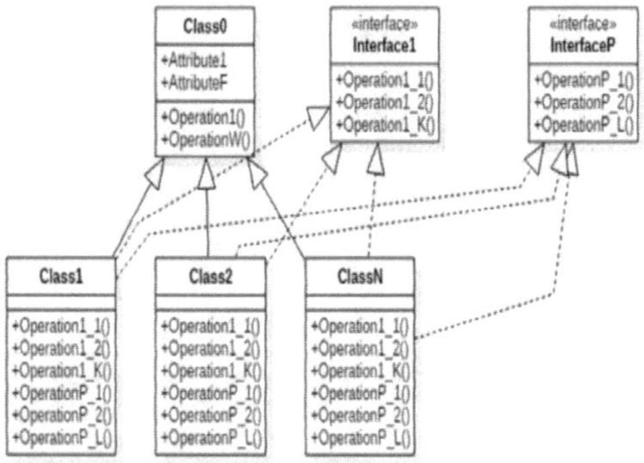

Fig. 2. Preconditions for the application of the Strategy transformation

Algorithm of searching sets of diagram elements E on which the Strategy transformation can be conducted can be described as follows:

1. For each class from the diagram d find those that have inheritors and add them to the hash map <Class, List<Class>> $l1 = \{c_i, \{c_{i1}, c_{i2}, \ldots\}, \ldots\}$.

2. For each class from the $l1$ check whether its inheritors implement any interfaces. If yes – add them to the hash map<Class,List<Class>> $l2 = \{c_i, \{i_{i1}, i_{i2}, \ldots\}, \ldots\}$.

DOI: 10.1051/itmconf/20171004002

3. For each class from $l2$ calculate $\Delta f(d)$. If $\Delta f(d)<0$ – add to the list $l3$ = {*parent_id*, {*child_classes_ids*}, {*interfaces_ids*}}.

4. Return $l3$.

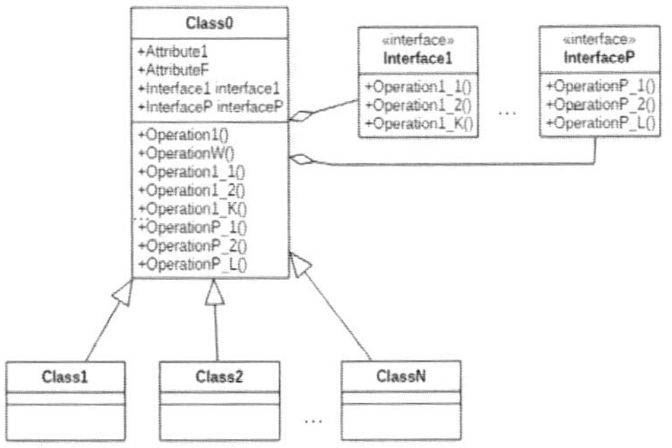

Fig. 3. The result of the Strategy transformation

For the abstract data structure UML Map, which stores hash maps of diagram classes, interfaces and relations, the algorithm can be described as follows:

```
for each c in classes
  inheritors = null
  for each r in relations
    if (r.getEndId() == c.getId())
      if (r.getType() == "generalization")
         inheritors.add(r.getStartId())
  l1.add(c.getId,inheritors)
for each c in l1
  interfaces = null
   for each r in relations
     if (r.getStartId() == c.getId())
       if (r.getType() == "realization")
         interfaces.add(r.getEndId())
   l2.add(c.getId, interfaces)
for each c in l2
   inheritors = l1.get(c.getId())
   interfaces = l2.get(c.getId())
   if (Δf(c,interfaces,inheritors,d)<0)
     l3.add(c,inheritors,interfaces)
return l3
```

A graph depicting the execution time of the algorithm depending on the UML class diagram size is shown in Fig. 4. The value of the execution time was calculated as the average execution time measured during 100 runs for each UML class diagram size. From the graph it follows that the algorithm time performance evaluation is $O(n)$.

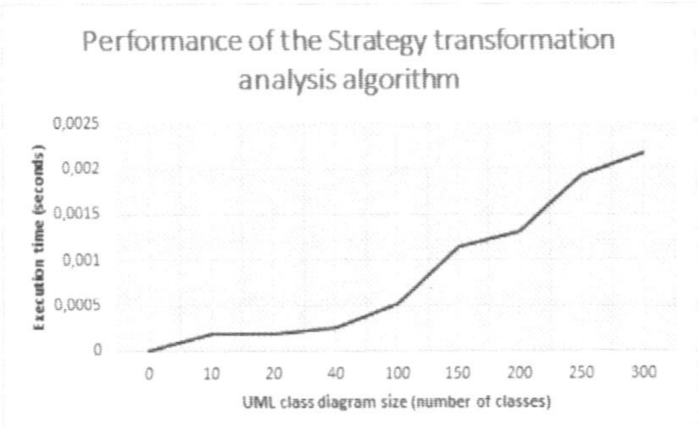

Fig. 4. Performance of the Strategy transformation analysis algorithm

5 Interface transformation analysis algorithm

The Interface insertion transformation involves the creation of an additional level between the classes, which realize a set of methods M, and the classes, which invoke these methods using dependency relations r_i.

Algorithm of searching sets of diagram elements E on which the Interface transformation can be conducted can be described for the abstract data structure UML Map as follows:

1. Find all classes $c_i \in d$, which do not implement any interfaces and add them to l_1.

2. Find among these classes c_i those that have dependency relations of the kind: $c_j \xrightarrow{dep} c_i$ and add them to l2.

3. For each c_i, calculate $\Delta f(d)$.

4. Return all c_i, where $\Delta f(d) < 0$.

For the abstract data structure UML Map the algorithm can be described as follows:

```
for each c in classes
  fl = false
  for each r in relations
    if (r.getStartId() == c.getId())
      if (r.getType()=="realization")
        fl = true
  if (!fl)
    l1.add(c)
for each c in l1
   fl = false
   for each r in relations
     if (r.getEndId() == c.getId())
       if (r.getType()=="dependency")
         fl = true
   if (fl)
     l2.add(c)
for each c in l2
   if (Δf(c,d)<0)
     l3.add(c)
return l3
```

A graph depicting the execution time of the algorithm depending on the UML class diagram size is shown in Fig. 5. The value of the execution time was calculated as the average execution time measured during 100 runs for each UML class diagram size. From the graph it follows that the algorithm time performance evaluation is $O(n)$.

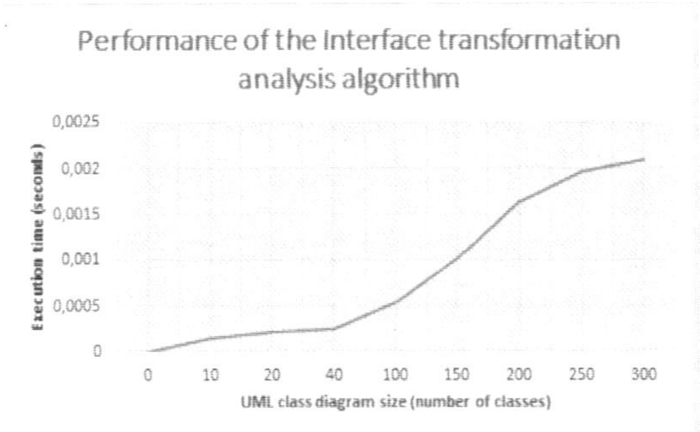

Fig. 5. Performance of the Interface transformation analysis algorithm

6 UML Refactoring tool

The introduced algorithms have become a part of the automated UML class diagram refactoring framework UML Refactoring Tool [16].

This tool allows analyzing UML class diagrams: it calculates various object-oriented metrics (such as Avg. DIT, Avg. CBO [20], DAC, SIZE2 [21], etc.) and proposes a list of transformations, which minimize a fitness function value. In addition, the tool applies the chosen transformation to the diagram. Framework can import/export projects from/to the XMI format.

7 Conclusions

The proposed UML Map abstract data structure makes it possible to analyze and transform UML class diagrams more convenient than in the XMI format.

The proposed algorithms of UML class diagram analysis allow searching elements of a UML class diagram, on which Strategy and Interface transformation can be applied in order to maximize/minimize fitness function value.

Time performance of the introduced algorithms has been evaluated with the help of the computational experiments. For both of them time performance evaluation is $O(n)$.

References

1. OMG Model Driven Architecture (http://www.omg.org/mda)
2. OMG Meta Object Facility Core Specification. Version 2.5.1. (http://www.omg.org/spec/MOF/2.5.1)
3. OMG Unified Modelling Language UML. Version 2.5 (http://www.omg.org/spec/UML/2.5)
4. XML Metadata Interchange (XMI) Specification. Version 2.4.2 (http://www.omg.org/spec/XMI/2.4.2)
5. M. Amoui, S. Mirarab, S. Ansari and C. Lucas, International Journal of Information Technology and Intelligent Computing, **1**, 235 (2006)
6. M. Bowman, L. Briand, and Y. Labiche, *Solving the class responsibility assignment problem in object-oriented analysis with multi-objective genetic algorithms* (2002)
7. O. Räihä, *Genetic Synthesis of Software Architecture* (2008)
8. O. A. Deryugina, Russian Technological Journal, **1**, 26 (2015)
9. R. Lutz, JSA, **47**, 613 (2001)
10. C. Simons C., I. Parmee, *Single and multi-objective genetic operators in object-oriented conceptual software design*", (GECCO, 2007)
11. S. Hadaytullah, Vathsavayi, O. Räihä, and K. Koskimies, *Tool support for software architecture design with genetic algorithms* (IEEE CS Press, 2010)
12. M. O'Keeffe and M. Ó Cinnéide, *Towards automated design improvements through combinatorial optimization* (W2S, 2004)
13. M. O'Keeffe and M. Ó Cinnéide, *Search-based software maintenance* (CSMR, 2006)
14. S. Mancoridis, B.S. Mitchell, C. Rorres, Y.F. Chen, and E.R. Gansner, *Using automatic clustering to produce high-level system organizations of source code* (IWPC, 1998)
15. J. McGregor, F. Bachmann, L. Bass, and P. Bianco, *Using ArchE in the classroom: one experience* (CMU/SEI, 2007)
16. E. Nikulchev, O. Deryugina, International Journal of Advanced Computer Science and Applications, **7**(12), 76 (2016)
17. D. Chamberlin, IBM systems journal, **4**, 2002
18. XSL Transformations (XSLT) v1.0. W3C Recommendation, Nov. 1999. http://www.w3.org/TR/xslt
19. Meta Object Facility (MOF) 2.0. Query/View/Transformation Specification. Version 1.3. http://www.omg.org/spec/QVT/1.3
20. S. R. Chidamber and C. F. Kemerer, IEEE Transaction on Software Engineering, **20**, 476 (1994)
21. W. Li and S. Henry, *Maintenance Metrics for the Object-Oriented Paradigm*" (ISMS, 1993)
22. B. Henderson-Sellers, *Object-oriented Metrics – Measures of Complexity* (New Jersey: Prentice-Hall, 1996)
23. M. Marchesi, *OOA Metrics for Unified Modelling Language* (Conference on Software Maintanance and Reengineering, 1998)
24. L. Briand, W. Devanbu and W. Melo, *An investigation into coupling measures for C++* (ICSE, 1997)
25. F. Brito e Abrue, W. Melo, *Evaluating the Impact of Object-Oriented Design on Software Quality* (International Metric Symposium1996)
26. M. Cartwright, *An Empirical View of Inheritance* (Information and Software Technology, 1998)
27. S. Chidamber, D. Darcy and C. Kemerer, IEEE Transactions on Software Engineering, **24**, 629 (1998)

ITM Web of Conferences **10**, 04003 (2017) DOI: 10.1051/itmconf/20171004003
2017 Seminar on Systems Analysis

The Hierarchical Distributed Agent Based Approach to a Modern Data Center Management

Andrey Gavrilov[1,*] and *Yury* Leokhin[1]

[1]National Research University Higher School of Economics (HSE), Moscow, Russian Federation

Abstract. This paper overviews and analyzes progressive trends in modern data center, and existing solutions to build the distributed cloud data center. Authors present the hierarchical distributed agent-based control plane architecture to build a web-scale control layer based on software-defined domains. The goal of this approach is to design the simple extensible agent that could be used for any management purposes, just by adding some specific code. Using of this approach makes easier the scalability and increases the efficiency of the management of a multi-site environment. There are five main use-cases of using this approach: distributed cloud, hybrid cloud, hyperscale data center, IoT, Continuous Integration.

1 Introduction

There is currently the growing concern among many companies for the digital transformation of business – the next step for companies to start leveraging digital and IT technologies in the prioritized way to improve the performance quantifiably [1,2]. This trend requires the business to actively implement information systems that support data analytics, the big data processing, the machine learning. At the same time to remain a competitive business in a rapidly changing world it is necessary to provide the operational flexibility and the adaptability of these IT systems.

The growing number of smart devices, the size and the variety of the network traffic [3], and as a result, the necessity to increase the storage capacity, the network bandwidth and the number of computing nodes forces companies to scale its IT infrastructure or, even, to build a new site. At the same time, the IT infrastructure in data centers typically is heterogeneous, resulting problems with the integration of individual devices or units.

Large enterprises and service providers with the geographically distributed infrastructure mainly focus on the service quality and resiliency [4], and the expense reduction. It is necessary not only to guarantee a secure and reliable data exchange between data centers, but also to provide the efficient management of entire infrastructure and services.

The number of hyperscale [5] data centers will continuously grow and will be doubled by 2020 [6]. These data centers will represent 47% of all installed servers by the same period. Additionally, the number of workloads that are processing by cloud data centers will reach 92% by 2020. Furthermore, the modular data centers and related equipment market will rapidly grow to $ 35,11 billion by 2020 [7].

The software-defined approach and related technologies make easier to implement "Infrastructure-as-a-Code" [8], providing the flexibility and dynamics of the IT infrastructure through the software control. Currently, most of the new data center designed as a software-defined [9].

The key issue for the analysis of data centers is the new paradigm, called the software-defined data center (SDDC) [10]. The core idea of this approach is that all possible elements of the infrastructure should be virtualized and can be configured via management applications. The SDDC involves five major components: the software-defined networking, the software defined storage, the virtualization technology, the automatization and the orchestration. The result is an extremely dynamic, manageable, cost-effective, and adaptable architecture that gives administrators improved programmability, automation, and control.

This approach makes a data center structure quite more complex and complicated, but at the same time, it gives more flexibility, agility, scalability, availability. However, the problem of the SDDC design has not yet received all the attention it deserves and should be continuously and carefully investigated. Nowadays the SDDC concept is young and immature, hence current solutions in this area still have many drawbacks and software vulnerabilities.

Taking all earlier mentioned into account, building the distributed cloud infrastructure become the subject matter to enter into the evolving "web-scale IT" world [11,12].

Tricircle [13] provides a cascading approach that has API gateway and many OpenStack instances. However, it only unites sites and unify the management. A microsegmentation of instances would require the

* Corresponding author: agavrilov@hse.ru

additional management overhead. Moreover, it is desirable to process some raw data and critical analytics locally on the site.

In this paper, we present the concept of the hierarchical distributed agent based control plane (HD-ABCP) approach that could be used to design modern cloud distributed data centers. HD-ABCP has many different agents that are centrally managed by the proxy and the management cluster. This approach makes a lot easier the scalability, gives all advantages of the fog computing (agents) and has the easy-to-understand architecture.

2 HD-ABCP

The core idea of HD-ABCP is to split the entire data center infrastructure into software-defined domains (SDD) that are under control of agents. The agent is the local management platform, the lightweight SDN-controller and an orchestration tool that could have some subordinate agents, which could have specific functions. The whole set of agents are controlled by "Local view" of the management cluster that implements the domain management and the local analytics. Furthermore, it is possible to use some additional management applications for custom policies or domain-specific operations. On the top level of the hierarchy, the proxy is placed, the central point that unites all domains and sites. It is controlled by "Global view" of the management cluster that processes summary data from agents and perform the global analysis. Figure 1 shows the illustration of this approach.

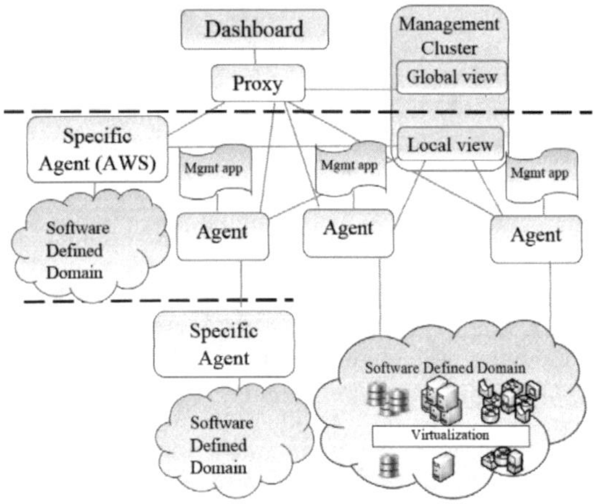

Fig. 1. HD-ABCP architecture.

2.1 SDD

SDD is composed of the physical and virtual infrastructure (including containers), hypervisors, management tools, that are managed by the agent.

Since all components are software-defined, mostly virtualized and hardware independent, we can use different platforms for specific needs. Such domains will form the distributed heterogeneous management level of the data center infrastructure that is easy-to-scale and easy-to-integrate. It allows us to use, for example, different hypervisors (MS Exchange and MS SQL Server are better to use with a Hyper-V virtualization, and Oracle databases - with the Oracle VM). Such zones will form the local software-level converged infrastructure. It is important to mention that SDD is not only the set of IT infrastructure, it is the set of components, including smart devices, applications, sensors and other elements, that should be monitored, managed and could be dynamically reconfigured via API.

2.2 Agent

The agent collects all the event and metric data from components of the domain via OpenStack API or different sources (directly, monitoring tools, 3rd party applications) to analyse the raw data, execute a set of commands, make retrospective reports for users and administrators and send a summary data to the proxy.

At the implementation level, agents are the set of microservices [14], like heartbeat service, self-healing service, agent-to-analytics service, agent-to-proxy service, etc.

Agents can be implemented in two ways: the thick agent and the thin agent that integrates with existing management platforms (OpenStack) The thick agent implements all needed management platforms to the proper control of distributed cloud data centers. The thin agent is placed on the top of local management platform hierarchy (integrates with existing local management stack) and control the domain via OpenStack REST API and other tools.

We can divide SDDs into smaller domains for specific purposes and operations. For example, the hypervisor with additional vendor management tools (VMware ESXi, MS Hyper-V, Oracle VM, KVM, Xen), the SDN-controller (OpenDaylight, Contrail, APIC), the computing type (bare-metal, virtual machine or container) or the public cloud (AWS, GCE, Rackspace). Furthermore, such domains could be used for specific type of services (SaaS, PaaS), workloads and applications.

2.3 Proxy

The main component in the control plane hierarchy that implements the centralized control of all agents and unites all sites to a single cloud/resource pool. It also process summary reports from agents for the global analytics ("Global View") and the visualization. It is also responsible for make a decision about deploying workload based on the client region, SDD's free space, SLA and other parameters. It collects all summary data from agents and perform analytics.

At the implementation level, the proxy is also the set of microservices, like heartbeat service, subscriber for data from agents service, proxy-to-analytics service, report service, proxy-to-dashboard service, etc.

2.4 Management Cluster

Management cluster implements IT operations analytics [15]. It is composed of two views: local and global. "Local View" implements capacity planning, dead VM, log analysis, uptime measuring, performance monitoring, health check. "Global View" implements WAN-optimization, workload balancing between DC/SDD, multi-SDD tenant's workload placing analytics, adding and relocating components between SDDs.

At the implementation level, the management cluster is a set of virtual machines or containers that run applications. It is recommended to have the additional management tool for this cluster due to its importance.

The number of local view instances depends on the number of sites, because it needs to be placed on every site (it needs to be local due to self-healing principles and additional regional policies). The number of global views may vary, but should be more than one due to the high availability (instances may be in both active/active and active/standby modes).

3 Proof of Concept

First of all, the interaction of agents with Openstack. It is necessary to use the cloud platform due to all advantages of the cloud computing and the growing number of workloads that are processed by cloud data centers [5,16]. OpenStack was chosen since it is the most popular cloud platform, it has the huge community, many commercial releases and, last but not least, it is opensource.

Second, the presented architecture. In our perspective, this pattern clearly illustrates all of control plane components and distinguish them with regard to their functions and purposes.

Mainly we focus on an agent like a favorable and convenient unit to build the big modern data center architecture. It is easy to customize due to the extensible architecture; we could add some additional code to improve the current functionality or develop own environment-specific agent. Furthermore, we can easily connect new sites to the existing distributed cloud, just by placing the new agent. If the thick agent will be used, building new site will become much easier since all needed platforms will be already integrated. Finally, we could always develop special agents for special purposes.

Additionally, agents are the realization of the fog computing. They process all raw data and send only summary to the proxy. Due to microservices realization, agents could self-heal and easily scale if it is necessary. Moreover, it is possible to build the distributed cloud with different version of OpenStack.

From the software-defined networking (SDN) [17,18] point of view, making the control plane distributed benefits to deploy less complicated management applications and services in data centers. This approach can make all important traffic isolated and simplify firewalls and internal devices configuration. Second, a hierarchy of controllers gives higher level of a scalability, an availability, a fault tolerance and less overhead; it makes easier disaster recover, because core configuration could be restored from the «parent» controller. In addition, it provides more efficient use of resources, since the pool of devices, which need to be controlled, greatly decreased. Finally, the customization of software-defined controllers by removing unnecessary components for a specific type of the cloud or a department reduces a management complexity and increases security, performance and availability of infrastructure and workloads.

However, this approach has some drawbacks: additional overhead in design planning and expenses on the security and the fault tolerance of agents. Notwithstanding, we believe that the advantages by far outweigh the disadvantages, and this concept may have potentially important influence on modern data center architecture design.

4 Use-cases

This part of the paper illustrates different types of the architecture pattern usage. There are five key use-cases: distributed cloud, hybrid cloud, hyperscale data center, IoT, Continuous Integration (CI).

The distributed DC (Cloud) is the typical realization of the HD-ABCP approach. The whole distributed infrastructure will be managed as a single resource pool that is split into domains. On every site, both agent(s) and management cluster's "Local view" should be placed [19]. Due to self-healing agents, losing connection to proxy will not disrupt the agent operation. As soon as the connection will be recovered, the agent will send all summary and crucial data of this period to the proxy.

For the hybrid cloud will be used specific agent for public cloud provider. Thereby we can easily have infrastructure in several different public clouds. The whole infrastructure could be managed from one console and automatically balance workloads between clouds. As it was said earlier, it is easy to add new sites and such distributed cloud could simply scale [20].

Nowadays, DevOps [21] is spreading across the world, and CI is significant step. We can use presented concept with respect to blue/green deployment [22]. Since we develop applications using microservices and containers, it is easy to have the same environment on all stages of development (dev, test, QA, deployment on customer site). Agent could simply reconfigure the current environment if changes are occurred and it is permitted to change to the new version.

Since the IoT world moving towards the edge computing, it is possible to use HD-ABCP approach to build a highly distributed IoT-infrastructure. According to [23], we can use the specific agent – cloud agent, fog agent and dew agent – for every IoT level. On each level of this hierarchy an agent could manage not only smart devices, but also level-specific applications.

Hyperscale data centers has the huge amount of devices [24] that generate plenty of management traffic and causes the overhead on the central management point. Since we would use smaller infrastructure areas (SDD), it is possible to localize the management traffic and increase the number of event checks. Furthermore, using vendor-specific domains may increase the service catalog of the cloud provider.

5 Conclusion

Nowadays, the building of multi-site and hypersclae environment is the hot topic. The data center infrastructure should have not only huge amount of processors, terabytes and gigabits per second, but also could be automatically reconfigured based on demand or occurred events, should be high available and match client's needs and expectations.

HD-ABCP will make the data center infrastructure easier to reconfigure and highly scalable. The findings of this investigation bring a software-defined domain design to the foreground and reveal the necessity of using a heterogeneous distributed control plane in IT environment. The results anticipated are intended to establish patterns of a data center design and highlight the potential of the software-defined approach. The result is an adaptive, cost-effective, easy-to-reconfigure infrastructure-as-a-code.

The verification of the proposed approach will be based on the data, obtained in experiments. The methodology obtained might dramatically change the way data centers will be designed.

References

1. K. O'Connell, K. Delaney, R. Moriarty. *Digital Business Transformation: Disrupt To Win* [Data file]. (2015) http://www.cisco.com/c/dam/en_us/about/business-insights/docs/digital-business-transformation.pdf.
2. K. Korpela, K. Mikkonen; J. Hallikas, M. Pynnönen, 2016 49th Hawaii International Conference on System Sciences (HICSS), 3959–3968 (2016).
3. *The Zettabyte Era — Trends and Analysis – Cisco.* (2016). http://www.cisco.com/c/en/us/solutions/collateral/service-provider/visual-networking-index-vni/vni-hyperconnectivity-wp.html
4. M. Alhamad, T. Dillon, C. Wu, E. Chang, iiWAS '10: Proceedings of the 12th International Conference on Information Integration and Web-based Applications & Services, 603-606 (2010)
5. L. Fang, F. Chiussi, D. Bansal, V. Gill, T. Lin, J. Cox, and G. Ratterree, Proceedings of the 1st ACM SIGCOMM Symposium on Software Defined Networking Research, SOSR'15, 1-13, (2015).
6. Cisco Global Cloud Index: Forecast and Methodology, 2015–2020 [Data file] (2016) http://www.cisco.com/c/dam/en/us/solutions/collateral/service-provider/global-cloud-index-gci/white-paper-c11-738085.pdf.
7. M. Smolkas, Modular data center market to triple its size by 2020 (2015) http://www.datacenterdynamics.com/content-tracks/power-cooling/modular-data-center-market-to-triple-its-size-by-2020/94114.fullarticle/
8. K. Morris, *Infrastructure as Code* (O'Reilly Media, 2016).
9. D. Adami, B. Martini, C. Callegari, et al. Spects '15: Proceedings of the International Symposium on Performance Evaluation of Computer and Telecommunication Systems, 1-6 (2015)
10. R. Buyya, R. N. Calheiros, J. Son, A. V. Dastjerdi, and Y. Yoon, Proceedings of the 3rd International Conference on Advances in Computing, Communications and Informatics (ICACCI 2014), IEEE. IEEE Press, 2014.
11. C. Haight, *Enter Web-scale IT* (2013) http://blogs.gartner.com/cameron_haight/2013/05/16/enter-web-scale-it
12. A.V. Gavrilov, Y.L. Leokhin, System Administrator, **11**, 76-80 (2016)
13. Tricircle. https://github.com/openstack/tricircle
14. A. Balalaie, A. Heydarnoori, P. Jamshidi, IEEE Software, **33**(3), 42-52 (2016)
15. IT Operations Analytics. https://en.wikipedia.org/wiki/IT_Operations_Analytics
16. E. Nikulchev, E. Pluzhnik, O. Lukyanchikov et al. International Journal of Advanced Computer Science and Applications, **6**(6), 22–26 (2015)
17. M. Casado , M. J. Freedman , J. Pettit et al. ACM SIGCOMM Computer Communication Review, **37**(4), 1-12 (2007)
18. N. McKeown , T. Anderson , H. Balakrishnan et al. ACM SIGCOMM Computer Communication Review, **38**(2), 69-74 (2008)
19. E. Nikulchev, E. Pluzhnik, O. Lukyanchikov et al. International Journal of Advanced Computer Science and Applications, 7(11), 165 (2016)
20. E. Nikulchev, E. Pluzhnik, O. Lukyanchikov et al. International Journal of Advanced Computer Science and Applications, **7**(1), 30-36 (2016)
21. M. Rajkumar, Anil Kumar Pole, Vittalraya Shenoy Adige, Prabal Mahanta, 2016 International Conference on Advances in Computing, Communication, & Automation (ICACCA) (Spring), 1-6 (2016)
22. M. Fowler, BlueGreenDeployment (2010) https://martinfowler.com/bliki/BlueGreenDeployment.html [Accessed 16 Jan. 2016].
23. K. Skala, D. Davidovic, E. Afgan, I. Sovic, Z. Sojat, Open Journal of Cloud Computing, **2**(1), 16 (2015)
24. AWS re:Invent 2014: AWS Innovation at Scale with James Hamilton (SPOT301) [Video file]. (2014). https://www.youtube.com/watch?v=JIQETrFC_SQ

DOI: 10.1051/itmconf/20171004004

Organization of Secured Data Transfer in Computers Using Sign-Value Notation

Shamil Magomedov[1,*]

[1] Moscow Technological University (MIREA), 119454 Moscow Russia

Abstract. In this paper, another approach to organization of secured data transfer between processor and random access memory is proposed, which includes two peculiarities: the use of residue number system (RNS) instead of standard positional notation as the basis of the closing data and an approach to organization of transfer process excluding the use of special subsystems within the framework of security system. With such an approach to the transferred data security process, there is no need for the subsystems mentioned above, what deprives potential attackers of opportunities to select the dispatching center as an object of attack and thereby increases data transfer process security.

1 Introduction

Traditional technology of restricted access information protection usually involves the use of encryption techniques. However, the requirements for such systems, are rather strict, and as a consequence, are bulky in the implementation and expensive in operation, what often makes it barely acceptable and cumbersome to use. The following is a procedure for the closure of the information, based on the use of residue number system. In addition, the traditional protection of the data exchange circuit lines as a necessary stage typically involves the distribution of a given task encryption key between the participants of data exchange, and when data transfer occurs, they are encrypted (or subscribed, in the case of an electronic signature) with this key. Control over the use of keys, update, formation and key distribution over existing technology, should be exercised by special control center in the system, in particular a special subsystem (or utility) in the interaction between the processor and RAM. Since all key information, including ciphers, concentrated in the center, the center becomes a potential target for malicious attacks. Due it is necessary to make special efforts to protect this center, what is a quite complex and costly task. The specifics of the problem as applied to data exchange between the CPU and RAM (this problem is the subject of our studies) is, in particular, to use as a basis RNS data closure technology as in [1–3], we consider processors, in which RNS is the basis of computer processor. That is why the use of RNS as a basis for the closure of these technologies in the process of exchange is seen as a natural extension of technologies perform computing operations in the processor.

We did not manage to find any works on the subject of the use of RNS as data closure technology basics. The closest one is our work, [1] where we describe the procedure of closing the data into the RAM, and [2] on the use of RNS in the process of data exchange between remote entities. Close to the procedure in question is the transferred data protection organization while the network sharing on the basis of frequent change of encryption keys is considered in [4].

2 The change frequency of the residue number system base

The implementation of the data transfer protection concept through the use of RNS, which is described in the introduction, at the stage of its formation [1], raises the question of the frequency of updates and even complete replacement of the base of RNS used for closing the data. Frequent change of RNS will require significant expenditure of computing resources of the processor, which is undesirable. In a rare change of RNS base, the risk of opening a base and, as a result, unauthorized entry into the data system significantly grow up. Consequently, there is an optimal value of the interval between consecutive shifts inception. As a result, the following problem arises: how often should I change the base of RNS so that the overall costs are minimized?

Below is a formalized model, in which the solution of a search task of the optimal value of the interval between successive moments of the key changes is offered. We analyze the problem of changing the base of RNS based on the construction of a formalized model of key changes and solutions, within the framework of this model, of the base change frequency task. Here is a formalized description of the problem.

As an optimality criterion we take the chance of theft of keys (i.e. the base of RNS) during a time interval not exceeding the interval between successive moments of

* Corresponding author: petrovich4you@gmail.com

change or update of RNS base (let's call this period an update period), minus the minimum time required to activate this key. We consider first, on what factors the probability of theft of the key within the task depends.

The probability of theft primarily depends on the strength of the closing procedure of the data (encryption) that, in turn, is determined by the number of numbers at the base and by their size: the larger the numbers of the base and the larger their values are, the generally more resistant will be the encryption procedure. Furthermore, among the numbers of the RNS base, there should not be relatively small ones, i. e. all numbers of the base should be approximately the same length. However, the closeness of the individual values may be regarded as a procedural parameter. We note that, typically, herewith, encryption time disproportionately increases.

Thus, the basic parameters of the model are:

a) the quantity of prime numbers included in the base of RNS;

b) the number of numbers in the base of RNS;

c) the minimum time required to restore data if there is the base of RNS;

d) the boundaries of the most preferred areas of possible values of prime numbers in the base of RNS;

e) the period of time of an key upgrade.

One of the basic parameters that must be evaluated in terms of the model, is the degree of resistance of these private keys. In this regard, first we describe the basic concept of the function that evaluates the stability of the system key. Evaluation of resistance should include an assessment of n key length and evaluation of resistance of each number in P_i in the base of RNS. To simplify evaluation, we shall restrict additive estimates according to preset settings of the key. Further, resistance numbers P_i are proposed to assess by means of functions that satisfy the following heuristic conditions conducing to improvement of resistance of RNS.

1. The function should give minimum values for P_i estimates beyond a certain value zone. The lower limit of the zone is determined by the minimum acceptable value of P_i – at lower values the probability of opening P_i greatly increases. The upper limit of the zone is determined by the computing power of the processor and the share of the allowable time for closing the data during processing – this share is determined while designing the processor.

2. Within the area of values, distribution of P_i values at full replacement of one RNS to another one may be determined by linear (horizontal) function, which corresponds to the equiprobable choice of any of the values included in this zone. However, if the numbers at the base of RNS are replaced partially, but not fully, it is desirable (from the perspective of the current data processing) by replacing, wherever possible, to maintain approximately the length of the replaced number and replacing one of the P_i numbers. In this case, a uniform distribution is not appropriate, in connection with what is proposed to use functions with data accumulation area, namely multi-peak functions. The following is proposed for this purpose, namely two-peak function class.

3. You must have parameters that define the degree of blur, data uncertainty *in separate ones* around each peak of multi-peak function. This will be an additional option to increase the resistance, making it difficult, at least acceptable, for an attacker to limit the enumeration area of possible key variants.

4. It is desirable to have a simpler function (to reduce the amount of computations when evaluating resistance) and relatively smooth (for computational stability).

With regard to function, which evaluates the length of a key resistance, it is possible to formulate similar requirements.

In view of the above, we propose the following formula for the initial evaluation of the resistance of the selected base of RNS as an encryption key:

$$S = S(\pi(n, \vec{P})) = \varphi(n) + \sum_{i=1}^{n} f(P_i), \qquad (1)$$

where

$$f(P) = y(P, a_1, b, c, d, \sigma, r) + y(P, a_2, b, c, -d, \sigma, r),$$
$$\varphi(P) = y(P, A, B, C, 0, s, R),$$

$$y(P, a, b, c, d, s, r) = \frac{a}{1 + b(P - (c - c \cdot d))^k}\left(1 - e^{-r \cdot \max(0; P-s)}\right) \qquad (2)$$

and either $k = 2$ or $k = 4$, and all the coefficients are positive numbers.

Let us clarify the content of all the coefficients included in the definition of the functions $f(P)$, $\varphi(n)$ and $y(P, a, b, c, d, \sigma, r)$. Function $y(P, a, b, c, d, \sigma, r)$, and together with it the function $\varphi(P)$ for any positive values of coefficients are one-peak ones. In particular, Fig. 1 shows an example of the function $\varphi(P)$ with the following parameter values: A = 3; B = 0.01; C = 7; s = 3; R = 1, k = 4.

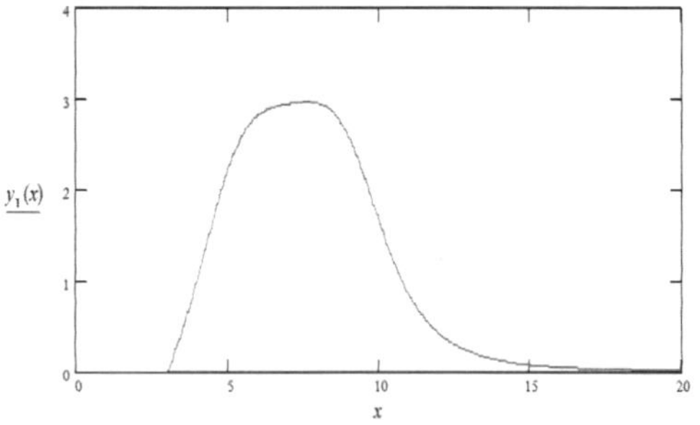

Fig. 1. Example of the function $\varphi(P)$ graph

A is a scale parameter characterizing the maximum value of the function $\varphi(P)$ and is selected at random, being based on reasons of clarity; B is determined by the degree of "stretch" of the function $\varphi(P)$ – the more is B, the more the function $\varphi(P)$ is one-peak, and the narrower is the range of permissible effective (i.e., the most frequent ones) values of the variable x (= n); in the example of Fig. 1, B is selected so that the effective value interval of n key length range from 3 to 15; C defines the central importance of n key length (in this case n = 10), around which the effective range of values is formed; s is the lower limit of the permissible n key length values; the example imposes limitation – the number of integers in the base of RNS should be less than 3 (corresponding to $s = 3$); R is intended to provide relative smoothness of the point $n = s$ (more precisely, to reduce the size of the jump function at the boundary point $x = s$); with an increase in R at a point $x = s$, the jump of k graphics increases; k firstly determines slope of graph rises to the top (left and right), and secondly, the length of the upper, relatively flat top of the graph – with $k = 4$, the upper part is longer and rises abruptly at $k = 2$, the function is more peaked.

With respect to the function $f(P)$, there is another parameter – d, and the parameter a is replaced into the other two – a_1 and a_2. We explain these parameters. We note that, as can be seen from the examples below showing graphs of the function $f(P)$, this function is two-peak ("two-hump") in the most interesting cases for us. The distance between the peaks is determined by $2cd$, and therefore, d is defined (for fixed c) by the degree of hump blur. Consequently, the parameter d is always less than 1; it is possible to estimate the percentage: how you should dilute the zone of the effective values of the variable x around its center c. Parameters a_1 and a_2 define the maximum value of each hump – of both the left and the right one.

It should be noted that the formula (1) and the function (2) satisfy the conditions listed above 1–3. At the same time, changing the parameter b, you can obtain the function with the desired depth of the pit between the humps, until the case of absence of the pit, and even with the tab instead of the pit (for small values of b). Regarding the choice of the parameter, we specify the following: the value of $k = 4$ is more preferable that provides a greater blur to the data in each hump, but at the same time it requires a larger number of calculation, what is essential while multiply (massively) calculating. To illustrate the positions of things said lower (in Fig. 2), an example of the function $fi(P)$ with $k = 2$ is brought; the rest parameters have the same values. Parameter values: $a_1 = 3.5$; $a_2 = 3$; $b = 10^{-6}$; $c = 400$; $d = 0.3$; $r = 0{,}005$; $s = 500$.

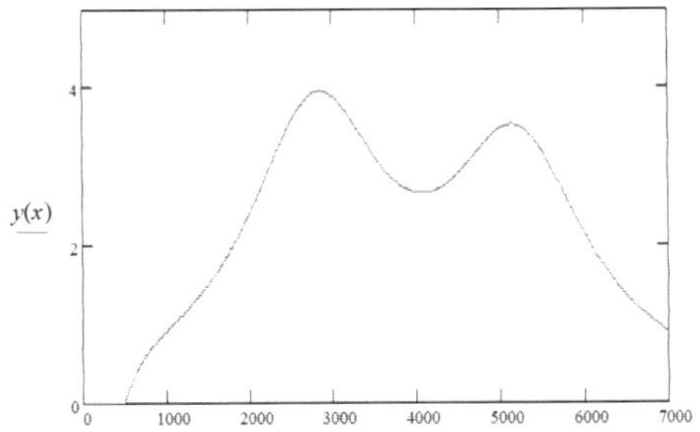

Fig. 2. Example of the evaluation function with $k = 2$

The function $f(P)$ describes the degree of unexpectedness (even unforeseeability) for an attacker to find the number P as part of the base of RNS: small values P are unlikely, because they are less resistant to cracking; larger values P are unlikely as well, because they greatly increase the time required for data processing when used as part of RNS; median values are also increasingly expected by the attacker, since in the median values, values of bases are generally arranged, and they are optimal for compromise requirements simultaneously to the key durability and acceptability of data processing time. The graph in Fig. 2 satisfies the mentioned intuitive reasons, so it is for these reasons, the coefficient S is considered above as the key resistance evaluation.

Based on the selection index S as an indicator of resistance, we can offer a key to select the key by accident, in accordance with its resistance, i.e., the probability of selecting the key $\pi(n,\vec{P})$ is considered equal to normalized value S.

$$q(\pi(n,\vec{P})) = \frac{S(\pi(n,\vec{P}))}{\sum_{\pi(n,\vec{U})} S(\pi(n,\vec{U}))}, \quad (3)$$

where the sum in the denominator is taken over keys $\pi(n,\vec{U})$ so that values of parameters n and P_i are in effective areas of these parameters. In order to prevent re-use of the key as well as the keys close to it, it is proposed, until the use of formula (3) and before the key update, to multiply the function $f(P)$ on the expression

$$\theta(P) = \prod_{i=1}^{n} (1 - y(P, 1, \Delta, P_i, 0, s, R).$$

The graph of function $1 - y(P, 1, \Delta, P_i, 0, s, R)$ (let's call it the excluding function) at $\Delta = 10^{-7}$, $P_i = 4000$, $s = 500$ and $R = 1$ is shown in Fig. 3.

Fig. 3 shows that the function $y(P, 1, \Delta, P_i, 0,)$ is almost everywhere equal to 1, and only in a narrow band about $1/(P_i \cdot \Delta) \approx 250$ wide it abruptly goes down to zero at $P = P_i$, and then just as abruptly rises. Thus, by multiplying the function $f(P)$ on $y(P, 1, \Delta, P_i, 0,)$ at the point $P = P_i$, the function $f(P)$ falls to zero, thereby excluding the value $P = P_i$ and all close to it values chosen at random while choosing the next value P_j based on the distribution density $q(\pi(n,\vec{P}))$.

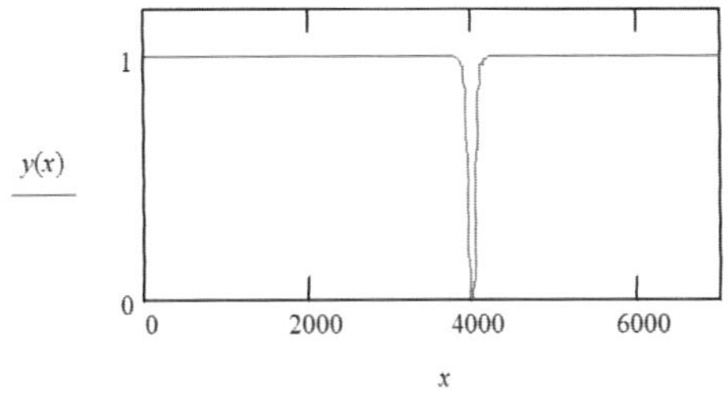

Fig. 3. Graph of excluding function

We should note that the probability $q(\pi(n,\vec{P}))$ can be regarded as the probability of key resistance, i.e. non-disclosure of key for the routine time T. Then, in the first approximation, we can assume that $\Pr(\pi(n,\vec{P}), T) = 1 - q(\pi(n,\vec{P}))$. Assuming that the

DOI: 10.1051/itmconf/20171004004

dependence of the probability of key non-disclose on time is exponential, i.e., $1-\Pr(\pi(n, \vec{P}), t) = \alpha \cdot e^{-\beta t}$ where α and β are constant, considering $\Pr(\pi(n,\vec{P}),0) = 0$ and $\Pr(\pi(n,\vec{P}),T) = 1 - q(\pi(n,\vec{P}))$, we obtain the following relationship: $\alpha = 1$ and $q(\pi(n,\vec{P})) = e^{-\beta T}$, from where we conclude $e^{-\beta} = \left(q(\pi(n,\vec{P}))^{1/T}\right)$ and

$$\Pr(\pi(n,\vec{P}), t) = 1-\left(q(\pi(n, \vec{P}))\right)^{t/T}. \quad (4)$$

To construct the model, we introduce the following notation: $\Pr(\pi(n,\vec{P}), t)$ is the likelihood of key disclosure, i.e., the base of RNS, at a time t; $C(\pi(n, \vec{P}))$ are costs of resources (especially, of time) on the formation of the key; $\tau(\pi(n, \vec{P}))$ is the time required for the activation key; $L(\pi(n, \vec{P}))$ is average loss because of disclosure of the key $\pi(n, \vec{P})$ in the exchange of data; $D(\pi(n, \vec{P}))$ are costs of key $\pi(n, \vec{P})$ update; T is routine during operation of the computer while data processing, taking into account the repeatability of data processed (for example, month, week, day); λ is the intensity of the exchange of data between the processor and RAM; δ is the interval between successive moments of the key update; N is the maximum acceptable amount of numbers at the base of RNS.

$$x(\pi(n,\vec{P})) = \begin{cases} 1, \text{ if key } \pi(n,\vec{P}); \\ 0 \text{ otherwise.} \end{cases}$$

We estimate the total loss associated with the use of a given set of encryption keys. During the routine time T, the average number of key updates is equal to T/δ. Then the average total costs associated with the upgrade key for the routine period are:

$$\rho_1 = \frac{T}{\delta}\sum_{n=s}^{N}\left(\sum_{\pi(n,\vec{P})}(1-q(\pi(n,\vec{P}))C(\pi(n,\vec{P}))x(\pi(n,\vec{P}))\right).$$

The second group of losses is associated with the key opening in the transfer process, resulting in losses. Since the probability of disclosing key is usually a very small value, the probability that during key life more than one key disclosure happens is practically zero. Assuming that the time of the attacker invasion on the network node is a random, it is natural to assume that the average time that a malicious user takes to use the disclosed key is equal to $\delta/2$. Then, for the magnitude of the losses associated with the disclosure of the key, in view of (4), we can write the expression

$$\rho_2 = \frac{T}{\delta}\sum_{n=s}^{N}\left(\sum_{\pi(n,\vec{P})}(1-\left(q(\pi(n,\vec{P}))^{\delta/(2T)}\right))L(\pi(n,\vec{P}))x(\pi(n,\vec{P}))\right)$$

Finally, the last group of the losses is related to costs to update the keys. Since the number of updates per routine period is on the average equal to T/δ, the total cost for the routine period of update of keys on the average are:

$$\rho_3 = \frac{T}{\delta}\sum_{n=s}^{N}\left(\sum_{\pi(n,\vec{P})}(1-\left(q(\pi(n,\vec{P}))^{\delta/(2T)}\right))D(\pi(n,\vec{P}))x(\pi(n,\vec{P}))\right).$$

Based on the obtained relations, we derive the following expression for the total costs and losses for the routine period of T:

$$w(T) = \rho_1 + \rho_2 + \rho_3 = \frac{T}{\delta}\sum_{n=s}^{N}\left(\sum_{\pi(n,\vec{P})}\left[\left(1-\left(q(\pi(n,\vec{P}))^{\delta/(2T)}\right)\right)\times \times\left(L(\pi(n,\vec{P})) + D(\pi(n,\vec{P}))\right) + (1-q(\pi(n,\vec{P}))C(\pi(n,\vec{P}))\right]\right)x(\pi(n,\vec{P})).$$

Since the key is always one (single), then the equality is relevant

$$\sum_{n=s}^{N}\left(\sum_{\pi(n,\vec{P})} x(\pi(n,\vec{P}))\right) = 1. \quad (5)$$

On the basis of the obtained relations, a task of selecting the optimum number of numbers in the base of RNS, and the composition of these bases can be formalized: to select key n length, the number $P_i(\,i=\overline{1;n}\,)$ and the period of key update τ so that the total costs $w(T)$ are minimal, i.e. the equality (5) holds.

$$w(T) \to \min \text{ on } x(\pi(n,\vec{P}))$$

$$\text{such that } x(\pi(n,\vec{P})) = 0 \vee 1. \quad (6)$$

In theoretical terms, the task (6) is a classical problem, which developed its own specific methods of solution [7]. Without consideration of this statement, the problem of partial update of RNS base remains.

One of the most difficult problems associated with the implementation of the above-described procedure for updating the key of closing the data using the RNS is the task of choosing the model parameters, in particular, parameters of the functions $\varphi(P)$ and $f(P)$. The solution of this problem is advisable to implement being based on the use of expert procedures.

This work was partially supported by motivational payments system faculty MIREA.

3 Conclusions

The analysis is carried out and a set of parameters that critically affect the efficiency of data security while processing in CPU using RNS is formed.

The model of the task of choosing the optimal interval of updating RNS base, a solution of which will minimize the total costs associated with the malicious theft of keys of closing the data, as well as the cost of resources for key update, is formed.

References

1. S. Magomedov, Vestnik of Astrakhan State Technical University. Series: Management, Computer Science and Informatics, **1**, 22-32 (2015)
2. S. Magomedov, Vestnik of Astrakhan State Technical University. Series: Marine engineering and technology, **2**, 44-46 (2010)

3. S. Magomedov, Caspian magazine. Management and high technology, **4**, 118-125 (2013)
4. V. Laptev, G. Popov, Vestnik of Astrakhan State Technical University. Series: Management, Computer Science and Informatics, **2**, 94-98, (2012)
5. N. Worms, S. Ryadnov et al. *Modular structure neuroprocessor parallel computing systems* (FIZMATLIT, 2003)
6. A. Omondi, B. Premkumar, *Residue number systems: theory and implementation Advances in Computer Science and Engineering* (London, Imperial College Press, 2007)
7. M. Belkin, S. Coogee, A. Sigov, Russian Journal of Technology, 1, 4-21 (2016)

ITM Web of Conferences **10**, 04005 (2017) DOI: 10.1051/itmconf/20171004005
2017 Seminar on Systems Analysis

Methods and Tools for Profiling and Control of Distributed Systems

Roman Sukharev[1], *Evgeniy* Pluzhnik[2], Oleg Lukyanchikov[1, *], and *Dmitry* Biryukov[1, 2]

[1]Moscow Technological University (MIREA), 119454 Moscow, Russia
[2]Moscow Technological Institute, 119334 Moscow, Russia

Abstract. The article analyzes and standardizes methods for profiling distributed systems that focus on simulation to conduct experiments and build a graph model of the system. The theory of queueing networks is used for simulation modeling of distributed systems, receiving and processing user requests. To automate the above method of profiling distributed systems the software application was developed with a modular structure and similar to a SCADA-system.

1 Introduction

All complex systems tend to be separated into smaller modules that perform autonomous tasks. Each developed software module may be included in different programs, if the conditions of its use are met, declared in the documentation for this module. Thus, a software module can be considered as a tool to deal with the complexity of the programs, and as a tool to combat duplication in programming. But modular programming has failed to fully implement all its concepts in full [1]. Therefore, with the development of networks and distributed systems, modules became separate network applications, which formed a service-oriented system Software-as-a-Service (SaaS) and more complex cloud systems. However, the complexity of the analysis of such systems also increased, since operations are performed on different computing nodes, and for each service a different load is applied. So today it is important to develop methods and tools for profiling and management of distributed systems.

All existing applications for the analysis of distributed systems are based on the analysis of logs gathered from all services, such as ELK [2, 3] or Dapper [4] by Google. Systems like SCADA (Supervisory Control And Data Acquisition) are preferred for profiling and management of distributed systems. The information systems produce a great amount of operations. In result, the operator is unable to keep up, so it is preferable to only show false and time-consuming operations, this will help finding the bottlenecks in the system and reconfigure it if necessary.

2 Methods for profiling of distributed systems

Today there is no widely accepted methods and tools for profiling of distributed systems, but there is a number of proposed methods in [5]. Both of these methods for analysis and profiling of distributed systems are focused on simulation to conduct experiments and build the graph model of a system. After combining these methods, it is possible to identify the main stages of profiling distributed systems:

To form the graph representation of the process of solving functional problems as a coherent set of query processing.

To build and configure the simulation model of query processing for a specific version of a computer network and the distributed data warehouse.

To carry out the experiment on the simulation model to evaluate the execution time of the queries.

To determine the bottlenecks in the system, dramatically affecting the performance of the distributed system.

In these methods the profiling results depend on the simulation model, which determines the load on the system with a certain requests' flow intensity. When profiling a distributed system using the calculation indicators for monitoring the system's effectiveness, following should be considered:

– a plurality of storage devices in the queuing systems (QS). This factor leads to a consideration of the QS as a system with a total lineup of applications, eliminating the receipt of the individual characteristics of the queues;

– generally non-deterministic time for the service of application unit. The time spent on application maintenance depends on the total volume of the package,

*Corresponding author: luk-it6@yandex.ru

with the result that there is a mutual dependence of the average time of service applications and the number of requests waiting for service;
– correlations between the time of receipt of applications coming from different elementary sources, leading to lack of steady-state flow.

Having calculated performance of individual QS's, it is possible to calculate the performance of stochastic queuing network (SQN).

After building the simulation model, for profiling of a distributed system it is necessary to conduct a series of experiments with different system architectures, in which the number of calculated nodes, their location, data flow, and other parameters change. SCADA-like software will allow automating the construction of these systems, immediate implementation and the collection of data based on the results of the experiment.

3 Development tools for control and profiling

Tools that automate profiling of distributed systems are implemented in hmiSCADA system (https://github.com/RSukharev/hmiSCADA), written in C++, using the Qt libraries. This application uses the principle of modular construction. The system consists of a main module, providing a complete set of basic functions for processing and visualization of information, as well as additional functional modules, implementing the data collection functions and optional monitoring and control functions in the application. Additional modules for data collection and management are included in the source code of the profiled system.

The core module's functionality includes: obtaining data from external modules; data visualization; options to manage the software profiling process; simulation.

Additional modules' functionality includes (Fig. 1):
– data collection on the times of start and end of the test piece of code;
– sending profiling data over the network to the main module of the system;
– execution of the commands, received from the visualization and control modules.

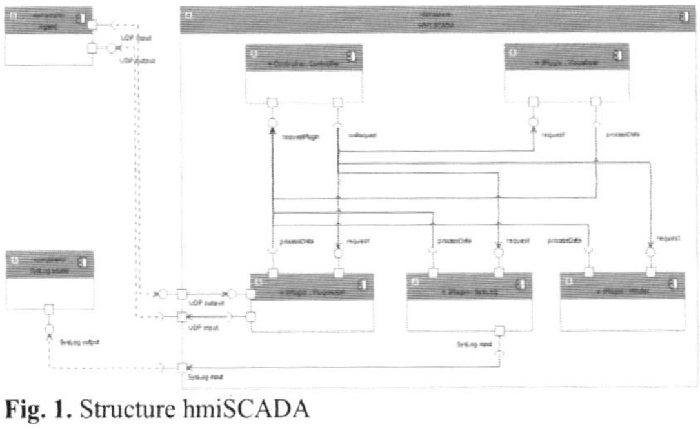

Fig. 1. Structure hmiSCADA

The main difference of this system from other SCADA systems is that to render data received from an operator, it is not required to build the mnemonic of what should be displayed in advance. The mnemonic is generated automatically based on the data obtained. However, due to the modular structure of the system it is possible in the future to bring the graphical user interface to a common standard. It is also possible to provide compatibility with the data transmission standards for SCADA systems (OPC UA). Enhanced system functionality occurs as new modules are written and connected.

The architecture of the system allows following the process, in which messages may pass through a series of modules, each of which performs its work on data processing and forwards the result further, modifying and extending the functionality of the system as a whole.

An example of profiling the two applications is shown in Fig. 2.

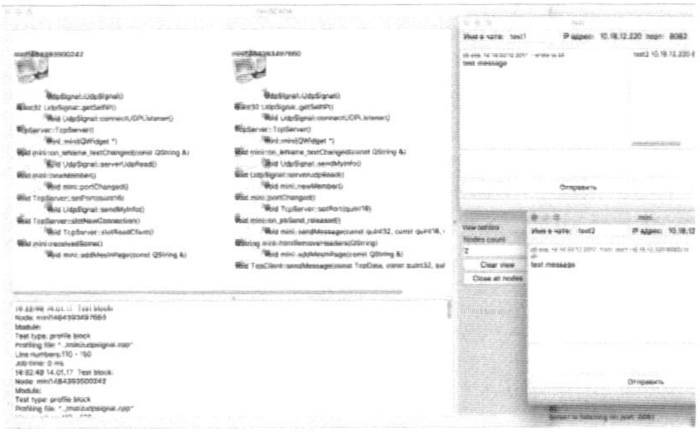

Fig. 2. An example of profiling

4 Conclusion

This article describes the methods and SCADA-like tools for profiling and management of distributed systems. Those allow automating the process of profiling systems, which makes it possible to locate bottlenecks and errors in the system.

An important factor in the development and promotion of these SCADA-like systems is the ability to integrate them into functioning distributed systems. That's why the prototype hmiSCADA proposes modular architecture. With this architecture, third-party developers can develop their modules for hmiSCADA. Costs for the development of these modules are easily compensated by the time saved on profiling and analysis of the system.

References

1. I.B. Bresler et al., Radio industry, **1**. 72-88 (2009)
2. A. Reelsen, *Using elasticsearch, logstash and kibana to create realtime dashboards* (2014)
3. S. Bagnasco et al. Journal of Physics: Conference Series, **608**, 012016 (2015)
4. B.H. Sigelman et al. *Dapper, a large-scale distributed systems tracing infrastructure* (2010)
5. O.I. Lukyanchikov, V.V. Filatov, Engineering Vestnik, **2** (2016)

Web-based Platform for Psychology Research

Ilya Zakharov[1], *Evgeny* Nikulchev[2], *Dmitry* Ilin[2,3], *Victoria* Ismatullina[1], and *Alexander* Fenin[1]

[1]Psychological Institute of Russian Academy of Education, 125009 Moscow, Russia
[2]Moscow Technological Institute, 199334, Moscow, Russia
[3]Moscow Technological University MIREA, 119454 Moscow, Russia

Abstract. This article is devoted to contemporary methods of risk management under the conditions of crisis on financial markets. The article deals with developing the new approaches to studying finance and financial markets. It outlays new methods to compare fundamental events and their technical interpretation shown on quotation charts. It also introduces recommendations as to improve the risk management's efficiency of financial markets' participants.

1 Introduction

During the last few decades psychological research is consistently moving from laboratories to internet and web-based studies. Web-technologies offer numerous advantages for psychologists. For example, according to Andrew Gelman and colleagues [1], psychological studies tend to be systematically underpowered, which is stated as one of the reasons for the replication crisis in psychology. An easy access to bigger samples through internet and social networks provides an opportunity to radically enlarge the study samples thus leading to more reliable results. However, web-technologies offer more than just an increase in the numbers of people involved. Another advantage is the possibility to individualize the outcome and feedback for participants. The amount of data is getting big enough to start using machine learning and other artificial intelligence approaches. In the present article we will review existing web-based technologies for psychological research around the world with an emphasis on the situation in Russia.

2 Analysis of platforms for psychological research

The first widely used web-based psychological tool was the "Amazon Mechanical Turk" (MTurk, [2]). It was a crowdsourcing internet marketplace where researchers were able to recruit subjects for taking part in online studies. Subjects got a small amount of money for participating. MTurk was used mostly by researchers from the US. It was shown that MTurk samples did not perfectly match the US population characteristics. For example, MTurk population was mostly white and female, and more educated and young than overall US population. However, the quality of the obtained data remained good enough [3]. MTurk was successfully used to study attention [4], creativity and dishonest behavior [5] or sexual attitudes [6]. It has been shown that MTurk can be a valuable tool even for working with clinical population [7] (Shapiro et al., 2013).

After the MTurk success new technologies started to appear. However, the framework has changed. While MTurk was a marketplace that accumulated its own audience, new tools only provided instruments to develop studies that could then be distributed through the web, but it was the responsibility of the researcher to find the sample. One of the most famous tool of that type became Google Forms (Google Inc.). This free software was intended to create web-surveys. Every researcher was able to create his questionnaire for which he was given a unique link that he was able to spread elsewhere in the internet. Google Forms also provided some simple analytics for the researchers. Its openness and Google brand made it ubiquitous for online surveys, especially among students. However, Google Forms lack some of the features that play an important role in psychological research. For example, the analysis of the amount of time spent for each part of the survey is hardly feasible with the Google Forms. There are also some concerns regarding the way the data is stored. To face the needs of the psychological society, some new products started to appear. Out of the most recognized, we can mention Survey Monkey [8], Qualtrics [9], LimeSurvey [10] or EnKlikAnketa [11]. Some of these products are proprietary or at least shareware (SurveyMonkey, Qualtrics), some are free (EnKlikAnketa).

These services tend to provide many new functions for researchers. The Slovenian EnKlikAnketa shows one of the non-mainstream way to improve online services. For example, it offers to fix the methodological flaws in the design of the surveys. Apart from being completely free, it has plenty of other useful advantages that are not implemented in other systems. First of all, it collects a lot of metadata, such as which site the respondent came from, how much time he or she spent in the survey and how many pages he actually visited, what browser and system he or she had and many other indicators. Secondly, it allows a much broader variety of item types, advanced preferences for every item (such as choosing the numeric/ordinal scale, showing statistics for this item to the respondent, returning the feedback after in-system computing etc.) and scenarios based upon the if-then scripts for several choices. Moreover, 1ka allows its users to save, copy and share questions through its library system, thus saving a lot of time that would be otherwise spent on rewriting the questions and categories. Finally, it has a wide range of built-in analytic instruments, computing frequencies, sums, contingency tables and much more, as well as a graphic constructor, that enables researchers to either generate fulldata descriptive statistics in several clicks or to flexibly adjust the diagrams for specific data reporting. Finally, 1ka allows the data export in many formats, including .sps for SPSS, that is widely used by psychologists around the world.

Today, these services have almost replaced the traditional pen-and-paper studies. However, they can be used only for the questionnaires or knowledge-type tests (q-type of data according to Cattell [12]) thus ignoring some areas of currently challenging psychological topics, such as, for example, individual differences in cognitive or executive functions. In these areas the modern technologies have already replaced the classical pen-and-paper approach. Here, the computerized automated tools are being developed [13, 14]. Computerized adminsitration of tests is convenient due to several factors. Firstly, it helps to monitor the administration process automatically thus reducing the errors related to human factor. Secondly, computerized tools of this type can record the aspects of performance with the precision that is difficult to achieve otherwise, and "these may reflect activity in developing neural networks with more sensitivity than can be achieved with traditional tests" [15].

Different cognitive tests are organized in batteries that are designed to assess the cognitive sphere integrally. The widely used cognitive characteristics include general cognitive abilities, working memory [16], spatial or mathematical abilities [17], recognition processes [18], and many others. Most of these batteries have been developed for the clinical use (NAB, CNTB, [19, 20]). However, they have also been successfully used to study the normative sample [15, 21, 22]. We have also showed its advantages in the behavioral genetics studies [23].

Cognitive tests are becoming more and more available to researchers. First, there are free software solutions, such as PsychoPy [24], that allows psychologists to develop their own tests without the need for advanced programming skills. Some of the applications of that type even include their own batteries of test. For example, though the Psychology Experiment Building Language (PEBL, [25]) requires more skills to create the test, it already has a large preprogrammed set of executables that allow to measure a wide range of characteristics.

Currently, the main limitation of the automated batteries is that they can only be administered offline with downloaded and pre-installed software. The psychological society tends not to trust the precision of tests administered online because of the potential confounding factors such as the technical properties of the personal computers or monitors of the respondents. However, the quantitative estimation of the noise added due to the differences in setup shows that at least for some type of tasks web-based experiments can be an acceptable source of data [26]. Thus, the next logical step for the computerized cognitive tests is to spread across the internet the same way it has happened to the questionnaires. According to it, the PsychoPy team, for example has recently presented the option to run experiments in a web browser.

The situation with web-technologies in psychological research can differ among the countries. In Russia one of the questions that arise is the localization of the services. The need for localization may concern Russian adaptation of questionnaires as well as translation of the test instructions. The other important factor is related to the data storage, which should be organized according to the local laws. Thus, it is important to develop Russian services that will be able to provide tools to conduct web-based studies. There are already several solutions that can be used (e.g., [27] or [28]) but they are limited to gathering q-type of data.

Web-technologies in psychology are important because they are related not only to the scientific community. According to the Russian federal law №273 and the requirements of the federal education standards, students must be provided with programs adapted to their psychophysiological development and health condition. Thus, educational policy should concern individual, age-related, psychological and physiological characteristics of the students. It is impossible to meet the requirements of the federal law without any continuous psychological assessment. Currently, the ongoing activity has only local nature and the need for the nation-wide projects is on the rise. Bigger scale projects are important because they give an opportunity to build national standards for the diagnostic tools. Web-technologies may play a key role for addressing these issues.

3 Architecture of the web-service

We have already started the project aiming to develop a web-based diagnostic tool for psychological, psychophysiological and cognitive assessment. This tool will combine the power of the online survey systems as well as the automated computerized batteries. It will include a wide range of generally acknowledged psychological methods. Given the rapid development of new methods it will also have the possibility to easily incorporate tools suggested by independent researchers.

From the end-user standpoint, the project will consist of two main components: researcher's private account (fig. 1) and applications for online and offline experiments (fig. 2).

DOI: 10.1051/itmconf/20171004006

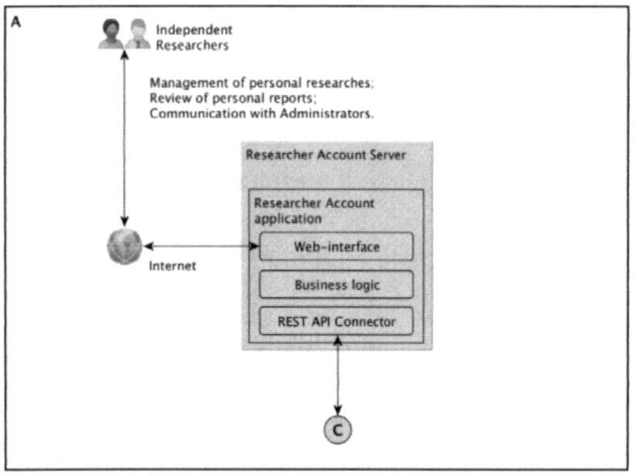

Fig. 1. Independent researcher's tool

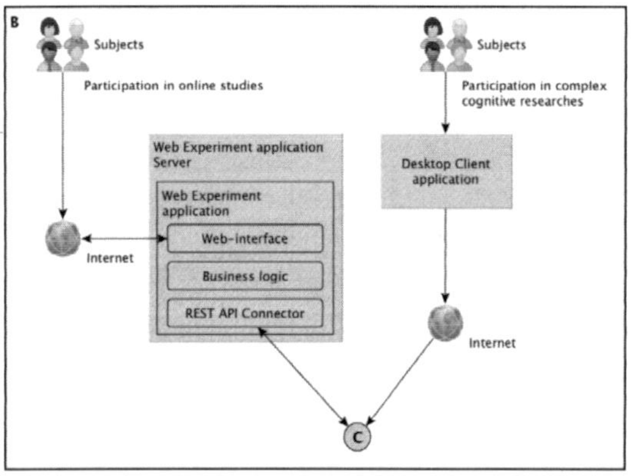

Fig. 2. Online and offline experiment tools

The main priority is the online survey tool as it covers most of possible use cases. Cognitive and psychophysiological assessments apply more requirements to the assessment environment. Thus, it is necessary to develop an offline tool as well.

Considering the fact, that the number of users will grow over time, the service has to be horizontally scalable (fig. 3). It is also essential for surveys with big samples. Each API node should incorporate layered architecture. In combination with the object-document mapping it will provide the service with better flexibility in comparison to monolithic architecture.

Experimental and data intense algorithms for population-base studies should be separated from the main service as well as the administration functionality (fig. 4). In addition, the administration panel can be used as an Intranet service for the security purposes.

In addition to the scaling of algorithmic part, the data storage should be scalable as well. The best fitting approach for the project is combination of sharding and replication (fig. 5). Sharding can provide the system with high I/O performance, while replication can help to ensure the service availability.

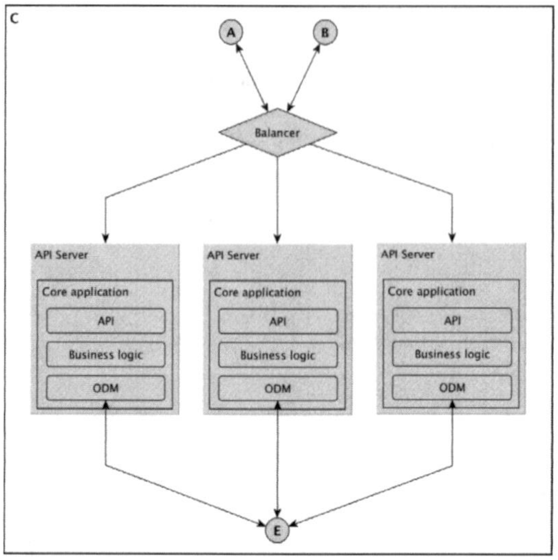

Fig. 3. Scalable API servers for uniform data access and management

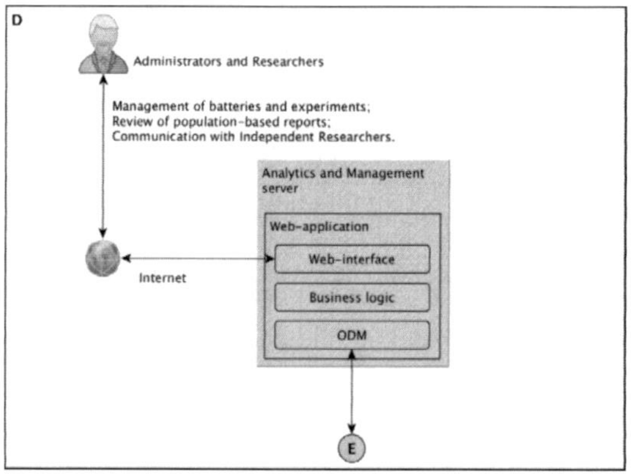

Fig. 4. Isolated analytic tools for population-based researches

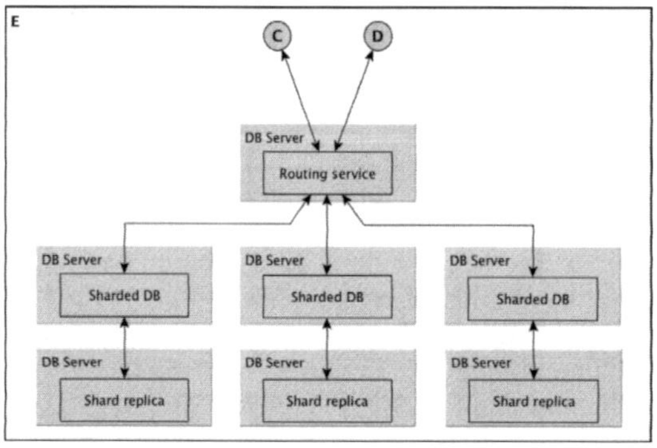

Fig. 5. Horizontal scaling of data storage through sharding

4 Conclusions

To conclude, web-based technologies have become much more than just a promising researcher tool. The future development of psychological studies depends on the implementation of new technologies to the same or even greater extent as on the new ideas, and it is essential for psychologists in Russia to have their own research tool.

References

1. http://andrewgelman.com/2016/09/22/why-is-the-scientific-replication-crisis-centered-on-psychology/)
2. https://www.mturk.com/mturk/welcome
3. M. Buhrmester, T. Kwang, S.D. Gosling, Perspectives on psychological science, **6**, 3 (2011)
4. D.J. Hauser, N. Schwarz, Behavior research methods, **48**, 400 (2016)
5. F. Gino, S.S. Wiltermuth, Psychological science, **25**, 973 (2014)
6. C. Perilloux, R. Kurzban, Psychological Science, **26**, 70 (2015)
7. D.N. Shapiro, J. Chandler, P.A. Mueller, Clinical Psychological Science, **1**, 213 (2013)
8. https://www.surveymonkey.com/
9. https://www.qualtrics.com/
10. https://www.limesurvey.org/
11. http://english.1ka.si/
12. R.B. Cattell, *Structured personality-learning theory: A wholistic multivariate research approach* (Praeger Publishers, 1983)
13. R.M. Bauer, G.L. Iverson, A.N. Cernich et al., Archives of Clinical Neuropsychology, **27**, 362 (2012)
14. V. Ismatullina, I. Zakharov, E. Nikulchev, S. Malykh, ITM Web of Conferences, **6**, 03005 (2016)
15. M. Luciana, Journal of Child Psychology and Psychiatry, **44**, 649 (2003)
16. V. Ismatullina, I. Voronin, A. Shelemetieva, S. Malykh, Procedia-Social and Behavioral Sciences, **146**, 353 (2014)
17. I. Zakharov, V. Ismatullina, I. Voronin, S. Malykh, Behavior genetics, **46**, 815 (2016)
18. I.M. Zakharov, M. Likhanov, Ju. Marakshina, L. Merzon, K. Poparenko, G.M. Vasin, The proceedings of the International Society for Intelligence Research (ISIR), 98 (2016.)
19. R.A. Stern, T. White, NAB, *Neuropsychological Assessment Battery: Administration, Scoring, and Interpretation Manual* (Psychological Assessment Resources, 2003)
20. A.E. Veroff, N.R. Cutler, J.J. Sramek et al. Topics in geriatrics, **4**, 211 (1991)
21. I.M. Zakharov, I.A. Voronin, V.I. Ismatullina, S.B. Malykh, Procedia-Social and Behavioral Sciences, **233**, 313 (2016)
22. I. Voronin, V. Ismatullina, I. Zaharov, S. Malykh SHS Web of Conferences 9, 02043 (2016)
23. I. Voronin, V. Ismatullina, I. Zakharov, G. Vasin, S. Malykh, ITM Web of Conferences, 6, 02010 (2016)
24. https://psychopy.org
25. S.T. Mueller, B.J. Piper, Journal of neuroscience methods, **222**, 250 (2014)
26. A. Chetverikov, P. Upravitelev, Behavior research methods, **48**, 1086 (2016)
27. http://webanketa.ru/
28. https://virtualexs.ru/

ITM Web of Conferences **10**, 04007 (2017) DOI: 10.1051/itmconf/20171004007
2017 Seminar on Systems Analysis

Use of Game Systems of Scaling for the Improvement of GIS Productivity

Kirill Zhigalov[1,2,*]

[1]V.A. Trapeznikov institute of Control Science of Russian Academy of Sciences, 117997 Moscow, Russia
[2]Moscow Technological Institute, 119334 Moscow, Russia

Abstract. The application of a game method of megatextures in GIS systems is considered in the article. The main attention is paid to the method usage not only in image display , but also in relief scaling and 3D models. The application of the method of relief megatextures will allow to significantly increase the image quality of a relief and the quality of the calculations of volumes and distances almost without losing system productivity. It is possible to use this technique in any modern GIS, that will allow to process much more basic data.

1 Introduction

Due to the recently increased data stream, the existing displaying mechanisms in the modern GIS systems don't cope with the task of high-quality display. In this connection, GIS operation is a constant compromise of minimum sufficient volume of basic data. Nevertheless, if not all the data participate in the processing, it will badly affect both mathematical and visual parameters. The companies, which are engaged in game development, solved this problem long ago. We will try to review briefly their idea with regard to GIS systems.

2 Textures' Optimization

Nowdays, game systems use so-called units of megatextures for image quality improvement, they allow to break textures into units and to use different permissions for their displaying, depending on the remoteness of an object, to which they belong, from the camera. As the aerial photography, used in GIS systems, have a high-resolution–, they occupy a considerable part of a video card memory in case of their loading, It may lead to failures of displaying them or to essential slowdown of system operation in general (see Tab. 1).

It was defined by practical considerations, that it is reasonable to use three-fold scaling. In other words, the area located as close as possible to the camera (in our case it was a square of 1 by 1 kilometer) boots using the maximum possible resolution, the next one – using the resolution of 70%. And all the remaining – using the resolution of 30% (see a Fig. 1) [1, 2].

Table 1. Dependence of the speed of application opening with a texture from its volume.

Video card memory size	Speed of application opening with a texture				
	0,5 Gb	1 Gb	2 Gb	4 Gb	8 Gb
0,5 Gb	30 sec	5 min	could not run	could not run	could not run
1 Gb	15 sec	1 min	5 min	could not run	could not run
2 Gb	15 sec	30 sec	1 min	5 min	could not run

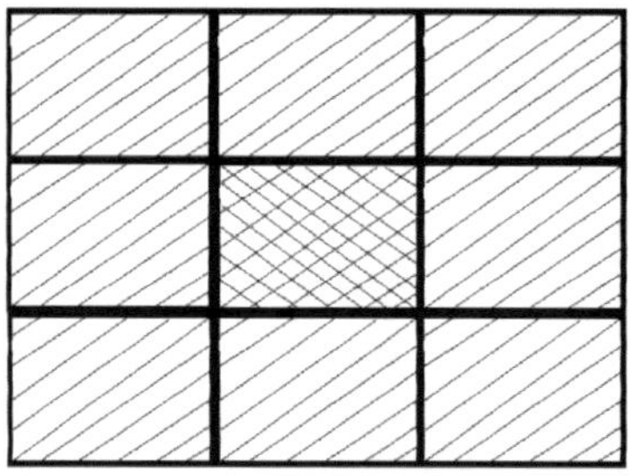

Fig. 1. Scheme of image scaling when using megatextures when a camera is placed in the middle of a map.

Such configuration allows to release video card resources on average for 60%, that positively influences the speed of the GIS 3D displaying in real time. At the same time, the general quality of displaying remains at rather high level (see Fig. 2) [2].

Nevertheless, this technology has also disadvantages [2]: (1) More space on the server or at the workstation for storage of additional copies of textures (It was

* Corresponding author: kshakalov@mail.ru

calculated that, the space is required twice more on average) is required; (2) The program needs time for the conversion of a GIS image or of a texture before displaying them.

Fig. 2. An example of displaying of megatextures in GIS.

3. Optimization of surface displaying

Similar kinds of megatexture system can also be used in case of surface displaying. The surface is built on the points, consisting of 3 coordinates (X, Y,Z). In case of large areas of GIS covering (for example, 20 by 20 kilometers) and large scale (for example 1:5000) there may be 2-3 000 000 of points. At the same time, single displaying of a surface consisting of more than 500 000 points significantly slows down the system (system response time is more than 1 second) [3].

According to the conducted research, it is necessary to discharge points in the ratio 1:4 (see Fig. 3) for the solution of the problem of speeding up the displaying.

There is a number of questions while using this method:

- Absence of a possibility of real-time computings;
- A possibility of appearance of "holes" in places of transition of the complete model into the discharged one of a surface.

Both of these issues are resolved by analogy with megatextures by the preliminary surface modeling with the maximum quantity of points. Then the surface is discharged and a surface with the thinned-out points is created. Further both surfaces are cut on squares (for example, equal to 1 on 1 sq. kilometer). In case of GIS displaying the program builds by default the surface discharged, and in the places as close as possible to the camera squares of a complete surface are displayed.

At the same time, the system does all calculations on a complete surface that allows saving accuracy at the original level. One of the disadvantages of the system displaying is the impossibility to edit surface in real time as it is connected with a large volume of calculations.

Nevertheless, such system is quite efficient for the majority of tasks without editing a surface.

According to the carried-out tests, the system allows to save up to 40% of the CPUs resources, 60% of resources of a RAM and to 35% of resources of the video card in case of the area of GIS spanning in 90 sq. kilometers and quantity of points of a surface equal 3 500 000.

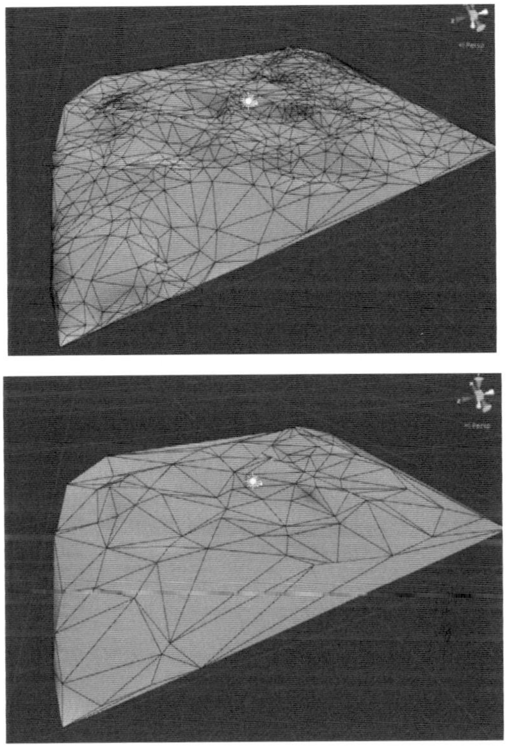

Fig 3. An example of displaying of the complete and discharged surface.

4. Conclusion

According to the conducted researches volumes of the data, displayed in GIS, permanently grow. Nevertheless, resources of users' computers are restricted. Besides, on average users update a computer once in 5-7 years. In this connection, vendors of GIS systems have a problem of optimization of geographic information systems themselves for the upcoming tasks. Megatextures and a megarelief can be one of the decisions. This combination of solutions can save up to 50% of resources of user machines or servers, that allows to re-distribute them on improving of systems of visualization.

References

1. A. Bhardwaja, L. Samb et al. Remote Sensing of Environment, **175**, 196–204 (2016)
2. K. Zhigalov, ITM Web of Conferences, **6**, 03018 (2016)
3. In-Ae Yeoa, Jurng-Jae Yee, Automation in Construction, **71**, 398–413(2016)

AUTHOR INDEX